EPINETS

Advance Praise for Epinets

"Cognition and behavior are increasingly used as variables in social network theory, but Moldoveanu and Baum leapfrog evolution to analyze the purely cognitive underpinnings of social networks. Your epinet refers to your understanding of how other people see you and one another within your network. Combining network analysis with the reflected self and emotional intelligence, *Epinets* serves up a buffet of innovation and insight."
—Ronald S. Burt, Booth School of Business, University of Chicago

"*Epinets* offers a really exciting new lens for social network analysis, grounded in excellent scholarly work. Mihnea Moldoveanu and Joel Baum's ideas are both intriguing and demanding, yet always presented in clear and accessible language."
—Woody Powell, Stanford University

"What your contacts really know remains one of the most intriguing and mysterious quandaries of a powerful social network. Moldoveanu and Baum offer a treasure of insights for solving this puzzle and one thing more—a system, called the 'epinet'—that illuminates how to grasp and authenticate hidden network knowledge and the competitive benefits of making the unknown known."
—Brian Uzzi, Kellogg School of Management, Northwestern University

"With *Epinets*, Mihnea Moldoveanu and Joel Baum have created a comprehensive epistemic paradigm, challenging the mechanisms behind well-established ideas in social network theory and research. It is a brilliant, fully thought-through tour-de-force, complete with theory, constructs, models, language, and empirics. Especially interesting for me is the conjoining of trust with epinets, producing original and sometimes startling findings."
—Aks Zaheer, Carlson School of Management, University of Minnesota

EPINETS

The Epistemic Structure and Dynamics of Social Networks

Mihnea C. Moldoveanu and Joel A.C. Baum

Rotman
a new way to think

STANFORD BUSINESS BOOKS
An Imprint of Stanford University Press
Stanford, California

Stanford University Press
Stanford, California

Special discounts for bulk quantities of Stanford Business Books are available to corporations, professional associations, and other organizations. For details and discount information, contact the special sales department of Stanford University Press. Tel: (650) 736-1782, Fax: (650) 736-1784.

Printed in the United States of America on acid-free, archival-quality paper

Library of Congress Cataloging-in-Publication Data

Moldoveanu, Mihnea C., author.
    Epinets : the epistemic structure and dynamics of social networks / Mihnea C. Moldoveanu and Joel A. C. Baum.
        pages cm
    Includes bibliographical references and index.
    ISBN 978-0-8047-7791-9 (cloth : alk. paper)
    1. Social networks.   2. Social interaction.   3. Knowledge, Sociology of.   4. Social sciences—Network analysis.   I. Baum, Joel A. C., author.   II. Title.   III. Title: Epistemic structure and dynamics of social networks.
    HM741.M65 2014
    302.3—dc23
                                2013032081

Designed by Bruce Lundquist

Typeset by Newgen in 10.5/15 Adobe Garamond Pro

Contents

Preface   vii

Chapter 1

Why We Need an Epistemic Model of Social Networks   1

Chapter 2

An Epistemic Description Language for Social Interactions and Networks   19

Chapter 3

"What Do You Think I Think You Think about It?":
Epinets as a Tool for the Study of Network Structure   51

Chapter 4

"I Think You Think I Think You're Lying":
Trust, Secrecy, Covertness, and Authentication in Social Networks   93

Chapter 5

"I Know You Think She Thinks I Trust You—But I Don't":
Moves, Tactics, and Strategies Defined and Played in Epinets   131

Chapter 6

"What You May Think We Think We Are Doing Here": By Way of Conclusion   156

Glossary   169

Notes   173

References   175

Index   181

Preface

This is not another book on network analysis, despite the fact that both "networks" and "analyses" figure prominently in its pages. We were motivated to write it by a gap that we observed in network analysis as it relates to the epistemic underpinnings of social networks—specifically, the gap in our understanding and in our representations of what networked human agents know or believe. Bridging this gap is necessary for network-based explanations of behavior and a genuine representation of network dynamics, but it cannot be straightforwardly done by work in fields such as epistemic game theory or artificial intelligence, which emphasize formal models for dealing with interactive states of knowledge and belief. For this reason, this book introduces a language that researchers can use to explain, predict, and intervene in the epistemic fabric of social networks and interactions.

Because we are building a language that is meant to be used (and perhaps sometimes abused), it is useful to think of this not only as a book but also as an "application"—or "app"—in the computer software sense of the term. An app is a set of representations and the procedures for manipulating them that allows users to accomplish new tasks. Think of Microsoft Excel, Google Chrome, or the video game Rock Band. An app should be both us*able* and use*ful*. Unlike a "theory," which lives in a purely representational space, an app is embodied and made useful through repeated use. Thus, our goal is not simply to introduce another way to describe the cognitive and epistemic states of networked agents but to do so in a way that is "plug-in compatible" with the discursive and empirical practices of the fields that study social networks.

We owe a debt of gratitude to several people who have given generously of their time and energy to help us build this edifice. In particular, we thank

Ron Burt, for his enthusiastic support and insightful commentary and suggestions throughout; Raluca Cojocariu, for her detailed, exacting, and attuned editorial and production assistance; Tim Rowley and Diederik van Liere for sharing network data and assisting with the collection of additional data used in the analysis of trust in Chapter 4; and two anonymous Stanford University Press reviewers for their detailed comments and suggestions for improvement.

Finally, this work would not have come to fruition at all but for the expert, caring, and patient guidance of our editor, Margo Beth Fleming, over the past three years. We thank her deeply.

MM and JB

EPINETS

Chapter 1

Why We Need an Epistemic Model
of Social Networks

Using examples and unstructured intuitions that highlight the importance of knowledge and of beliefs, both individual and mutual, to the outcomes of social situations and interpersonal relations, we argue for the usefulness of explicit epistemic models of human interactions and networks. We introduce the notions of an epistemic state—that is, a link between individuals and propositions they may know or believe—and of an epistemic tie—that is, a connection between individuals' epistemic states: if Alpha knows Beta knows Gamma knows that the park is closed after dark, then there is a set of epistemic ties connecting Alpha, Beta, Gamma, and the proposition that the park is closed after dark, which is part of the epistemic structure of the situation. We show how the structure of epistemic networks— epinets—formed by such links among individuals and their beliefs is relevant to the dynamics of human interactions, and how the dynamics of these networks are critical elements of complex interpersonal narratives.

What must human agents know about what other humans—with whom they are connected—know in order for the resulting patchwork of ties among them to *function* as a social network? Suppose that an anonymous survey of the friendship network of a seven-person executive team reveals that Beth, Harry, and Martha form a clique, with each describing the others as "friends." We designate the triad as a clique, rather than as a patchwork of ties, because we expect these three to exhibit some special forms of cohesion that may be evidenced by, for example, an above-average ability to coordinate, collaborate, communicate, and collude. In other words, we expect the triad to *function* as a clique: we expect each member to know—and know that the other two know—sensitive information about an event of mutual importance, or we expect that such sensitive information will quickly propagate within the triad.

What each knows of and about the others and their knowledge is the "epistemic glue" of the clique; it is what allows Beth to react to an unforeseen disaster in ways she knows Harry and Martha will find justifiable, and it is what allows her to make sense of their intentions based on observing their reactions and knowing what they think about what she knows. The grammar is somewhat complicated, but its complexity closely tracks that of the phenomena we expect a clique to exhibit. This epistemic superstructure is what makes the clique a clique—an identifiable network substructure with very specific expected properties—rather than a patchwork of ties and connections that can offer no further insight or predictive value.

At a more fundamental level, what must human agents know or believe about what others know or believe for their interactions to have joint or shared sense and meaning and to lead to stable patterns of interpersonal behavior? Game theory has contributed a basic canon of coordination, cooperation, and collaboration "games" that require coherent mutual beliefs (players' beliefs about other players' beliefs, about other players' beliefs about their own beliefs, and so on) whose "epistemic structures" can be analyzed to arrive at the preconditions for coordination, cooperation, collaboration, and even coherent communication. However, these neat analytical structures come at the cost of oversimplifying what humans believe and how they believe it as well as what they know and how they know it. States of knowing, like "oblivion" (not knowing and not knowing you do not know) or "forgetting" (knowing but not recalling what you know), are ruled out by assumptions such as those of "common priors" and "common knowledge," even though these states are all important to the unfolding of real human interactions. Moreover, because the event spaces of game theory do not admit interpretations and shadings, the resulting analyses lack the subtlety required to understand that humans interpret "Can I pray while I smoke?" very differently from the way they interpret "Can I smoke while I pray?" The conjunctive "while" functions very differently in first-order logic from the way it functions in plain English.

The contemporary importance of epistemic moves and games to an understanding of social interactions is clear from the direction of technological progress and innovation. *Homo sapiens* is *Homo communicans* and makes use of the full range of methods for passing information-bearing signals to shape, control, and predict the social milieu of being in the world. Consider the "cc" (carbon copy) and "bcc" (blind carbon copy) functions of everyday e-mail, which act as levers for shaping the informational structure of an interaction: "cc" creates pools of mutual knowledge about the contents of a message and serves as an aggregation tool; "bcc" oppositely brackets cliques that are "in the know" from individuals outside a circle of trust or power. But these are just the rudiments: new technologies allow senders to control a message after they have sent it—and possibly delete it—making it possible for them to deny ever having sent such a message even though they know the recipients know its contents; to "hack" into each other's e-mail servers to access a critical message without the message's author or recipient knowing that the hacker knows its contents; and to encrypt a message so that only intended recipients can decode it on the basis of access to the public or private key with which it has been encoded. The complexity of "interactive epistemology" has multiplied over the past few decades and continues to do so. A new language and new models are needed to understand the epistemic glue of human social interactions.

Although we are interested in building intuitive, yet precise, models of this epistemic glue, we are assuredly not pioneers of the epistemic dimension of social interactions. Nuanced treatments of epistemic structures and effects have appeared in the fields of artificial intelligence (Fagin et al. 1995), epistemic game theory (Aumann 1989), and analytic philosophy (Kripke 2011). Nor are we the first to point out that social networks (and social structures more generally) require descriptions sensitive to differences between what social agents think, and what we think social agents think, about such structures (Krackhardt 1987). What we are after is a tool kit for modeling, measuring, and manipulating the *epistemic glue* of human interactions and networks in ways that are as accessible to social network analysts as they are engaging to logicians, epistemic game theorists, and artificial intelligence researchers. We are building an application—an "app"—as much as we are theorizing, modeling, or philosophizing.

The Epistemic Structure of a "Friendship Tie"

Because we are building an app as much as a theory, we need to become intimate with "user requirements"—that is, the kinds of uses to which our modeling tool kit may be put. To that end, consider the friendship tie between Beth and Harry in our earlier example. Beth "knows" Harry: she sees him daily, is familiar with his latest setbacks and successes, works with him on a joint project, and sees him socially about every other week. That is her longhand unpacking of the shorthand answer "Harry is my friend," which she gave on the anonymous survey. Now what we want to know is this: when Beth needs

Harry to convey to her, quickly and covertly, a sensitive piece of information she believes he has received from one of his acquaintances with whom Beth has no connection, what must Beth know about Harry for her to have good reason to believe that he will come through with it?

The minimal set of beliefs about Harry that Beth needs to rationalize her expectations may include the following: she believes that Harry knows the information is useful to her, that it is important to her that their office mate, Martha, does not know Beth has come to know it, and perhaps that Harry knows Beth will not divulge her source after he has passed along the information. Complications can arise: if Beth knows Harry's boss knows of Harry's ties to Beth and is monitoring Beth's actions to detect any sign that Harry has leaked to Beth the information he was entrusted to hold in confidence, then Beth may have to believe Harry knows of this threat and trusts in her integrity and competence not to "blow his cover." Alternatively, she may have to believe Harry does *not* know about this threat (in which case she may choose to inform him of it as befits the level of trust she assumes they share).

In each case, there is a structure to the knowledge that these social agents "share" that is both intelligible and intuitive, although it grows quickly in logical complexity with the addition of new information and people. The structure of this "epistemic glue" is rendered intuitive and intelligible by the recursive and interactive nature of what this "social knowledge," as it should properly be called, relates to, which is often knowledge *about* knowledge: Beth's knowledge about Harry's knowledge, which includes Harry's knowledge about Beth's knowledge about Harry's knowledge, and so on. The structure of the epistemic glue is "interactive": it links not only an agent's mind to a proposition but also one agent's mind to a proposition via another agent's mind: Beth knows Harry knows that his boss is monitoring Beth's actions for any sign of information leaked by Harry.

Of course, it is not only knowledge but beliefs, conjectures, and even barely articulated hunches that we want to capture and address with our language. Beth may not know—by any acceptable use of the term "knowing"—that Harry knows that the piece of information he possesses should be transmitted to her in a way that guards against eavesdropping—but she may simply believe it for reasons having to do with a complex of other prior beliefs. Harry may merely "sense" that Beth needs him to transmit the information covertly, without really having fully articulated that hunch as a proposition.

All of these are legitimate objects of modeling, measurement, and manipulation for our app. We need a comprehensive conceptual framework to engage the range of states in which humans find themselves vis-à-vis propositions about the world. To study the gamut of mental objects playing pivotal roles in the relationships that form the fabric of human networks, we use the covering term *epistemic states* and represent these states as directed ties between social agents and propositions, which are grammatically correct sentences in natural language or well-formed formulas in propositional logic. And we use the term *epistemic networks* or *epinets* to refer to the networks that comprise a group of social agents, potentially true or possibly true propositions, and the interactive ("I think you think . . .") and recursive ("I know I know . . .") epistemic ties among them.

Let us give meaning to these words through usage. If Beth knows Harry knows that she needs him to convey a piece of sensitive information to her quickly and covertly, there is an epistemic sequence of ties connecting Beth to Harry to the fact that she needs him to act in such and such a way: as an agent to another agent to a proposition. If Harry knows that Beth knows this, then there is an epistemic tie sequence that connects Harry to Beth to Harry to the proposition in question; if Beth knows Harry knows she knows this, then there is a further epistemic tie sequence representing the correspondent connections; and so on. One can add agents (Martha, Harry's boss) and propositions (the boss's vigilance) to the epistemic network, as well as additional interactive epistemic ties involving one agent ("Beth knows that she knows what she knows"), two agents ("Beth knows Harry knows she knows . . ."), or more ("Beth believes Harry believes that his boss believes that she believes . . .").

Epinets in Shakespeare, Kesselring, and Durrenmatt. Epinets evolve and, as they do, "things happen," socially speaking. Far from being epiphenomenal—appearances *sine* consequences—changes in epistemic networks are those on which "the plots turn."

In Shakespeare's *Othello* (circa 1603; Ridley 1963), epinets representing the epistemic states of Othello, Desdemona, Iago, and the audience are essential to the interpretive schemata that allow the audience to understand and become involved in the play. The drama can be understood as the evolution of the epistemic states of its lead protagonist, Othello, from one of oblivion and trust through those of doubt and suspicion to one of certainty about a false belief regarding Desdemona's infidelity. The epistemic state changes can be traced to manipulations by Othello's lieutenant, Iago, that make careful use of the structure of interactive epistemic states—what Othello thinks Desdemona thinks when she says what she says; what he thinks she thinks he thinks; and so on).

At the beginning of the play, Othello believes unconditionally in Desdemona's loyalty and faithfulness. He trusts her, in the sense of believing that she could not evince fidelity and love if she did not have these feelings. Also, Othello is oblivious to the possibility that Desdemona is attracted to the young Cassio—one of his lieutenants and a rival to his chief lieutenant and schemer, Iago—in the sense that he gives this possibility no thought. It is not that, if asked about Desdemona's putative relationship with Cassio, he would say, "I do not know" or "I do not believe it is true"; rather, he would be shocked by Iago's presumption and by the suggestion of such a possibility. At the same time, Othello is jealous of Desdemona, yet not aware of his jealousy, and so is an easy target for Iago, who seeds doubt in Othello's mind regarding Desdemona's fidelity and manages to augment it by playing with what Othello thinks Desdemona thinks and with what Othello thinks Desdemona thinks he thinks: when Desdemona realizes that Othello is now both jealous and suspicious, she attempts to endear herself through loving entreaties. However, Iago has also managed to plant in Othello's mind that Desdemona is a master dissembler, and therefore Othello interprets these entreaties as masterful dissimulations of faithlessness rather than avowals of love.

Some outright lying and trickery are required of Iago to wean Othello from his trust of Desdemona, but his deceit succeeds because of his prior success in setting up the right epistemic states among Othello, Desdemona, Cassio, and himself. In particular, Othello believes Desdemona is unfaithful; he knows she does not know with whom he suspects her of being unfaithful; he believes she knows he is suspicious; and therefore he thinks she is likely to exaggeratedly "protest" her love for him, Othello, so as to lay his suspicions to rest. When Desdemona—oblivious to much of this epistemic structure—intervenes in favor of her presumed lover, Cassio (who has in the meantime fallen from Othello's grace after a contretemps into which he has been cunningly pulled by Iago), the epistemic trap Iago has set for Othello springs exactly as planned. Othello sees the situation as one of figuring out with whom his wife is cheating rather than whether or not she is cheating at all. Iago's soliloquies keep the audience informed of the dynamics of Othello's epistemic states, contributing to the indignation the audience feels as it witnesses the epistemically trapped Othello smother Desdemona in a fit of jealous rage—an indignation that is assuaged, though perhaps only partly, when a finally awakened Othello at last sees Iago for the vile manipulator he has become and attempts, unsuccessfully, to kill him.

In Joseph Kesselring's *Arsenic and Old Lace* (1942), Mortimer Brewster, the central character, is deciding whether or not to fulfill his promise to marry the woman he loves, within the complicated emotional landscape of his family, which includes two elderly spinsters, Abby and Martha—who, while passing as "good Christians," specialize in poisoning lonely old men with a home brew of elderberry wine laced with cyanide and arsenic; his brother Teddy, who believes he is Teddy Roosevelt and digs graves for the spinsters' victims in Mortimer's cellar thinking he is digging locks for the Panama Canal; and a murderous brother, Jonathan. The characters are oblivious to each others' beliefs and intentions—they do not know and do not know they do not know—and the only bits of information that are common knowledge are either false (the spinsters are good Christians) or relatively useless (Teddy thinks he is Roosevelt). It is this oblivion—of which the audience is aware—that creates the tension between what the characters say, do, and cause one another to think, and what the audience knows they know, as illustrated in Figure 1.1.

Friedrich Durrenmatt takes the strategy of building dramatic tension based on interactive epistemic knots and tangles to a higher level in *The Physicists* (Die Physiker) written in 1961 (Kirkup 1994). The play is set in a sanatorium for the mentally ill run by Dr. Mathilde von Zahnd, a famed psychiatrist, and features three patients—Beutler (who "believes" he is Sir Isaac Newton), Ernesti (who "believes" he is Albert Einstein), and Mobius (who "believes" he is visited regularly by King Solomon). "Einstein" has just murdered one of his nurses, and the police investigation turns up the fact that Newton had earlier murdered another nurse. "Believes" is in quotation marks because it represents a far more complex interactive epistemic state than we expect, which the second act elucidates—specifically, the fact that each inmate *pretends* to believe in a false identity for the benefit of the staff and Dr. von Zahnd to more convincingly feign the madness required to cover up his true identity and so allow him to stay in the asylum. Mobius *is* a renowned physicist who has checked in to protect his inventions from government exploitation, and he is being tracked by two foreign spies—"Newton" and "Einstein"—who are

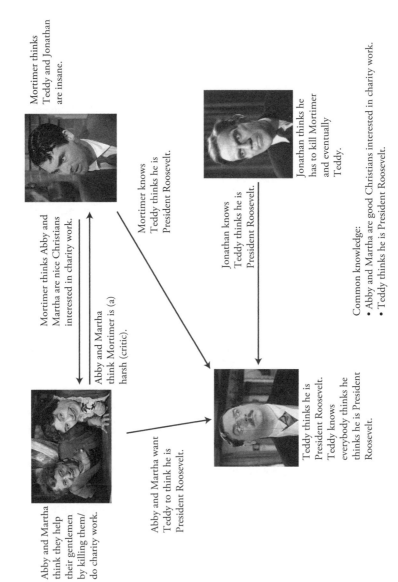

Mortimer thinks
Teddy and Jonathan
are insane.

Mortimer thinks Abby and
Martha are nice Christians
interested in charity work.

Abby and Martha
think Mortimer is (a)
harsh (critic).

Mortimer knows
Teddy thinks he is
President Roosevelt.

Abby and Martha
think they help
their gentlemen
by killing them/
do charity work.

Abby and Martha want
Teddy to think he is
President Roosevelt.

Teddy thinks he is
President Roosevelt.
Teddy knows
everybody thinks he
thinks he is President
Roosevelt.

Jonathan knows
Teddy thinks he is
President Roosevelt.

Jonathan thinks he
has to kill Mortimer
and eventually
Teddy.

Common knowledge:
• Abby and Martha are good Christians interested in charity work.
• Teddy thinks he is President Roosevelt.

FIGURE 1.1 Epinet: *Arsenic and Old Lace*

interested in appropriating one of his inventions to their statist ends. Meanwhile, Dr. von Zahnd, in order to appropriate Mobius's invention for herself, *pretends* to believe that "Newton" and "Einstein" are who they say they are and that Mobius is deranged.

As illustrated in Figures 1.2 and 1.3, the plot of *The Physicists* turns not only on an epistemic network that includes states of knowledge, uncertainty, and oblivion regarding both facts and intentions, but also on an evolution of that network—between the two acts—even though the facts remain consistent. These facts are the murders of the nurses and the unfolding action in an asylum. However, this network upends the viewer's interpretation of these facts (e.g., that "Einstein" and "Newton" are mad and that Dr. von Zahnd is their caregiver).

"Everyday" Epistemic State Tangles

If we are correct that interactive and reflective epistemic states make a large difference in explaining and understanding human social behavior, we should be able to show how epistemic states and the epistemic links that connect them produce insight into common interactive situations and predicaments. We do so through the following vignettes.

Vignette 1. Alice is seeking a job in Bob's firm. She is being interviewed by Bob for this purpose. Alice made some false statements on her resume, which Bob has before him while the interview is proceeding—a notable one about having won an engineering contest in college in 2010. Alice is unaware of the fact that Bob knows that his own son had actually won an engineering contest that year at the same college. And she does not know (or know she does not know) that Bob suspects—though he does not know—that the contest he knows his son to have won is the very *same* contest Alice claims to have won. Thus, the credential that Alice has given on her resume is suspect to Bob—who also comes to suspect Alice of lying—but Alice believes her deception is working.

As the interview unfolds, Alice thinks Bob believes her. Bob does not believe her. He also knows, from her facial expression, that she believes her deception has been successful. Because she is certain of this success, Alice does not obsess any further about who thinks what about whom and proceeds oblivious to the inferential dynamics that are developing. Bob manages to keep his conjectures about Alice's sincerity hidden, which leaves Alice in her turn deceived about the success of her own deception.

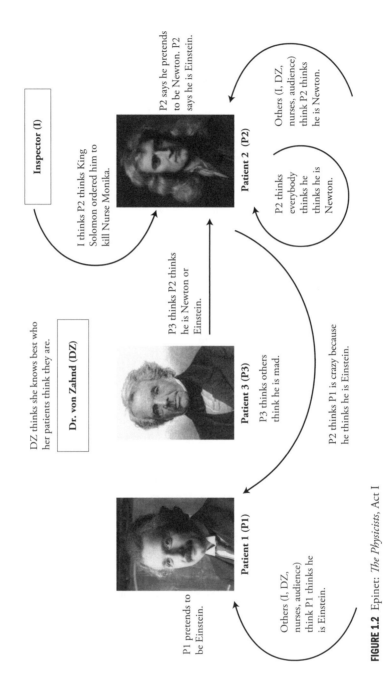

FIGURE 1.2 Epinet: *The Physicists*, Act I

DZ thinks she knows best who her patients think they are.

Dr. von Zahnd (DZ)

Inspector (I)

I thinks P2 thinks King Solomon ordered him to kill Nurse Monika.

P2 says he pretends to be Newton. P2 says he is Einstein.

Patient 2 (P2)

Others (I, DZ, nurses, audience) think P2 is Newton.

P2 thinks everybody thinks he thinks he is Newton.

P3 thinks P2 thinks he is Newton or Einstein.

Patient 3 (P3)

P3 thinks others think he is mad.

P2 thinks P1 is crazy because he thinks he is Einstein.

Patient 1 (P1)

P1 pretends to be Einstein.

Others (I, DZ, nurses, audience) think P1 thinks he is Einstein.

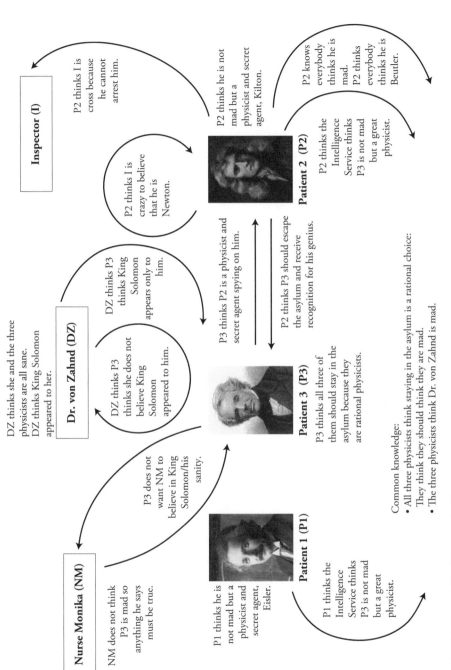

FIGURE 1.3 Epinet: *The Physicists*, Act II

Inspector (I)

P2 thinks I is cross because he cannot arrest him.

P2 thinks he is not mad but a physicist and secret agent, Kilton.

P2 knows everybody thinks he is mad. P2 thinks everybody thinks he is Beutler.

P2 thinks I is crazy to believe that he is Newton.

Patient 2 (P2)

P2 thinks the Intelligence Service thinks P3 is not mad but a great physicist.

DZ thinks she and the three physicists are all sane. DZ thinks King Solomon appeared to her.

Dr. von Zahnd (DZ)

DZ thinks P3 thinks King Solomon appears only to him.

DZ thinks P3 thinks she does not believe King Solomon appeared to him.

P3 thinks P2 is a physicist and secret agent spying on him.

P2 thinks P3 should escape the asylum and receive recognition for his genius.

Patient 3 (P3)

P3 thinks all three of them should stay in the asylum because they are rational physicists.

P3 does not want NM to believe in King Solomon/his sanity.

Nurse Monika (NM)

NM does not think P3 is mad so anything he says must be true.

Patient 1 (P1)

P1 thinks he is not mad but a physicist and secret agent, Eisler.

P1 thinks the Intelligence Service thinks P3 is not mad but a great physicist.

Common knowledge:
• All three physicists think staying in the asylum is a rational choice: They think they should think they are mad.
• The three physicists think Dr. von Zahnd is mad.

Vignette 2. Alan sends an electronic message to Belinda and, without specifying that he is sending it anywhere else, also sends the message to Charles, who is Belinda's boss, via a "bcc." Thus, Alan thinks Belinda knows the contents of the message, and Belinda thinks Alan thinks she knows (absent any other considerations); Alan thinks Charles knows, and Charles thinks Alan knows (absent any other considerations). However, Belinda does not think Charles knows—otherwise, the "cc" would have appeared in the message, even though Charles thinks she knows and also thinks she does not think he knows. Charles can therefore "play" with Belinda, assuming that she does not think he knows. Charles also knows Alan thinks Belinda does not think Charles knows, and therefore can also wield some power over Alan by credibly threatening to respond to Alan's message with a "cc" of the response to Belinda, on which Belinda's original "bcc" will appear.

Vignette 3. The CEOs of three large consumer goods firms selling undifferentiated products to a homogeneous market decide to coordinate their pricing of a particular product in order to prevent a new competitor from entering their market space. Because they do not want to get together and explicitly set prices for the critical period in which the new competitor's threat of entry is high—lest they be found out and pursued by antitrust authorities—they must coordinate tacitly. Accordingly, by a series of sequential cuts or hikes, they aim to arrive at a mutually agreeable price. The *goal* of the exercise is common knowledge among the oligopolists—every one of them knows it, knows that every other one knows it, and so forth, ad infinitum. Also, common knowledge is the fact that any oligopolist can use the disguise of a rational response to the threat of entry by a new competitor to steal business from incumbent rivals. Should one oligopolist implement a severe price cut (down to or below his marginal cost, for instance), the others will infer a breach of trust that they would not have inferred had the structure of the preemption game—as well as the possible excuse given by the renegade oligopolist—not been common knowledge among them.

Trust, in this case, keeps the price-fixing game from turning into a "Bertrand game" in which the oligopolists dissipate their profits by bidding all of the prices down to their marginal costs. This trust is predicated on a base of mutually shared facts and premises that each oligopolist knows all of the others know, as well as a set of shared premises that allows each oligopolist to make sense of every other oligopolist's actions in the context of the price-setting game (such as the fact that an oligopolist can fake panic at an imminent new threat and slash prices in response, but would do so only provided that every other incumbent takes the same view of the threat).

Vignette 4. The board of directors of XYZ Corporation has reached the decision to terminate the employment of the firm's CEO at a board meeting that did not include him. The date of the public announcement of his departure has been set. The firm is in a delicate financial and organizational state, with many key employees on the verge of resignation, and with key accounts at stake upon the departure of key employees, some of whom are loyal to the outgoing CEO. The board expects the mode, manner, and timing of the announcement to play a key role in determining the ongoing viability of XYZ. To quell rumors and speculations that could lead the outgoing CEO to break confidence and detrimentally communicate the impending changes, a controlled and well-timed release of the announcement is desired, with some key employees being brought into a "circle of trust" that can manage the firm on a daily basis in advance of a public announcement.

Because of the board's fragmentary and sporadic access to the firm's everyday communications, it is important for the leadership to be able to anticipate, in advance, the social paths along which the news will propagate in order to predict the response and to control possible side effects. It is well known to the directors that conveying the news "in confidence" to key employees may generate an informational cascade in which each recipient also conveys the news "in confidence" to a few trusted employees, to show connectedness, signal their importance, or simply out of a conspiratorial inclination. Thus, the question for the board is this: Who at XYZ can be trusted, and who trusts whom? The trust is not "generalized": it is not merely the inclination to act cooperatively. Rather, what the board needs is a depiction of the social relationships within XYZ that will enable the news to be communicated precisely, reliably, and securely. Clearly, a trust relationship turns on what each party thinks the other thinks—or knows—at a moment in time, and on what the relationship is between what someone says and what is actually the case. The trust that employee A will place in any employee B will turn both on A's confidence in B's integrity (safeguarding the source and content of the information) and on A's confidence in B's competence (saying no more and no less than what is true and relevant at a particular point in time, without colorful distortions or purposeful omissions). Such confidence may need to be safeguarded by *A*'s expectation of *B*'s own trust in *A* ("only the trusting can be trusted"), which in turn generates new complications in the description of what a trusting relationship is.

"Information games" of the type we have constructed in these vignettes are entertaining because the moves they comprise produce changes—potentially very significant changes—in a larger pattern of interactive epistemic states that also overturn the emotional landscape of the situation. Baseline assumptions that social agents make about each other—cooperativeness, trustworthiness, rationality, docility—are uprooted by single and often involuntarily conveyed signals. *Ex*formation—what the sender of a message *does not say* but is nevertheless relevant to the receiver precisely because it goes unsaid—can be as informative as *in*formation, provided that the right "epistemic tangle" is in place: if Alice thinks Bob knows that Alice is about to be fired and Bob says nothing to Alice when they have lunch together, the absence of a signal from Bob will influence Alice's trust in him and her estimate of his support.

Ambiguous or complex epistemic states can be useful for either creating or breaking the trust required for information to flow freely; the local and temporary topology of an epinet can change the meaning of signals exchanged between the agents within it. Differences among the epistemic states of agents and among the relationships between them—which are what epinets are designed to capture—make a difference, and often a very large one, in the ensuing dynamics of the relationships or of the network.

Epistemic States and Epistemic Networks as Explanation Generators

The epistemic glue whose microstructure we aim to model via epistemic networks is intimately and ubiquitously involved in empirical studies of network phenomena. Networks of interorganizational collaboration (Powell, Koput, and Smith-Doerr 1996) rest on shared knowledge about tasks, technologies, and capabilities of other organizations in the same network, as do interpersonal networks of collaborative creative work (Uzzi and Spiro 2005). The cohesiveness and robustness of such networks hinge on regimes of trust among agents that often make possible "private games" (Burt and Knez 1995) that may be "too dangerous" (Burt 1999) in their absence. Co-mobilization in networks is sensitively dependent on what agents believe other agents will do if the former decide to mobilize (Chwe 1999, 2000, 2001), as well as on the fact that they know what other agents (validly) know they believe.

Nevertheless, their own social networks often confront agents with "horizons of observability" (Friedkin 1983) that constrain their knowledge of agents in the network to those corresponding to adjacent or alter-adjacent "nodes," thus limiting the explanatory power of models of affiliative behavior predicated on an agent's knowledge of the position of every other agent within the network (Gould 1993; Jackson 2005). The explanatory success of network theories of interpersonal and interorganizational phenomena thus depend on researchers' assumptions about what agents know, what they know about what other agents know, and to what extent they trust what they and others know.

We are about to develop a precise way of representing states of knowledge, awareness, ignorance, and the like—jointly known as *epistemic states*—of agents in a social network. This representation will permit development of a new theory about the relevance and importance of epistemic states to the structure and dynamics of (interpersonal and interorganizational) networks (henceforth networks *tout court*), as well as development of more precise measurement instruments and techniques for testing and validating the theory. When we model a social structure as a social or economic network of agents, we pay a price in explanatory depth and generality when we omit an epistemic model of that structure. Consider the problem of predicting *which* among a large number of possible exchange networks will form among a set of agents interested in net-benefit-of-affiliation maximization (Jackson 2005; Ryall and Sorenson 2007). Existing analyses typically assume that the value associated with the formation of different ties is given and known to all agents, and they concern themselves with the calculation of the feasible or efficient networks that emerge as a result of different agents forming the ties that are most beneficial to them. However, if we assume that agents form ties on the basis of cost-benefit calculations of the relative values of possible ties that are in turn based on their knowledge of the value of each possible tie they could form, then we see that the set of possible ties must be conditioned by what agents know or believe about the value of forming any one tie in particular. In order for the most efficient of possible networks to form, the function that assigns values to each possible tie also has, itself, to be known to all network agents.

Two options are available to the realistically minded modeler who wants to examine the conditions under which this assumption is valid. One is to posit that, even though not all agents are informed about the value of all possible ties they can form, they can become informed over a finite period of time. In this case, the explanatory problem shifts to the *mechanisms* by which a full-knowledge state can be achieved. Different mechanisms for information dissemination are likely to create different knowledge regimes within the network. Broadcasting the value function, for instance, achieves full knowledge provided that (1) every agent is tuned in to the broadcaster and (2) every agent considers the presence of the broadcaster's signal to be sufficient reason for believing the signal to be valid. Stipulation 1 raises questions about the marginal proclivity of agents to tune in to the broadcaster (e.g., it assumes that they believe the broadcaster can and has reason to supply information that is useful to them, and that they are aware that they are ignorant of, not oblivious to, the information). Stipulation 2 raises questions about the *trustworthiness* of the broadcasting source. Alternatively, the value function can be assumed to "percolate" through the network through word of mouth and rumor. The relative success of this explanation hinges on the marginal proclivity of agents (1) to inform each other truthfully and (2) to believe each other authentically; that is, success hinges on the trustworthiness and trustingness of network agents—qualities that are likely to be heterogeneous.

The second option is to assume that not all agents under examination know the value function. This creates a different explanatory agenda, one aimed at figuring out "who knows what" at any point in time. One possibility is to "survey the field," but this has the disadvantage of (1) assuming that agents know what they believe or (2) inducing knowledge states that these agents would not otherwise have and that therefore cannot function as valid explanatory variables for what "would have happened had there been no intervention" (see Seidel and Westphal (2004) for evidence of such researcher-initiated information contagion). Since, moreover, we are interested in predicting what *actions* agents are likely to take by virtue of their knowledge, it is also important to understand whether or not different agents "believe or trust what they know," which leads to the need to make finer distinctions in what we mean about "knowledge" in terms of the credibility or trustworthiness of the knowledge source.

What emerges from this discussion is the need to be precise about knowledge even when trying to explain a relatively simple network phenomenon such as purposeful tie formation. Being precise about knowledge requires more than just an effort to specify a function that maps bits of knowledge to individual network agents; the ways in which these agents know what they know are also relevant. Higher-level epistemic states such as awareness, oblivion, and ignorance are as important as first order states such as risky and uncertain belief. Moreover, interactive epistemic states such as trust, trustworthiness, trustingness, and credibility are crucially important to the kinds of plausible and testable stories that we can devise about network formation. By distinguishing epistemic differences likely to make a material difference, we aim to make the study of network epistemics an important component of social network modeling and inquiry.

The Way Forward

In this chapter, we have introduced the notion of *epistemic glue* as a prerequisite for the explanatory power of network models of social interaction and social action. We have shown that this glue has structure, comprising the epistemic states and ties among networked agents. We have illustrated how the evolution of this structure produces changes in the outcomes of interactions ("narratives") and taken this to be a telling sign of the causal significance of such structures. We have defined *epinets* as symbolic representations of the glue underlying social networks and established that they matter and, more loosely, how they matter.

The investment to be made in appropriating a new language for modeling and representing phenomena is substantial. In spite of what we hope is a persuasive argument for considering epistemic states in detail and incorporating them systematically into the apparatus of social network analysis, we recognize that some *surplus* of insight and explanatory power is likely required to generate the necessary inducement to compensate for the required cognitive effort. To this end, we summarize here and elaborate in subsequent chapters the applications that epistemic imagery enables in key areas of social network theory and research. Figure 1.4 illustrates the organization of the book. We begin in Chapter 2 with an outline of the primitives of an epistemic description language (EDL) that can be used to describe epinets comprising

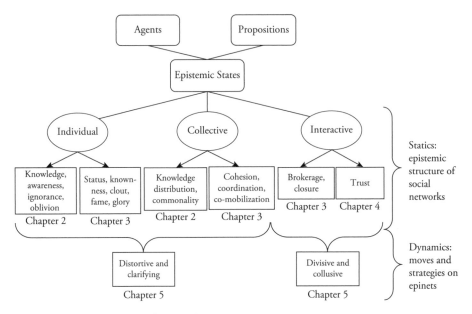

FIGURE 1.4 Organization of the Book

individual agents, propositional beliefs, and epistemic states and ties. In Chapter 3, we deploy the EDL to show how interactive epistemic states (what agents think about what other agents think) can be used to understand fundamental network phenomena such as brokerage and closure via the epistemic analysis of basic mechanisms of network formation, co-mobilization, coordination, and communication. In Chapter 3, we show how self-referential epistemic states (beliefs about the structure of the network itself) can be used to analyze components of status, including knownness, fame, glory, and clout. In Chapter 4, we examine in detail how interactive epistemic states can be used to unpack and analyze trust-based relationships and network structures, such as "circles of trust" and superconductivity. We transition from epinet structure to dynamics in Chapter 5, introducing a series of moves and strategies that are defined as operations that agents perform on the structures of epinets of which they are part. We also introduce concepts that function in a manner similar to that of *equilibrium* in game-theoretic accounts, and we show how these concepts can be used to understand the long-run dynamics of epinets.

Chapter 2

An Epistemic Description Language
for Social Interactions and Networks

We introduce a modeling language for representing the epistemic states of networked human agents at both individual and collective levels. The new "epistemic description language," or "EDL," has a graphical component (diagrams for describing relationships among agents and relevant propositions) and a syntactical component (an epistemic logic that allows us to track epistemic states of linked agents and their dynamics). We use the EDL to articulate both the relationships between individuals and those individuals' beliefs as the building blocks of epinets—for example, "Alice knows (the cat is on the mat)"—and the basic relationships among individuals' epistemic states as the elementary building blocks of interactive epistemic networks—for example, "Bob knows (Alice knows (the cat is on the mat))." We show how epinets can be used to capture causally relevant states of social networks, and we argue for an epistemic description language for social networks and interactions.

The study of (human) epistemic states is not new to social theorizing. Thomas Schelling's (1960) original insight—that mutually consistent belief sets are required as antecedent conditions for strategic or coordinative equilibrium-based explanations of social behavior—was developed by David Lewis (1969) into a framework for the analysis of conventions, which Robert Aumann (1976) then used to build an interactive epistemology for strategic interactions that yields sufficient conditions for game-theoretic explanations of social interactions (Brandenburger 1992; Aumann and Brandenburger 1995). "Interactive epistemology" is now a branch of game theory concerned with elucidating the role of epistemic structures as the glue of social networks and interactions. It asks questions like these: "What are the epistemic conditions under which two or more agents arrive at a Nash equilibrium in their strategic interaction?" (Answer: mutual knowledge of game structure, strategies, payoffs, and rationality for two agents; common knowledge of same for all N players.) and "What are the epistemic conditions under which two or more agents can exclude, through iterative reasoning, the dominated strategies in a strategic game?" (Answer: almost common knowledge of game structure, strategies, payoffs, and rationality.)

These questions are relevant to our endeavor; however, the formalism of interactive epistemology is based on a particular set of modeling choices that researchers committed to the quasi-realism inherent in much social network analysis find empirically problematic and pragmatically uncomfortable. Relationally interesting and relevant epistemic states such as *awareness* (knowledge of one's own knowledge of X), *oblivion* (lack of knowledge of X and lack of knowledge about that lack) and *subconsciousness* (knowledge of X without awareness of that knowledge) are largely uncharted in this framework. Whatever we have now that might qualify as an epistemic theory of relationality can be significantly improved on, albeit at the cost of introducing a more complex modeling language. What, then, are the objectives that such a language should aim to fulfill?

Desiderata for an Epistemic Description Language and an Epistemic Theory of Networks

What we are after is a modeling framework that maximizes the following objectives.

Precision and Subtlety. Unlike the standard economic modeling approach, wherein parsimony is sought through the enforcement of standard probabilistic representations of epistemic states (in which degrees of belief and structural uncertainty are represented by probability distributions and in which strategic uncertainty is represented by conjectures about other probability distributions (Harsanyi 1968a, 1968b; Mertens and Zamir 1985)), our EDL must be able to represent *noninteractive* epistemic states of individual agents such as awareness, oblivion, and subconsciousness, as well as more conventional epistemic states of knowledge and ignorance. We must also be able to represent the *interactive* epistemic states of networks and subnetworks in a way that is consistent with the representation of the self-referential epistemic states of individual agents.

The reason for these requirements is that, unlike economic analysis, which has been the source of theorizing about epistemic states in formalized games, network analysis originates in the *realist* epistemological tradition of sociology, where the interest is in representing epistemic states that closely track perceived ontological or conceptual differences. We aspire to an epistemic theory of networks that fits the epistemological tradition of sociology or artificial intelligence, even as it aims for a logical structure more commonly associated with economic theorizing that rests on an *instrumentalist* epistemology.

Operationalizability. Related to the requirement of representational precision is the requirement that the constructs that make up the EDL be operationalizable. Thus, we need to be able to demonstrate that trust—defined parsimoniously by some network researchers as a mutual expectation of cooperation (e.g., Burt and Knez 1995)—can be understood as a precisely specified epistemic structure that can be independently measured in a noncircular fashion—that is, not by questionnaires that merely ask, "Do you trust *X*?" or "Whom do you trust?" but by inquiry into conditions causally linked to trust. Similarly, the EDL we introduce should make it possible to give precise, tractable meanings to such terms as *fame* and *glory*, which are important to social network theorists interested in status (e.g., Benjamin and Podolny 1999) but remain under-analyzed.

Logical Auditability. Arguably, logical auditability is a vital aim of any formal model or theory (Saloner 1991; Moldoveanu 2002) and a potent reason for engaging in formal modeling in the first place (Oxley, Rivkin, and Ryall 2010). For a model of interactions to be logically auditable, it must allow us to track how changes in individuals' beliefs and knowledge affect others' beliefs and knowledge on the basis of the logical structures we use to represent these states. For instance, if *A* thinks *B* thinks that today is Tuesday when in fact it is Wednesday, and *B* finds out that he is wrong and communicates this to *A*, who trusts in *B*'s competence, then we should be able to track the change in *A*'s and *B*'s beliefs following the flow of information, all the way from the experience that allowed *B* to discover his error to the modification of *A*'s belief about *B*'s belief.

Our EDL and theory of epistemic networks must also make it possible to check for logical consistency between hypotheses regarding the epistemic states of networked agents and axiomatic assumptions linking these individual states to interactive epistemic states of subnetworks of agents and the kinds of network phenomena we are likely to observe. Such a theory should allow us to derive *sufficient* epistemic conditions for certain types of network behaviors (e.g., mobilization, exchange, and formation of trust conduits or structural holes), as well as to derive hypotheses about these network phenomena that are *theorems* of the basic axioms of our epistemic theory and *syntactically correct* constructions in the basic EDL we advance.

Fit with Other Network Agent Models. An important characteristic of any new theory is the interfaces it allows its users for communicating with developers of other theories and models. Specifically, it is important for the theory to offer a sufficiently broad conceptual space in which findings from other models of network behavior can be included. Our epistemic theory of networks and accompanying EDL must permit the incorporation of psychological biases that affect how agents process information in the form of *operators* working on agents' epistemic states. *Simplification biases*, for instance, can be incorporated via *contraction operators* acting on first-order knowledge structures. *Attribution biases* can be incorporated via *distortion* or *deletion operators* acting on first- or higher-order knowledge structures. Our theory should also "dialogue" with game-theoretic approaches for investigating epistemic states and epistemic conditions for equilibria in games (Aumann 1987; Binmore and Brandenburger 1990; Aumann and Brandenburger 1995).

Fit with Empirical Approaches to Networks. The study of networks has evolved as an empirical craft as much as it has as a science or a set of theories: network researchers have specialized tools and techniques for representing, visualizing, and measuring variables of interest, along with a set of theories that function as prediction- and explanation-generating engines. Our EDL and epistemic theory of networks must be engineered both for a pragmatic fit with these tools of the trade and for a logical and conceptual fit with existing theories of network formation, structure, and dynamics.

Epinets are themselves networks. Therefore, standard network analysis tools can be employed to analyze links among agents and their epistemic states in ways that are already familiar to network researchers. For example, if $\{P_j\}$ is a set of propositions that are mutually relevant to agents i and j, we can employ the basic strategy of representing networks as adjacency matrices to create N *cognitive adjacency matrices* around the beliefs $\{P_j\}$, with matrix $\{M_1\}_{k,l=1,...,J}$ defined by the relation $m_{kl} = 1$ iff i knows P_k and j knows P_k and 0 otherwise; matrix $\{M_2\}_{k,l=1,...,J}$ defined by the relation $m_{k2} = 1$ iff i knows j knows P_k and j knows i knows P_k and 0 otherwise; and so on. In this way, we extend the adjacency matrix tool kit of standard network analysis to the epistemic realm.

An Epistemic Description Language

Our epistemic description language features a graphical tool that maps agents and what they believe or know, and a syntactical tool that allows us to analyze the content and structure of an epinet. The graphical tool is based on a set of building blocks, depicted in Figure 2.1, for intuitively representing what one or more agents know or believe. A node in an epinet is either an agent (Alice, Bob) or a proposition, which can be a well-formed formula of first-order logic (*For all x, iff x = g, then Fx = Fg*) or a well-formed sentence of a natural language ("There are no black swans on this pond").

Links in epinets are directed: they travel from an agent (Alice) to a proposition (*Today is Tuesday*) and encode epistemic relations like "knows" and "believes." In Figure 2.1, part (a) represents the epistemic state *Alice knows P* or, more compactly, *AkP*, and part (b) represents the epistemic state *Alice believes P*, or *AbP*. Epinets also allow us to represent intuitive epistemic states such as awareness, oblivion, and ignorance via directed ties linking Alice to the relevant proposition (*P*) and to her epistemic state about the proposition, as illustrated in Figure 2.1, parts (c)–(e) respectively.

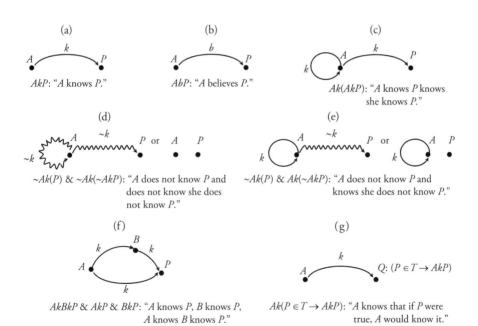

FIGURE 2.1 Simple and Compound Epistemic States via Epinets

We can add both agents and propositions describing what agents might believe to epinets via additional nodes that represent them and further directed ties that link agents to propositions and agents' epistemic states to one another. For instance, part (f) in Figure 2.1 shows an epinet comprising two agents and a proposition, where Alice knows *P* and knows Bob knows *P*, which he in fact does, even though he does not know that Alice knows *P*. Finally, epinets allow us to graph—and the accompanying syntax allows us to express—more subtle epistemic states such as confidence in one's ability to know the truth. As shown in part (g) in the figure, Alice's confidence in her beliefs about *P*, for instance, may rest on her knowledge that if *P* *were* true, then she *would* know it—call this proposition *Q*: *Ak*(*P* ∈ *T* → *AkP*)—which establishes that her knowledge is truth tracking. Together, these building blocks allow us to construct epinets to represent in microstructure the epistemic glue of an interaction or relationship, and to build an analogous set of statements (using our epistemic syntax) to track and audit the epistemic structure and dynamics of a network.

Primitives and Kernels for an Epistemic Description Language

Now that we have an intuitive sense of the EDL, let us introduce, unpack, and justify some of its main components in greater detail, to explicate our choice of epistemic relations and the logical relationships among them.

Individual Epistemic States. We begin with a basic set of *individual* epistemic states, as follows.

*Knowledge (*K*). A knows P*: *AkP*, for some agent *A* and some proposition *P*. If agent *A* knows that, say, *P* = *A judgment in favor of the defendant was entered today*, then *A* will, ceteris paribus, act as if *P* is true in those cases in which (1) *P* is relevant and (2) *A* sees *P* as relevant (in which case we say that *P* is salient to *A*). *k* is a simple binary relation (either *AkP* or ~ ["not" in propositional logic] *AkP*) between an agent (or his mind) and a proposition *P* that is characterized by the following necessary conditions: (1) *A* believes *P* for a valid reason *R*, and (2) *P* is true. Note that these are not *sufficient* conditions for knowledge (Gettier 1963). *A* may believe *P* = *There is a quarter in my pocket* on the basis of the vague sensation of a weight in his left pocket, and, indeed, there is a quarter in *A*'s pocket but in his right one. In this case, *A* does *not* know *P*, even though he has a valid reason for a true belief. What counts is having the *right* reason for holding that belief.

A question may be raised at this point regarding our focus on *propositions*—subject-predicate sentences constructed according to syntactic rules that are more or less "self-evident," rather than "states of the world," as the proper arguments of knowledge states. Since Savage (1954), states of the world have been treated as the fundamental building blocks of what decision theorists call semantic state spaces (Aumann 1976, 1989, 1999a, 1999b). If we use semantic state spaces, we say that "*A* knows *e*, knows that $f \in e$"—that is, "Agent *A* knows that event *e* has come to pass, knows that event *e* will occur only if *f* occurs and therefore knows that event *f* has occurred." Describing what an agent knows in terms of his or her degrees of belief regarding states of the world— rather than propositions *referring to* objects and events or propositions that are *true or false* as a function of certain states of the world—is attractive because it seems to eliminate the need to consider syntactic properties of the arguments, such as the grammatical form of propositions. Yet states of the world show up in our speaking about agents and their beliefs in ways that are categorized and expressed by propositions such as *It is raining, This car is blue, You are here and now lying*. Agreement or disagreement with such propositions is the "data" produced when we investigate agents' states of knowledge via surveys and questionnaires. These propositions—not the underlying events to which they refer or seem to refer—are the most immediate phenomena with which we deal and which our models should explain. They are bound by rules of predication and syntax on the one hand and by criteria of verification or corroboration on the other.

It will *not* do, as some suggest (Aumann 1989; Samet 1990), to describe a state of the world as *the set of all of the propositions that are true of or "at" it*, because doing so ignores the problem of ascertaining whether or not propositions *refer* to the events about which they seem to speak. Think of all of the ways to describe the conditions under which *It is raining today* holds true, thus rendering intractable the enumeration of the propositional representation of a state—or the epistemic state of an agent who *knows* that state. The problem with Samet's proposal is not only one of enumeration but also one of relevance: there is no way to delimit the range of true propositions warrantedly assertible about the set of conditions that constitute a rainy day that are also relevant to a particular situation or context and therefore properly uttered or believed by an agent in that context.

The problem of reference extends beyond relevance. Epistemic game theorists do not see a radical distinction between syntactic (propositions) and semantic (events and collections of events) approaches to modeling the arguments of agents' knowledge (Aumann 1999a, 1999b). Their view appears to stem from an implicit belief that the truth value of a proposition fixes the reference to (or "meaning" of) the objects to which the proposition's words refer. The word *rain* thus refers to the composite set of raw feelings and subjective experiences of "rain," and this correspondence is (supposedly) fixed by a reference relation that is determined by the truth value of propositions like *It is raining today*. But this assumption is false: truth conditions of propositions involving referent terms *do not* fix the reference of those terms (Putnam 1981). There is thus a conceptual and a practical distance between syntactic and semantic approaches that cannot be bridged simply by mirroring the apparatus of set theory, which we use to represent and symbolically manipulate events, in the apparatus of first-order logic, which we use to represent and symbolically manipulate propositions.

We thus distinguish between the raw qualia—that is, instances of subjective conscious experience or perceptions that correspond to an event or object—and a proposition (a fact, say) that refers to that event or object. The distinction is critically important to our description language because the language does not work on state spaces of events whose interpretation is self-evident—like those of game theory and standard decision theory. The language works on propositions that are true or false, depending on both states of the world and characteristics of the observer (such as her perceptual apparatus and the language she uses to represent and communicate).

Pragmatically, probing the epistemic states of agents—through questionnaires or surveys, for example, or through elicitation of forced choices among lotteries with outcomes determined by the truth value of certain propositions—is based on the specification and enumeration of propositions that we expect to have well-defined truth values for the agents in question. Whether or not an agent's state space contains *It is raining today* as a possible state depends on whether or not *It is raining today* is an intelligible proposition *for that agent*, where "intelligible" means "with a known set of truth conditions." Because we have access to an agent's personal state space only through propositions that describe either the space or the way in which the agent describes it, it makes sense for an EDL to be based on the set of propositions that the agent considers to have truth conditions, rather than on a set of events that refer to "raw" percepts but are only accessible or describable using propositions.

Consequently, we employ propositions that refer to events and objects rather than to states of the world as the arguments of the epistemic states of an agent, and we accept the challenge that different agents may propositionalize their raw experiences differently and in ways that are intersubjectively untranslatable because they use different languages or language systems to represent perceptions in propositional form. For instance, *It is raining today* is a proposition that represents a set of "raw perceptions"—cloudy skies, wet pavement, drops falling from the sky—that may be put into words differently by different agents. One person's rain can be another's drizzle and yet another's mist. Agents need agree only on whether or not they disagree about the truth of a proposition, not on the right way to refer to an event via a particular one. This approach discards "states of the world" and "events" in favor of propositions, their truth values, and agents' epistemic states regarding the content of the propositions and their truth values. Thus, an agent's actions have consequences that are not the standard set of outcomes of decision theory and game theory (events constituted by subsets of states of the world) but are rather the result of changes in the truth value of certain propositions and changes in the epistemic states of agents about the truth value of these propositions and about each other's epistemic states regarding them.

For example, the fact that Alice defects rather than cooperates in a one-shot prisoner's dilemma game with Bob induces a change in the truth value of the proposition *Alice defect(ed)*—a change for Alice, provided she is aware of her own intentions and their link to her actions and their outcomes; a change for Bob, provided he makes the right inference from the observed outcome of Alice's intentions; and a change for no one if Alice and Bob are unaware of or oblivious to each other's behavior and/or intentions. Moreover, the truth value for Bob of *Alice defected* is not necessitated by his observation of the outcome of the game. Bob can put into language his observation of the outcome as "A suboptimal outcome was realized" without further attribution or interpretation. Whether or not the way Bob puts experiences into language influences how he remembers them is naturally a relevant and interesting topic of inquiry that is already pursued in cognitive psychology (Loftus 1979).

Awareness and Awareness of Level n *(k^n).* The state "A knows P; A knows she knows P" is one that we refer to as awareness. "A knows she knows P, and so forth, to n levels": AkP, $Ak(AkP)$, $Ak(Ak(AkP))$, $Ak(\ldots AkP)\ldots)$, abbreviated as Ak^nP, generalizes awareness to a state in which A knows P, knows that she knows it, and so forth, ad infinitum. This epistemic state relates to an agent's introspective insight into the contents of his/her own knowledge. Not all agents know they know what they know: they may have imperfect or unreliable recall, and such infelicities of introspection are clearly relevant in social interactions.

Level 2 awareness (i.e., Ak^2P) denotes the situation in which an agent knows P and knows that he knows P. A may know $P = $ *Profits are nondecreasing in industry concentration* in the sense that A says "yes" when asked, "Is it true that profits are nondecreasing in industry concentration?" But A may not *know*^{2} P in the sense of being able to take unprompted action guided by a plan that rests on P when P is relevant to the situation. In this case, P is always-already salient to A, who does not need to be prompted in order to recognize its relevance to situations in which P is relevant. Knowledge of P does not guarantee to A the salience of P, but only guarantees that A will act as if P is true if P already is or is made salient. Level 2 awareness of P *guarantees* that A acts on P where P is *relevant*—that is, A *finds* P to be salient where P is relevant.

Via axioms that formalize commonsense intuitions about epistemic states and epistemic rationality, the literature on epistemic game theory, dating back to Aumann (1976), attempts to force certain properties on the epistemic states of agents. *Positive introspection* requires that if an agent knows P, s/he knows that s/he knows P (Modica and Rustichini 1999). However, this requirement is too strong and weakens a distinction—between knowledge and level 2 awareness—that is often relevant to modeling social interactions among real agents who may be prone to temporarily *imperfect recall* of what they know.

For instance, one agent may purposefully ask another agent questions that remind the latter about what s/he (really) knows, as a way of manipulating him or her into a particular thought or action. Harry could ask Sally an open-ended question about how the last quarter went, expecting Sally to interpret the question as about revenue and costs and not about technology, but (Harry knows and knows that Sally knows) there has been a major technical delay, and he makes use of her lack of awareness of the delay to demonstrate her ineptness as a manager. One way to represent this set of conditions is to claim that Sally's recall is imperfect, but doing so establishes *perfect recall* as a precondition for epistemic rationality that is too strong. Human agents differ with respect to their knowledge of what they know (or believe); their memory can be affected by the pragmatics of their interactions and their situational constraints in ways that are adaptive and useful, and should therefore not be deemed irrational or un-rationalizable without further inquiry.

In contrast to positive introspection, *negative introspection* requires that an agent know that s/he does not know something that s/he in fact does not know (Modica and Rustichini 1994). This condition is also too strong, for it requires that there be no *unknown unknowns* that are nevertheless relevant to an interaction. This is a counterintuitive and unappealing requirement. Think of the proposition *He is about to kill us* as part of the epistemic space of Heather, the young wife of Robert, a serial killer who has successfully played a model husband at home. It is possible—though strained, odd, and unrealistic—to say that Heather knows that she does not know that Robert is about to kill her and her children; it seems far more realistic and useful to say that Heather knows neither that *He is about to kill us* nor that she does not know it. Rather, she is *oblivious* of it: the proposition is simply not part of her (propositional) "state space."

We distinguish between states of awareness (positive introspection) and states of ignorance (negative introspection), unawareness, and oblivion as follows.

Ignorance. A does not know P, but knows he does not know P: $\sim(AkP)$ & $Ak(\sim AkP)$. Ignorance of P (which can also be more loosely understood as un-certainty about P) is such that A pays attention to the values of variables that are relevant to the truth value of P, but does not actually know those values or know the truth value of P. Ron does not know whether or not $P =$ *Industry profits rise with industry concentration* is true or false if he is ignorant about P, but, in a situation where the truth value of P is relevant, he seeks out signals that inform the truth or falsity of the proposition (because he knows he does not know it and wishes to determine its truth value).

Unawareness. A knows P but does not know she knows it: AkP & $\sim Ak(AkP))$. In this state, A may have temporarily forgotten that she knows P—although she may well answer "yes" if asked whether or not P is true. For example, Lynda may answer "yes" to the question "Is it true that it was raining last Wednesday?" but may have answered "I do not know" to the question "What was the weather like last Wednesday?" In this case, there is a leading aspect to the question that affects the information known to the agent; however, it is not correct to say that the agent does not know what the weather was like last Wednesday. It is then possible—and potentially highly relevant—that A knows P but does not know s/he knows P (i.e., AkP & $\sim(Ak(AkP))$).

On the other hand, lack of knowledge combined with the lack of knowledge about the lack of knowledge is represented as follows.

Oblivion. A does not know P and does not know that he does not know it: $\sim(AkP)$ & $\sim(Ak(\sim AkP))$ & . . . . In this state, A neither knows P nor is *heedful*, in any way, of P or of information that can inform A about the truth value of P: he does not pay attention to variables or experiences that can affect P's truth value. If technology T_1 is relevant to a future dominant product in industry I but completely irrelevant to the current product set, then an incumbent A may be said to be oblivious of the proposition $P = T_1$ *will supply the next I-dominant product design* if he does not ask himself, when exposed to T_1, "What difference will T_1 make to P?" Oblivion is fundamentally different from ignorance: an ignorant A raises questions about the subject P when P is relevant (and made salient), and an A who is level 2–aware of his ignorance of P raises questions about P when P is relevant, but an A who is oblivious of P does neither: P is outside of A's possible "zone of heed."

Degree of Belief. Agents' epistemic commitments to propositions about the world may be uncertain and risky. We can relax the stringent requirement that *knowledge* (or *ignorance*) imposes on an agent's epistemic state by referring to his/her *beliefs* regarding the truth value of a proposition, which can be measured via a *degree of belief* that can itself be either a probability (mathematical, statistical, or subjective) or some other weight (a fuzzy logic weight that does not have to satisfy the axioms of probability theory). In this case, we denote the epistemic state of agent A who *believes P* as AbP and the state of an agent who attaches degree of credence w to the truth of proposition P as Ab_wP. In the introduction of basic epistemic states that follows, we refer to states of *knowledge* by A of P, with the understanding that states of knowledge can be replaced by states of belief or w-strong belief without loss of generality.

Our definition of knowledge states can be further usefully augmented by an *epistemic qualifier* that safeguards an agent's epistemic state and function as a warrant for action predicated on that state. An agent may believe that a proposition, P, is true to a certain degree, w, but within the set of beliefs to which an agent attaches a similar degree of credence, there is an important distinction between a w-strong belief and a belief that "*were P* true (or false), then the agent would know it or come to know it." This *subjunctive* epistemic state relates to the confidence that the agent has in her own epistemic rationality. Instead of modeling this state as a second-order probability—a level of credence in the degree to which the agent lends credence to the weight with which he believes P, which gives rise to a regress—we model it as a special propositional belief. In its most basic form, this *meta*-epistemic state can be defined as follows.

Confidence (Con). *A knows that if P were (not) true, A would (not) know* P: $Ak("P \in T \rightarrow AkP")$, where the double quotation marks signify the subjunctive form of the enclosed phrase. *Con* captures A's belief about her own epistemic capabilities and virtues relative to a particular proposition. A binary measure, which can be rendered continuous if necessary, *Con* can determine A's belief in her own epistemic states and answer the question "Does A believe what she knows?" Note that the converse question—"Does A know what she believes?"—is captured by A's awareness, as described previously.

Collective Epistemic States. Thus far, we have presented our descriptive tool kit for a core of *individual* epistemic states—the basic palette of states from which to construct an EDL for networked agents and from which to build an epistemic framework for studying relationality and sociality more generally. To complete the palette, we need a set of *collective* epistemic states that describe ensembles and groups of interrelated agents, networked or otherwise. We consider a network of agents and propositions—an *epinet*—modeled by a graph, G, not necessarily fully connected, and we distinguish the following *collective*, or *network-level*, epistemic states.

Distribution or Sharedness. *A knows P and B knows P and C knows P . . . :* AkP & BkP & CkP . . . Distribution measures the spread of P throughout a network of agents, G, either in absolute terms (the total number of agents that know P) or in relative terms (the proportion of agents in the network G that know P).

Collective Awareness of Level n. *A knows^n P and B knows^n P and C knows^n P . . . :* Ak^nP & Bk^nP & Ck^nP . . . Collective awareness measures the degree of level n awareness about P in network G, either in absolute terms, as the number of agents that *know^n* P, or in relative terms, as the proportion of agents in G that *know^n* P. Level 2 collective awareness (k^2) guarantees that the agents in G that know P also find P salient when P is relevant (because they know that they know P). As is the case with knowledge distribution, awareness is not an interactive epistemic property of a network: it simply guarantees that the agents in a network know *P* and *find P salient when P is relevant*. Awareness *aids* coordinated action in mobilization-type models, but cannot vouchsafe it because an interactive knowledge structure is still required to induce action. To streamline the discussion, henceforth we refer to "knowledge" rather than "awareness" unless otherwise noted.

Near-Commonality of Level n *(*NC^n*)*. *A knows P* and *B knows P* and *A knows B knows P* and *B knows A knows P*, and so forth, to level *n*: *AkP* & *BkP* & *AkBkP* & *BkAkP* & . . . abbreviated as $(AkBk)^n(P)$ & $(BkAk)^n(P)$. Commonality of level *n* measures the level of mutual knowledge relative to *P* of the agents in network *G*. It is a measure of the *coordinative potential* of the network in the sense that many coordination scenarios not only require agent-level knowledge of focal points or coordinative equilibria and a selection criterion among them; they also require agent-level knowledge about the knowledge of other agents and about the knowledge that other agents have of the agent's own knowledge (Schelling 1978). Level 2 commonality (mutual knowledge) and level 3 commonality of knowledge about some proposition *P* (i.e., *AkBkAkP* & *BkAkBkP*) are therefore particularly important for studying network-level mobilization and coordination. The value of closure to agents in a densely connected network is materially affected by the agents' ability to accurately and reliably co-mobilize and coordinate their activities for a common purpose.

Commonality (C). NC^n with *n* = ∞. *A knows P* and *B knows P* and *A knows B knows P* and *B knows A knows P*, and so forth, as *n* increases without bound: $(AkBk)^\infty(P)$ & $(BkAk)^\infty(P)$. This is the full-common-knowledge state typically assumed to be a precondition for the deployment of game-theoretic analyses (Brandenburger 1992)—usually without postulating a mechanism or process by which knowledge becomes common or almost common.

Drawing on the building blocks illustrated in Figure 2.1, a basic notational form for epinets is illustrated in Figure 2.2 for a range of the individual and collective epistemic states just introduced. *Nodes* in an epinet are human agents (circles), propositions in subject-qualifier-predicate form (squares) that may be reflexive (i.e., about the state and structure of the network), and *edges* (links) represent the "knows that," "believes that," "conjectures that," and so forth, relations that link agents to propositions (*AkP*) or agents to other agents to propositions (*AkBkP*). The epinet as a whole is a directed graph,

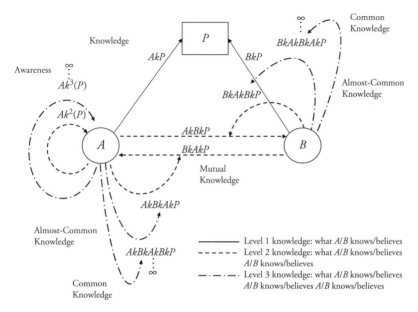

FIGURE 2.2 Epinet with Epistemic States
SOURCE: Adapted from Moldoveanu and Baum, 2011.

G ({*agents, propositions*}; {*epistemic links*}), that encodes the relevant agents and epistemic links among them and the set of propositions relevant to their behavior and interaction.

The Significance of Epistemic Levels

The perceptive reader will have noticed that the epinet in Figure 2.2 makes distinctions that are not customary in traditional game-theoretic analyses. She might ask, "Why distinguish degrees of commonality of knowledge and belief among agents in a network when representing their interactive epistemic states?" As Ayres and Nalebuff (1997) observe, traditional game-theoretic analyses have hampered themselves by assuming that information is either private (one and only one agent knows it, knows s/he knows it, etc.) or common knowledge (all agents know it, know they all know it, etc.). Yet many of the most interesting phenomena that arise in social interactions involve a finite level of interactive knowledge: agents' beliefs about other agents' beliefs (level 2) or agents' beliefs about other agents' beliefs about their own beliefs (level 3).

Ayres and Nalebuff consider a labor–management dispute that has resulted in a strike. The strike costs labor $10,000 per day and costs management $30,000 per day. Management has a total "strike budget" of $3,000,000; labor, one of $700,000. Management can thus hold out for 100 days, while labor can hold out for only 70 days (assuming that the party whose funds have run out will have to concede and accept the other's terms and conditions). If management agrees to labor's demands, its total cost will be $1,000,000; if the strike lasts for more than 33 days, management should give in today. If labor "wins," it stands to gain the equivalent of an additional $600,000 in job security–related pay, so it should be willing to strike for at most 60 days.

To render this negotiation "tractable" to analysis from a "rational agent" perspective in which labor and management act in their best interest and know the logical consequences of what they already know, we usually make an assumption about the structure of information. Specifically, we assume that all the figures just given are "common knowledge" between labor and management: labor knows it, management knows it, labor knows management knows it, and so forth, ad infinitum. But what if one bit of information is *not* common knowledge in this way? In particular, suppose that the size of the labor's strike fund is not common knowledge. How do successively higher levels of knowledge of this fact affect the dynamics of the negotiation? Ayres and Nalebuff's analysis of this scenario reveals the dependence of the negotiation on "beliefs about beliefs" by working backward from the point past which labor can no longer hold out—day 70.

- *Level 1:* Suppose that management knows the size of labor's strike fund. On day 70, then, management rationally should not concede because it knows that labor has to concede the following day, giving management a $1,000,000 benefit for the $30,000 cost of another day. In fact, the same logic applies on any day after day 37 because, after that day, management can wait for 33 days to register a positive gain.
- *Level 2:* If labor knows that management knows the size of labor's strike fund, then it is rational for labor to plan on quitting immediately after day 37, if that point in the strike is reached.
- *Level 3:* If management knows that labor knows that management knows the size of labor's strike fund, then it should not quit any day after day 4 of the strike, as its payoff to maintaining its position will be net-positive.

- *Level 4:* If labor knows that management knows that labor knows that management knows the size of labor's strike fund, then labor will realize that it should quit on day 4 of the strike because management has no incentive to give in thereafter.

- *Level 5:* If management knows that labor knows that management knows that labor knows that management knows the size of labor's strike fund, then management will not concede on any of the first four days, as all it has to do for labor to feel compelled to concede is wait a maximum of four days.

- *Level 6:* If labor knows that management knows that labor knows that management knows that labor knows that management knows the size of labor's strike fund, then labor should rationally decide to concede right away.

The analysis appears to "solve" the game by a six-fold iteration of the *knows* operator, coupled with some (possibly optimistic) assumptions about the rationality and logical prowess of the agents. The important thing is that every (interactive) iteration of the *knows* operator produces a new and important bit of information about what a rational agent endowed with the resulting epistemic state should do. Each difference in epistemic state generated by such an iteration makes a difference in the structure of the game and, contingent on the participants being rational in at least the two ways specified previously, each difference in epistemic states should also make a difference in their actions.

Now consider how one can explain what "actually happens" in a real negotiation that has the same payoff structure as that described. Suppose labor concedes to management's demands on day 6 of the negotiation. What do we make of this? The conservative interpretation from the standpoint of preserving the rational agent assumption is to posit that labor "did not think far enough ahead"; it "did not get to level 4" in the belief hierarchy outlined earlier. This interpretation has the advantage that we can still operate comfortably within the bounds of a rational agent model, parameterized according to the number of logical operations (in this case, iterations of the *believes* or *knows* operator, and the logical consequents of applying either operator to some propositional belief) that an agent can be presumed to be capable of performing. Of course, this does not explain why labor conceded on, say, day 6 rather than day 5, 7, or 15, but, of course, that is what "noise" is for in all such explanations. So far, we are both well inside the rational choice mode of modeling agents and making full use of the interactive belief hierarchy: differences in what an agent believes about what another agent believe ok make a real difference in the explanation and in our understanding of the situation.

Suppose further that we want to determine if our overall explanatory framework is on the right path and that we are open to the possibility that the rational choice model, along with some additional informational and meta-informational assumptions, is not in fact the right explanatory framework. If we interview and survey members of labor's negotiating team, we can design a protocol for probing both their rationality and their degree of "logical prowess." Suppose that such a protocol, once implemented, reveals that members of the team have not thought about what management believes labor knows about the size of labor's strike fund, and that they are genuinely surprised that such a thing matters. Suppose further that the interview and survey results show that labor conceded because of an internal quarrel within the negotiating team that might have undermined the cohesion and credibility of its negotiating position.

There is, of course, no need to "throw out" either the rational actor or the belief hierarchies model: all things considered, it may be rational to allocate our attention and cognitive resources to issues that are imminent and impactful, and it may well be that within the negotiating team an interactive belief hierarchy is nevertheless of explanatory value regarding the internecine conflict that has destabilized labor's collective resolve. We do, however, need to augment our model of the agents' epistemic states in order to account for labor's apparent state of *oblivion* regarding management's knowledge of the size of labor's strike fund.

Suppose, instead, that the interviews and questionnaires reveal that the negotiating team had known, on day 1, all the way up to level 6 of our belief hierarchy, but after day 1, caught up in the venomous negativity of the dispute, acted as if had forgotten that they knew it but then conceded as soon as they remembered it. Here again, we would be well advised to introduce language to help us make sense of a situation in which an agent knows a proposition and also knows that s/he knows it, at all relevant times, which we can call awareness of that proposition. The rational agent model usually constrains us to assume that agents always know what they know and that they can recall it "on cue" whenever that knowledge becomes relevant. So, although the imperfect recall scenario violates at least some versions of such a model, the epinets are nevertheless useful in spite of the fact that the explanations they produce deviate from normative requirements of perfect recall.

The foregoing analysis illustrates two basic points. The first is that epistemic states and belief hierarchies make significant differences both in how we analyze and in how we explain social behavior, even if we stray from rational agent and game-theoretic models of behavior that have traditionally been associated with interactive belief hierarchies. The second point is that it is clearly helpful to augment the vernacular of traditional rational agent and game-theoretic models to include more complex states such as awareness and oblivion.

The same kind of epistemic levels analysis can be applied to the interaction structure and plot dynamics of the plays we considered as intuitive motivating examples in Chapter 1. For instance, in *Arsenic and Old Lace*, Kesselring sets up an initial epistemic network (from the perspective of the audience), presented in Figure 2.3, that has all of the trappings of an "unusual, but nothing more serious than that" contemporary family. The epinet evolves to new state, shown in Figure 2.4, that is nevertheless coherent for each character, with new information revealed by the plot: the discovery of the first body in the basement, and, with the discovery of yet another body, evolves to the further set of interconnected epistemic states presented in Figure 2.5.

The agents play out, for the audience's benefit, a sort of "epistemic nightmare" that can be tracked through the changes in the state of the epinet that describes the group of agents as a whole. It is important for the epinet to comprise both the specific characters and a specific and dynamically changing set of propositions about which they have beliefs (even though very different beliefs). This is because several characters are ex ante oblivious of several different facts (called out by propositions), and it would be inaccurate to introduce these propositions (even with probability zero) in the description of the epistemic states of the characters at the beginning of the play. Changing the epistemic state of an agent from oblivion to awareness is very different (and this is where most of the dramatic impact accrues) from changing the agent's epistemic state from ignorance to knowledge. Moreover, as social life resembles drama far more often than it does chess, there is much that a modeler can learn from the epistemic state dynamics of a dramatic production.

LEVEL 1

Abby and Martha think they do charity work.
Abby and Martha think Mortimer is (a) harsh (critic).
Abby and Martha think Teddy is happy to be President Roosevelt.

Mortimer thinks Abby and Martha are his nice old aunts concerned with charity work.
Mortimer thinks Teddy is harmless as President Roosevelt.

Teddy thinks he is President Roosevelt.

LEVEL 2

Abby and Martha think Mortimer thinks they do charity work.
Abby and Martha think Teddy thinks he is President Roosevelt.

Mortimer thinks Abby and Martha think helping the community is important.
Mortimer thinks Teddy thinks he is President Roosevelt.

Teddy thinks Abby and Martha think he is President Roosevelt.
Teddy thinks Mortimer thinks he is President Roosevelt.

LEVEL 3

Abby and Martha think Mortimer thinks they think helping the community is important.
Abby and Martha think Teddy thinks they think he is President Roosevelt.

Mortimer thinks Abby and Martha think they do charity work.
Mortimer thinks Teddy thinks Mortimer thinks he is President Roosevelt.

Teddy thinks Abby and Martha think he thinks he is President Roosevelt.
Teddy thinks Mortimer thinks he thinks he is President Roosevelt.
Teddy knows he thinks he is President Roosevelt.

FIGURE 2.3 Epinet: *Arsenic and Old Lace*—Initial

			L E V E L 1
Abby and Martha know Abby killed Mr. Hoskins, but still think they do charity work. Abby and Martha think Mortimer is (a) harsh (critic). Abby and Martha think Teddy is happy to be President Roosevelt.	*Mortimer thinks Teddy killed Mr. Hoskins.* *Mortimer thinks Abby and Martha are nice, but have developed a very bad habit.* *Mortimer thinks Teddy is dangerous.*	Teddy thinks he is President Roosevelt. *Teddy thinks Mr. Hoskins is a victim of yellow fever.*	

			L E V E L 2
Abby and Martha think Mortimer thinks they do charity work. Abby and Martha think Teddy thinks he is President Roosevelt.	Mortimer thinks Teddy thinks he is President Roosevelt. *Mortimer thinks Abby and Martha think they help their gentlemen.*	Teddy thinks Abby and Martha think he is President Roosevelt and *has to bury the yellow fever victim in the Panama Canal.* Teddy thinks Mortimer thinks he is President Roosevelt.	

			L E V E L 3
Abby and Martha think Mortimer thinks they think they helped Mr. Hoskins and wants to attend his funeral. Abby and Martha think Teddy thinks they think he is President Roosevelt.	Mortimer thinks Abby and Martha think he thinks they do charity work. Mortimer thinks Teddy thinks he is President Roosevelt.	Teddy thinks Abby and Martha think he thinks he is President Roosevelt and has to bury the *yellow fever victim in the Panama Canal.* Teddy thinks Mortimer thinks he thinks he is President Roosevelt. Teddy knows he thinks he is President Roosevelt.	

FIGURE 2.4 Epinet: *Arsenic and Old Lace* — Discovery of the First Body

NOTE: Italicized text indicates changes from initial epistemic states described in Figure 2.3.

Abby and Martha think they do charity work helping selected gentlemen.
Abby and Martha think Mortimer is (a) harsh (critic).
Abby and Martha think Teddy is happy to be President Roosevelt.

Mortimer thinks Abby and Martha killed Mr. Spenalzo.
Mortimer thinks Teddy pretends to be President Roosevelt.
Mortimer thinks he is going insane (insanity gallops in the family).

Teddy thinks he is President Roosevelt and Mr. Spenalzo is another yellow fever victim.

LEVEL 1

Abby and Martha think Mortimer thinks they do charity work.
Abby and Martha think Teddy thinks he is President Roosevelt.

Mortimer thinks Teddy thinks he is President Roosevelt.
Mortimer thinks Abby and Martha think they help their gentlemen.

Teddy thinks Mortimer thinks he is President Roosevelt.
Teddy thinks Abby and Martha think he is President Roosevelt.

LEVEL 2

Abby and Martha think Mortimer thinks they help their gentlemen, but not strangers like Mr. Spenalzo.
Abby and Martha think Teddy thinks they think he is President Roosevelt.

Mortimer thinks Abby and Martha think he thinks they do charity work.
Mortimer thinks Teddy thinks Mortimer thinks he is President Roosevelt.

Teddy thinks Abby and Martha think he thinks he is President Roosevelt.
Teddy thinks Mortimer thinks he thinks he is President Roosevelt.
Teddy knows he thinks he is President Roosevelt.

LEVEL 3

FIGURE 2.5 Epinet: *Arsenic and Old Lace*—Discovery of the Second Body

NOTE: Italicized text indicates changes from epistemic states at the time the first body is discovered described in Figure 2.4.

Using Epinets to Describe the Epistemic Glue of Everyday Social Interactions

The everyday epistemic tangles we considered in Chapter 1 can also be mapped out as epinets to lay bare the logical structure of each situation. Doing so allows us, in many cases, to understand the various consequences of epistemic mismatches and other *malentendus*.

Vignette 1. Recall that Alice is seeking a job in Bob's firm and is being interviewed by Bob for this purpose. Alice has made some false statements on her resume, such as that she won an engineering contest in college; let this be statement q. The statement "Alice did not win the engineering contest" can be denoted p. Unknown to Alice, Bob knows that his son won an engineering contest that year at the same college, and he suspects—but does not know—that it is the *same* contest that Alice claims to have won. So we have that Alice believes p, as does Bob. Alice believes her deception is successful, so she believes that Bob believes q, and Bob believes she believes she has succeeded, so he believes that Alice believes he believes q. However, Bob believes Alice believes p. Because she is quite certain of the success of her deception, Alice does not go through any further levels of interactive reasoning; Bob, because he believes she is deceived about his being deceived, is able to avoid revealing his doubts, leaving Alice deceived. Alice and Bob's epistemic states are illustrated graphically in Figure 2.6.

How forgivable is Alice's deception? Believing that Alice is deceiving him, Bob seeks evidence in Alice's behavior of "tricks" and "maneuvers" that are meant to lead him astray. He may even interpret some of her nondeceptive behaviors as being inspired by a deceptive intent. All of these bits of evidence

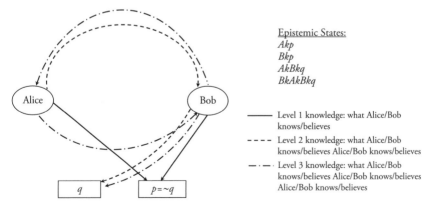

Epistemic States:
Akp
Bkp
AkBkq
BkAkBkq

——— Level 1 knowledge: what Alice/Bob knows/believes

– – – – Level 2 knowledge: what Alice/Bob knows/believes Alice/Bob knows/believes

— · — · Level 3 knowledge: what Alice/Bob knows/believes Alice/Bob knows/believes Alice/Bob knows/believes

FIGURE 2.6 Epinet for Vignette 1

may stack up against Alice to the point at which Bob decides to call her bluff, and they figure in Bob's decision to punish Alice without first confronting her with the discrepancy in order to determine whether or not what seems to him to be a lie is in fact a misunderstanding.

Vignette 2. Alan sends an electronic message, p, to Belinda and also sends it to Charles, who is Belinda's boss, as a "blind carbon copy." (bcc). Thus, Alan believes Belinda believes p, Belinda believes Alan believes p, Alan believes Charles believes p, and Charles believes Alan believes p. However, Belinda does not believe that Charles believes p—otherwise, the "carbon copy" (cc) would have appeared on the message, even though Charles believes Belinda believes p and moreover believes that Belinda does not believe that Charles believes p. Charles can therefore "play with" Belinda, assuming that she does not believe that he believes p. Charles also knows that Alan believes that Belinda does not believe that Charles believes p and therefore can also wield some power over Alan by credibly threatening to respond to Alan's message p and sending a copy of the response to Belinda, on which Belinda's original "bcc" appears. These epistemic states of Alan, Belinda, and Charles are mapped out in Figure 2.7.

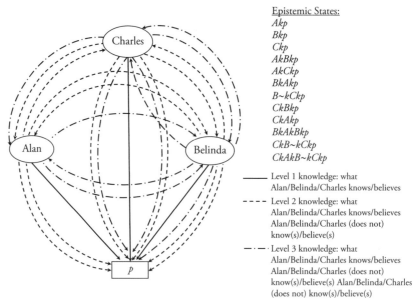

Epistemic States:
Akp
Bkp
Ckp
$AkBkp$
$AkCkp$
$BkAkp$
$B{\sim}kCkp$
$CkBkp$
$CkAkp$
$BkAkBkp$
$CkB{\sim}kCkp$
$CkAkB{\sim}kCkp$

——— Level 1 knowledge: what Alan/Belinda/Charles knows/believes

- - - - Level 2 knowledge: what Alan/Belinda/Charles knows/believes Alan/Belinda/Charles (does not) know(s)/believe(s)

—·—· Level 3 knowledge: what Alan/Belinda/Charles knows/believes Alan/Belinda/Charles (does not) know(s)/believe(s) Alan/Belinda/Charles (does not) know(s)/believe(s)

FIGURE 2.7 Epinet for Vignette 2

Using Epinets to Describe the Epistemic Structure of Social Networks

The elements of the EDL we have introduced allow us to refer to parts of a social network in terms of the degree to which agents comprising it share epistemically coherent belief hierarchies. The logical (syntactical) and semantic coherence of underlying beliefs has for some time been known to function not only as an important logical precondition for the achievement of equilibria in games but also as an important facilitator of coordination and co-mobilization (Chwe 1999, 2001). These forms of coherence have been used as explanatory concepts in *reverse* models that seek to explain observed patterns of interaction as outcomes of an equilibrium set of strategies selected by a group of interacting agents given a set of beliefs and utilities. However, they have not been used in *forward* models to make predictions about the specific sets of agents most likely to successfully coordinate and co-mobilize. That is the use we first make of epistemic states and the epinets they form. In particular, we use the states of epistemically linked agents to describe a set of structures (defined by agents, what they know, and what they know others know) for making predictions about achievable coordination and co-mobilization regimes. The set of structures include the following.

Mutual Knowledge Neighborhood $(N_{Kn}(G))$. Subnetwork SG of network G that shares level 2 almost-common knowledge of P. Mutual knowledge neighborhoods can be used to describe networks in which there is knowledge about shared knowledge. Deliberations of professional associations (e.g., the American Medical Association, the Institute of Electrical and Electronics Engineers) can be understood as turning shared knowledge into mutual and sometimes common knowledge as they unfold: each participant discloses by communicating what he or she knows, which in turn becomes known to the other participants. Mutual knowledge undergirds subnetwork mobilization in situations characterized by "I'll go if you go" scenarios (Chwe 1999, 2000). Suppose A knows "I'll go iff B goes" and B knows "I'll go iff A goes." A will *not* mobilize unless she also knows of B that he'll go iff she goes and B will not mobilize unless he knows of A that she'll go iff he goes. If A does indeed know that B will mobilize if and only if she mobilizes, and B knows that A will mobilize if and only if he mobilizes, then mobilization can take place in the two-agent neighborhood (A, B).

Almost-Common Knowledge Neighborhood $(N_{SE}(G))$. Linked subnetwork SG of network G that shares level n common knowledge of P. "Full-common knowledge" neighborhoods ($n = \infty$) can be used to model networks in which relevant knowledge P is self-evident. This condition obtains, for instance, in a situation in which P is uttered by one agent in the presence of all other agents, resulting in an epistemic condition where everyone knows P, everyone knows that everyone knows P, and so forth, ad infinitum. Almost-common knowledge of a finite level n is always a weaker condition than full-common knowledge. If a proposition is common knowledge, it is also mutual knowledge (level 2) and almost-common knowledge (level 3) but not vice versa.

Because commonality of knowledge about relevant facts and about the ways in which agents think about these facts is such an essential condition for network coordination phenomena, and because it can (at least in theory) be established through face-to-face communication (e-mail trails and exchanges can at best establish almost-common knowledge of level n, as Rubinstein (1986) demonstrates), understanding it as an epistemic condition that enables coordination highlights the importance of such otherwise curious phenomena as face-to-face meetings in the age of ubiquitous untethered broadband communications. However, almost-common knowledge is often a sufficient condition for coordination among agents. If Amy and Ben are trying to meet one another on a small island that has a single large hill, but neglect to establish a meeting place beforehand, then a sufficient condition for them to solve their coordination problem is that (1) Amy knows Ben knows Amy knows Ben will head for the hill and (2) Ben knows Amy knows Ben knows Amy will head for the hill (i.e., $n = 3$). Level 2 and level 3 almost-common knowledge represents important conditions for co-mobilization and coordination in networks and, accordingly, preconditions for turning network closure into social capital whose value resides in enabling co-mobilization and coordination.

Figure 2.8 graphically depicts the different "epistemic regions" of a network—in terms of the sharedness (distribution, commonality of various degrees) of agents within the network with respect to a proposition (or a set of propositions), P—that encode facts of joint relevance to the epistemically connected agents.

Network Epistemics and the Explanation of Social Network Phenomena

The epistemic landscape and the topology of epinets describing the beliefs relevant to a set of networked agents seem crucial to social network analysis; the structure and dynamics of the landscape constitutes a critical set of

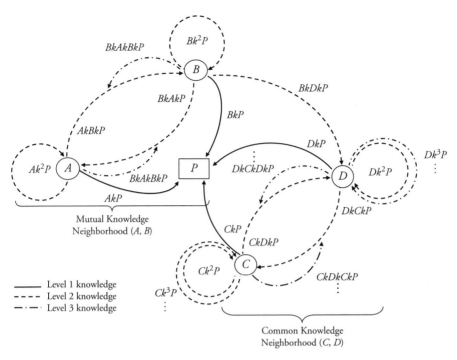

FIGURE 2.8 Epinet Describing a Social Network in Terms of Epistemic States
SOURCE: Adapted from Moldoveanu and Baum, 2011.

explanatory mechanisms for well-established social network effects such as coordination, brokerage, and closure. Let us now briefly consider a variety of familiar network problems—network formation, coordinated mobilization, status, trust, and information spread—in order to illustrate, in a preliminary manner, the ways in which our EDL and a theory of network epistemics can help deepen and sharpen the explanatory power of social network analysis. We emphasize the logical dependence of existing explanatory models on assumptions about the underlying epistemic states of connected agents.

Network Formation. Economic treatments of network formation typically ask which networks tend to form when self-interested agents are free to associate with any other agents; such treatments also inquire about the relative efficiency of different patterns of association as a function of (1) the *value function* mapping each trade or sequence of trades to a value metric and (2) an *allocation rule R* that maps each $(n + 1)$-*tuple* made up of the value v associated with an n-agent interaction and the specific n agents that participated in the interaction into an n-tuple comprising the fractions of v claimed ex post by each of the n agents (Hendricks, Piccione, and Tan 1999; Jackson 2005). Empirically minded networks researchers have reason to ask, "What are the epistemic conditions that support the resulting predictions of efficient network formation?"

At the oblivious end of the epistemic spectrum, if there is a value v to be realized by agents j and k by transacting, but they are not *both* aware of it, we expect that the transaction will be foregone, in spite of the fact that it would have been advantageous for both agents to engage in it. If only j knows of v, then, to be able to predict that v will materialize, we need to posit a mechanism by which j will credibly inform k of it. Not any mechanism will do, as the large body of literature on cheap talk illustrates (Farrell 1996): only one will make j's communication of v credible to k. Postulating such a mechanism involves us in the conjecture of additional epistemic conditions on j and k: k must either trust j (raising questions about the epistemic conditions under which trust obtains) or have a communicative interaction that makes j's transmission of v to k self-reinforcing, which *also* involves a set of assumptions about k's epistemic states on behalf of j.

Coordinated Mobilization. Chwe (1999, 2000) considers a model for social mobilization in which agents are connected in a communication/interaction network whose structure is common knowledge among them. Each agent has two options—mobilize (M) and do not mobilize (NM)—and a utility function that associates a payoff with each of the possible consequences of that agent's actions. These consequences depend on whether or not a sufficient number of *other* agents in the same network mobilize, and this condition holds for each in turn. Chwe (2000) argues that common knowledge of payoffs at the level of a minimum mobilization unit determines the minimum sufficient network that mobilizes: an agent mobilizes (as measured by the net benefit) iff at least two of his neighbors mobilize as well, and each neighbor knows this and knows that every one of the three neighbors knows it. In this way, mobilization takes place.

Interactive epistemic states are crucial to mobilization models of this kind. One can take cliques (fully connected subnetworks) to be synonymous with pockets of local common knowledge. But they need not be synonymous, as members of a clique need not all *trust* one another to the level required for communication establishing that common knowledge will take place. Consider a situation in which there is a clique-wide shared suspicion that one group member is a spy—a suspicion that is mutual knowledge, but not common knowledge, among all members but the putative spy. Establishing common knowledge of the spy without tipping him/her off requires precisely the kind of communicative trust that the clique does not enjoy. Nor is full-common knowledge *necessary* in many mobilization scenarios. *Mutual knowledge* of co-mobilization conditions may suffice.

One may communicate with several others who are all communicating with each other (i.e., be part of a clique), yet the mobilizability profile of each agent may not come to be common knowledge among clique members. The implication is that we cannot infer common knowledge of mobilization thresholds from clique membership and that we need tools that help us describe epistemic states and events in networks in greater detail (i.e., in terms of level 1, 2, 3 . . . *almost-common knowledge* and more complex epistemic conditions like trust) The tools required must build leading indicators of mobilization potential within a network.

Status. The status of an agent in a network is an important explanatory variable in theories of interorganizational networks (Podolny 1993; Benjamin and Podolny 1999) and is sometimes defined by the agent's Bonacich centrality (Bonacich 1987), which measures the relative connectedness of agents to other agents in the network who are themselves well-connected. The Bonacich measure is easily applied to networks in cases where agents are (well-) cited, referenced, publicized, and so forth, in forums that are (well-) attended—hence, its shorthand description as an agent-specific measure of *connectedness to the well-connected* or of *knownness to the well-known*.

Bonacich centrality does not, however, capture many of the ways in which status differences matter, because (1) it does not admit any semantic content (i.e., one is well connected to the well-connected or not, rather than *known for positive/negative quality P by those who are themselves known for positive/negative quality P*); and (2) it does not easily allow for an intuitive recursive generalization to higher levels of connectedness that may matter (i.e., knownness to those who are themselves well known for their well-knownness to well-known others). A precise description language for epistemic states accommodates useful extensions of classical status measures, and it allows us to posit mechanisms by which agents can change their status through the strategic manipulation of the semantic contents of their measures of relative knownness (i.e., in the structure of what they are known for).

Trust. Trust, a tricky variable that can benefit from detailed epistemic analysis, is often defined as "the mutual expectation of cooperative behavior" (Burt and Knez 1995). More detailed definitions are possible, but let us unpack this common one. We focus on "mutual": j expects k to act cooperatively and vice versa. But if j does not expect k to expect her to act cooperatively, there will be situations (e.g., a finite-horizon prisoner's dilemma game payoff structure) in which it is logically incorrect for j to expect k to behave cooperatively. This induces a belief structure for the pair in which (1) j trusts k but (2) j does not expect k to trust her and therefore (3) j finds it irrational to trust k, by the definition of mutual expectation of cooperation, which may or may not lead to a reversal of (1), depending on how j resolves the inconsistency that results. Persevering in believing (1) has costs for j, who must come to grips with the resulting proposition: (4) *I am irrational*, absent some other reason for continuing to trust k while knowing that k does not trust her. To avoid such problems, the expectation of cooperative behavior must be at least *mutual knowledge* between j and k: each must know the other knows it lest we run into problems of logical coherence.

Now we focus on "cooperative": j can have cooperative *intentions* that are causally linked to behavior that k may deem counter-cooperative: j may intend to help k, for example, but produce behavior that hurts him. Thus, the precise mapping of observable states of the world onto imputed intentions should be mutual knowledge between j and k as well: j and k should impute the same "intentionality" to the same observable behaviors they see each other produce.

This is complicated but by itself still insufficient: the expectation of cooperative behavior is not restricted to observed behaviors, but also involves *unobserved* behaviors. If I trust you (by the standard definition), I am confident that you will act cooperatively in circumstances that neither of us has experienced before: I know that "whatever happens, you will act cooperatively."

Finally, we focus on "whatever happens": to infer that you have acted cooperatively in a situation *neither one of us had anticipated*, the rules that you use to map a "behavior" onto an "intention" must be known to me and the rules that I use to accomplish the same feat must be known to you: they must also be mutual knowledge. No doubt, trust is an elusive phenomenon. Indeed, it is elusive in part because it is an epistemically complicated phenomenon but nevertheless an intelligible one that can be elucidated through analysis of its epistemic structure. The epistemic analysis of trust aims to turn an elusive phenomenon into a merely "complicated" one.

Information Spread. Decay functions are standard ways in which network theorists produce (network-distance-weighted) measures of inter-agent separation (Burt 1992). If j is distance D away from k (in network terms, D is usually denoted by the number of network edges that j must traverse to get to k), then a plausible "decay function" that can be used to discount the strength of the tie between j and k is e^{-rD}, where r is some constant. The *conductivity* of the network is usually poor and almost always assumed to be isotropic, or identical in all directions. Information is distorted, misreported, unreported, and *dis-* or *mis*trusted as it makes its way through the "grapevine," but these informational decays are modeled as similar across different grapevines.

Is decay an inevitable function of network distance? If so, under what conditions is it isotropic? Can we not have *superconductive* paths and sub-networks within a network that preserve both the accuracy and trustworthiness of the information reported? If such superconductive paths exist, then we can expect to find different levels of conductivity—and, accordingly, *network anisotropy*—similar to the variety we see at the levels of cliques, brokers, and center-periphery networks (Burt 1992). The keys to a more precise model of network conductivity are the usual suspects for an applied epistemologist: trust and status (or reputation), each of which needs an epistemic undergirding.

Does the Epistemic Description Language Deliver on Our Desiderata?

We began this chapter with a set of objectives that our EDL should deliver on, and this is a good time to take stock and appraise its performance under the rubrics we introduced:

Precision and Subtlety. The EDL supplies a syntax that represents the various ways in which human agents relate to (truth-functional) propositions in a precise way, but it does not restrict, ex hypothesi, the range of epistemic states that they can be represented as holding. Unlike standard state space models in game theory, our EDL does not preclude agents' states of ignorance and oblivion vis-à-vis propositions; also, it allows us to distinguish between agents' epistemic models—what they think is true and what they think others think is true—and our models of agents' epistemic models—what we think is true and what we think agents think other agents think is true. The resulting epistemic logic is also sufficiently flexible to accommodate more subtle epistemic states—such as subjunctive beliefs underlying intuitions about confidence—for which standard epistemic models do not have "conceptual room."

Operationalizability. The EDL's conceptual and graphical description tool kit makes it quickly operationalizable for rapid mapping of arbitrarily sized epinets. It does not require complex "translation" between the standard tools of network researchers (surveys, questionnaires) and the language in which agents and their epistemic states are represented—as is required, for instance, by Harsanyi's (1967, 1968a, 1968b) theory of types.

Logical Auditability. The EDL maps epinets onto a set of statements (e.g., $AkBkAkP$) that represent propositions whose truth values can be independently ascertained and that, moreover, can form the basis of higher-level epistemic states. The resulting statements allow us to describe "who knows what about whom, and when" in a social network and to derive hypotheses about the logical implications of the epistemic states of each agent.

Fit with Theoretical and Empirical Models. Because epinets are themselves networks, they permit treatment using the basic analytical tools employed by network researchers generally. These tools typically specify and measure the topological properties of a network—clustering, closure, centrality, diameter—and make predictions about the evolution of the network on the basis of such properties. Because it is an expanded, directed graph, an epinet is amenable to precisely the same analyses. Moreover, because epinets are representable as statements using epistemic logic operators, they are also compatible with the tools for analyzing human interactions through the precise representation of "everyday" insights in a formal language.

Summary

We have introduced a language for describing the epistemic states of human agents and the relationships among them. This language, EDL, allows researchers to measure and represent epistemic states and structures based on surveys and empirical research instruments with which they are familiar, and it allows modelers to symbolically manipulate epistemic state descriptors to derive predictions (or to create proofs regarding epistemic preconditions) regarding the statics and dynamics of epistemic structures in social networks. We are now in possession of an epistemic network modelers' tool kit that we will use to illuminate and deepen our understanding of a variety of network relations, structures, and phenomena.

Chapter 3

"What Do You Think I Think You Think about It?"

Epinets as a Tool for the Study of Network Structure

We show how epinets ground the analysis of social network phenomena such as broker-age and closure: epinets associated with coordination, communication, and collaboration phenomena constitute the "epistemic glue" that renders social network structures robustly identifiable and causally relevant. "Coordination" and "collaboration"—important capabili-ties or propensities of cohesive social networks—are enabled by an epistemic coherence that epinets help us to unpack and render precise. Epinets also bring into relief informa-tional and epistemic properties of "brokerage" and the epistemic operations that are neces-sarily embedded in brokers. We empirically examine the logical and epistemic preconditions for co-mobilization and coordination, finding that they are lacking in a situation in which we would expect them to be found, on the basis of the network's structure. We introduce a language for analyzing coordination and co-mobilization, which we use to describe the epistemic properties of agents who are pivotal to coordination and co-mobilization ("coor-dinators" and "mobilizers") and to describe those of the central propositions that form the epistemic core of coordination and co-mobilization processes ("coordinata"). We extend our epistemic approach to the analysis of status, where the EDL allows us to make more precise distinctions among levels of knownness and fame of connected agents.

Social capital—the advantages an agent accrues by virtue of her position in a social network—"works" through a host of mechanisms loosely categorized under the rubrics of brokerage and closure (Coleman 1988c; Burt 1992, 2005). Brokers "broker" ideas, trust, and goodwill by establishing a bidirec-tional channel that bridges at least two disconnected subnetworks, each of which is in some sense internally cohesive.

The cohesiveness of the brokered subnetworks is critical to what brokering means: if there are no identifiable, separate subnetworks to be spanned, there is no brokerage. A broker can broker ideas between economic sociologists and neoclassical economists only if these two groups are sufficiently cohesive to be identifiable (and self-identifying) as subnetworks in the broader com-munity of social scientists, and if the broker somehow succeeds in channeling information credibly from one group to the other. Of course, information and knowledge ("ideas") are not the only brokerable epistemic objects. One can broker trust, awareness, higher-order knowledge, and confidence, all of which can be understood as more complicated—yet intelligible—epistemic objects.

Closure "closes" the network footprint of an agent who has relationships with other agents, who in turn have relationships with one another. The advantages of closure depend on the specific structure and topology of the network and on the cohesiveness of the subnetwork that is "closed" by closure. High-closure networks "echo" (Burt 2005) the actions and words of the individual agent, making it more difficult for her to unilaterally deviate from the network's implicit and explicit norms and commitments. Cohesion is critical to how closure closes or forecloses the network footprint of the agent because it is only by virtue of a commonly held set of beliefs, norms, and commitments that individual deviations and departures can be measured, monitored, and sanctioned.

Cohesion and the Realization of Social Capital from Brokerage and Closure

Cohesion is critical to understanding both brokerage and closure. We use the term "cohesion" rather than "tie density" or "agent connectedness" or "network diameter," purposely. Cohesion is not tainted (yet) by reductive structural analyses and simplifying representations, yet it has an air of rigor. An "air of rigor" does not mean "rigor," however, and this is where the analysis of epinets can contribute.

At the cost of some complexity, epistemic representations of networked agents allow us to illuminate brokerage and closure in a way that makes the cohesion required for each more precise. Epistemically, cohesion is coherence among the interactive epistemic states of two or more agents. Alice and Bob are cohesive in the epistemic sense if what Alice thinks about a matter of mutual relevance, what Bob thinks, what he thinks Alice thinks, what she thinks Bob thinks, what she thinks he thinks she thinks, and so forth, are all coherent.

We have defined cohesion as coherence, but have not yet defined coherence. Here we have several options. Recall that we used propositions and propositional beliefs (*It is raining*) as arguments of epistemic states (*Alice knows it is raining*). Propositions, unlike names of objects and collections of "states of the world," can stand in relationships of logical entailment, negation, and independence relative to one another. Thus, it is possible to define cohesion in terms of coherence among epistemic states, provided that we have a satisfactory account of coherence. In this regard, we have at least two options.

One option is to limit coherence to deductive logical consistency and compatibility and to limit "logical" to first-order logic. This has the advantage that we can "do" network epistemics in the same way we "do" game theory: by establishing an informational base from which we can prove various hypotheses as deductive theorems. It has the disadvantage that everyday human discourse is not structured by deductive logic alone, but makes use of several other forms of inference. First-order logic also has several well-known lacunae in terms of being able to represent certain eminently sensible patterns of judgment that humans reliably produce.

A second option is to define coherence as logical consistency and compatibility but to expand what we mean by logic to include *deductive, inductive,* and *abductive* forms of logical inference among the set of syntactical rules by which we adjudicate coherence—as well as "fuzzy" and "deviant" logics, including three- and four-valued logics. This option has the advantage of making epistemic network analysis more intuitive and congenial as a tool for making empirical inquiries. However, it also reduces the sharpness of the predictions we can make as a result of understanding the epistemic structure of a network—the interactive belief hierarchies it forms around one or more relevant propositions.

We pursue here the first option on grounds of parsimony; however, without loss of generality of the epistemic approach, we can augment the extension of "logic" to include other forms of inference and other logics altogether.

Understood as the logical coherence of first- and higher-order beliefs regarding the truth value of mutually relevant propositions, epistemic cohesion is necessary but not sufficient for adequately analyzing "network cohesion." The kind of cohesion worthy of characterizing an identifiable group is more than just the logical coherence of interpersonal beliefs about a set of propositions.

For instance, Alice and Bob are friends. They interact copiously at the level of gossip and sporting events. On these topics, their beliefs may synchronize perfectly: each knows the scores of the last 10 Wimbledon finals and knows the other knows them and so forth. But they may not be able to successfully coordinate their actions in certain domains because they belong to different disciplines. Alice is an economist; Bob is a programmer. She represents human behavior in terms of choices, preferences, and beliefs. He thinks of humans as imperfect executors of algorithmic routines and procedures. To her, a person's preferences do not change—though that person's beliefs about how best to satisfy them might; he, on the other hand, sees the very essence of humanity in a person's ability to change the algorithms that describe his or her behavior in adaptive ways. Producing a joint article on the mathematical analysis of behavior will be a difficult enterprise for Alice and Bob, both in the sense that it will be laborious and in the sense that the probability is small that a truly collaborative and successful piece of joint work will result.

Many of the difficulties Alice and Bob will encounter undertaking such a project arise from the fact that they differ radically in their interpretations of what appear to be "the same" sense data. These differences, along with Alice's and Bob's ignorance and sometimes obliviousness of them, will give rise to repeated failures of coordination. They will violate each other's expectations when they try to interact around the meaning of a particular word ("decisions," say).

The coordinative difficulties that Alice and Bob will encounter are not limited to concepts and "the meaning of theoretical terms." Given their different backgrounds, they will likely follow different communication norms, particularly those of argumentation, justification, validity, and persuasiveness. She may insist on provability from a set of axioms as a norm or goal of justification. He may care about provability but not about any particular set of axioms. The two will attempt to communicate, but will find that they can neither agree to a set of norms of justification nor successfully agree to disagree about them since these norms are a prerequisite to further communication.

This is not a case in which private games, being too dangerous, can be salvaged by a third party acting as a monitor (Burt and Knez 1995), because this particular game is a language game. Charlie, connected individually to both Alice and Bob through regular interactions in different domains (ballet and golf, say) but significantly different from each of them in terms of epistemic commitments, will not be able to exercise the right kind of monitoring and sanctioning of agreements that Alice and Bob have made to each other in the domain of "uses of language and justification norms." This is not because Charlie will not "see" that some failure of coordination has occurred but rather because he will ascribe and impute agency and responsibility for that problem in a language that is alien and therefore binding to neither Alice nor Bob.

The interactive epistemic preconditions for shared understanding are likely brought into sharpest relief by the "natural language" school of analytic philosophy that culminated in the works of Austin (1961, 1962) and Grice (1968, 1969) and particularly in Grice's (1969) work on "conversational implicature" and the role of a cooperative principle of communication that must be common knowledge among interlocutors if they are to understand each other. Grice argued that the way to make sense of what people say to one another in many—perhaps most—settings is to ascribe to them shared, common knowledge of a cooperative principle that allows them to ascribe meaning to each other's words. This principle comprises a set of maxims: *informativeness* (say neither no more nor no less than necessary; be neither cryptic nor redundant; make your contribution relevant to the subject and context of the conversation), *validity* and *sincerity* (do not say what you believe to be untrue; do not say anything for which you lack sufficient evidence), and *expressivity* (avoid ambiguity and obscurity of expression).

In this case, proposition *P* is conversationally implied to agent *B* by proposition *Q* uttered by agent *A* iff the maxims of cooperative communication, together with proposition *P*, logically entail proposition *Q*. For example, if a bellman sees a guest loaded down with luggage and with a quizzical look on her face, and says to her, "It is to the left" to indicate the drop-off room, the speech act works for three reasons: (1) it fits the shared background that both guest and bellman know (and that each knows the other knows); (2) the fact that the drop-off room is to the left follows from the utterance; and (3) both interlocutors hold common knowledge of the norms of conversational implicature, which allows them to interpret the utterance as informative and relevant (she looks quizzical and has luggage in her hands), efficient (short), and valid (it is true, and he knows she knows he has reason to know where the drop-off room is).

Conversational implicature—the fabric not only of lay social interactions but also of the ritualized interactions of academic research and teaching—gives us a way of further unpacking the *epistemic glue* that holds various disciplinary subfields together. The statement "This does not satisfy the completeness axiom"— uttered by one rational choice theorist to another in a seminar in which the first presents a new model of choice under uncertainty—"works" because each understands (and knows the other understands) both the nature of the completeness axiom in rational choice theory and its relevance to the model at hand.

The same utterance, however, would not work if one of the interlocutors were a network sociologist trying to "describe" the behavior of a social agent with no intent to build an axiomatic model or to criticize the axiomatic base of another. The epistemic preconditions for felicitous conversational inferences—inferences that work to the effect desired by both interlocutors—can thus be traced to a base of shared propositions (axioms, methodological principles) that enable speakers to make sense of each other's speech acts via some version of a cooperation principle that is itself common knowledge among them.

The Epistemic Structure of Cohesion: Co-mobilization and Coordination

What makes a network the one it is must be related to the distribution and commonality of certain types of knowledge and information among the agents that make up the group to which the network corresponds. And however we define "ties" among networked agents—interaction frequency, self-reported perception of friendship, objectively ascertained patterns of collaboration—they matter to the dynamics of the network to the extent that they matter to its epistemic structure.

We are concerned with making the epistemic conception of a network more accessible to both analytical modeling and empirical study. To do so, we focus on the epistemic preconditions for two processes central to social groups generally and social networks in particular: co-mobilization and co-ordination. Whatever makes a group cohesive must make coordination and co-mobilization among its members easier—that is, more likely to happen, in a shorter period of time and at a lower average and total expected cost.

Co-mobilization. Co-mobilization is a kind of coordinative process, but it has a simpler epistemic structure than does coordination (Chwe 1999, 2000). In a co-mobilization scenario, several people must decide, independently, whether or not to mobilize—say to oust a dictator or CEO or some other dominant agent. Everyone would prefer to see the dominant agent (DA) fall (or leave) rather than remain in power (or stay). But no one wants to be the only one, or one of a very few, to mobilize: the probability of a violent reaction from the DA is too great and the private consequences too costly. Thus, each agent operates according to a simple private rule: *I will go if (at least n percent of the) others go.*

If Alice and Bob are among the would-be mobilizers and their threshold for mobilizing is low (each will mobilize if at least one other person does so), then what is required for *both* Alice and Bob to mobilize is for each to know that the other will operate according to the rule *R*: *I will mobilize if at least one other person mobilizes*. *Mutual* knowledge of *R* (that is, level 2 almost-common knowledge), in other words, suffices for co-mobilization because it turns the conditional rule *R* into a biconditional rule: *I will mobilize iff at least one other person mobilizes*; that is, *I will mobilize if at least one other person mobilizes* and *At least one other person will mobilize if I mobilize*.

Note that this is not a *necessary* condition for co-mobilization, especially given how we define knowledge: Alice may believe with probability *p* (*p-believe*) that Bob will mobilize if she does, and Bob (with probability *q*), may *q-believe* that Alice will mobilize if he does; moreover, although the probabilities in question are jointly too low to justify co-mobilization, some mishap—such as an action by Alice that leads Bob to overestimate *q*—may cause some action by Bob that induces Alice to overestimate *p*, resulting in co-mobilization in spite of the fact that neither *knows* the other will follow *R*.

Mutual knowledge of the private mobilization rule *R*, then—including each agent's co-mobilization threshold—is an all-else-equal sufficient condition for co-mobilization. "Sufficient" means logically sufficient, which need not be equivalent to causal or material sufficiency. Whether or not logical sufficiency is a good proxy for material and causal sufficiency is an empirical question, and its pursuit is enabled by mapping the epistemic networks in co-mobilization scenarios and the correlation between the epinets of the relevant subnetwork and the probability that it will co-mobilize.

For instance, perhaps Alice knows that Belinda intends to follow rule *R* and has a co-mobilization threshold of 1, but she does not trust Belinda's ability to follow that rule in practice because of "weakness of the will" or poor connectivity between normative thought and purposive action. Such issues can be addressed by introducing *modal* and *subjunctive* epistemic structures (Alice's beliefs about what Belinda *would* do *if* certain events were to come to pass), which we introduce in Chapter 4 to support our analysis of the epistemics of trust. But suppose for now that intertemporal coherence of preferences and performative rationality are valid assumptions regarding networked agents. Then we can posit that co-mobilizability is a good behavioral measure of the cohesiveness of a network, and that a sound epistemic precondition of co-mobilizability is *mutual knowledge of co-mobilization rules and thresholds*. This allows us to link an epistemic measure of network cohesiveness (mutual knowledge) to a behavioral measure of it (the ability of network agents to co-mobilize in a situation of common interest).

Chwe (1999) studied how the topology of a network influences the probability of achieving co-mobilization as a function of individual agents' co-mobilization thresholds. If each agent is connected to at most two other agents, for instance, and the co-mobilization threshold of each agent is 3 or greater, then, given that each agent follows rule R with a threshold of 3 or higher, the network will never mobilize in spite of all agents' mutual knowledge of R and their co-mobilization thresholds. This adds an important qualifier to the relevance of mutual knowledge for co-mobilization: even in the presence of mutual knowledge, co-mobilization is dependent on network structure. If agents in a network know this, however, and if they also know the structure of the network—or even their own small neighborhood in it—then they can seek to adapt by enlarging their own subnetwork to the point where co-mobilization *can* occur *if* other agents also engage in or respond favorably to such "network prospecting."

Suppose that this prospecting requires some form of co-mobilization, such as investing in a common web site, answering invitations to connect, and sharing personal information. Then mutual knowledge of personal network structure (*I know your subnetwork and you know my subnetwork*) will facilitate the mobilization required for each agent to engage in the prospecting required to determine if the structure of his/her personal subnetwork, rather than the preferences of everyone in the network, is the factor impeding co-mobilization (and eventual removal of the DA).

If the network is fully connected and knowledge of an agent's subnetwork entails holding true beliefs about it, then the condition that the personal subnetwork structure be mutual knowledge among network agents requires that every agent know the structure of the entire network (which comprises the collective personal subnetworks). This, again, is a logical condition that functions as a network self-discovery protocol, as illustrated in Figure 3.1. If the neighborhoods of agents A and E overlap that of agent D, and if agents A and E know their own neighborhoods and the neighborhoods of the agents to whom they are connected, then both will come to know of each other's neighborhood as well as the neighborhood of agent D, who is in their respective neighborhoods. Their knowledge of the network will therefore expand

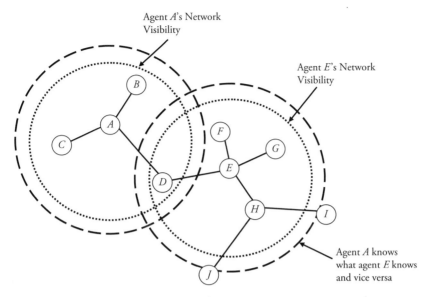

Agent A's Network
Visibility

Agent E's Network
Visibility

Agent A knows
what agent E knows
and vice versa

FIGURE 3.1 Network Self-Discovery Protocol

incrementally as agents come to know the neighborhoods of agents that overlap with their own.

Whether or not agents know the structure of their own networks is an
empirical question (which we take up soon) whose investigation can shed
light on the link between the epistemic states of networked agents and the
probability of collective action enabled by these states.

Coordination. Coordination problems are varied, as are their epistemic preconditions. Consider the "simple" problem of confirming the time and place
of a meeting arranged through an e-mail exchange—a problem formally posed
by Rubinstein (1989) in his "e-mail game" model but also one that arises daily
between interacting agents. Alex proposes to Beth that the two of them meet
at five o'clock on Thursday afternoon in Harvard Square. She writes back
electronically to confirm. If Alex receives her confirmation, he knows that she
knows he intends to meet her at the appointed time and place and, provided
that she knows he knows that she also knows this—which he does not—she
will be there. He does not know this because she does not know that he has
opened and read her e-mail confirmation, and he knows that she does not
know this. Suppose now that he confirms her confirmation. Once again, he

does not know that she has received and opened his e-mail, so he does not know that she knows of his confirmation. And so forth.

Full common knowledge is required for both Alex and Beth to be in epistemic states that warrant certainty—at least about intent—regarding their meeting. And full common knowledge is not achievable by a series of e-mail exchanges, which will never be able to re-create the epistemic landscape of a face-to-face meeting. Logically speaking, given all of the epistemic and logical requirements for coordination, Alex and Beth will not meet.

However, meetings set up successfully by e-mail are commonplace and often require no more than one confirmation because there is common knowledge of the fact that the communication channel—e-mail—is sufficiently reliable for one confirmation to represent an epistemic shortcut that proxies for full-common knowledge. Real human agents, in contrast to idealized rational agents, treat e-mail exchanges similarly to face-to-face communication, which establishes common knowledge in virtue of co-presence. And, if asked, agents can rationalize this shortcut based on the reliability of the communication channel, which itself is common knowledge.

Morris and Shin (1993) realized that coordination problems are solvable even by idealized rational agents, provided they make their decisions on the basis of the expected value of the gains and losses of coordinative successes and failures. For Alex, the downside to showing up at the appointed time and place and not finding Beth has to be weighed against the probability he assigns to her not having received his message, which may be further decomposed into the probability of a technical glitch that prevented his e-mail from reaching her inbox and the probability that she did not open his message and read it (but which may exclude the probability that she has a sudden lapse of memory or that she derives pleasure from standing him up). In turn, the expected value of these coordination failure costs should be weighed against the expected value of successfully meeting at the appointed time and place, and both weighted by the probability that the meeting will take place conditional on his background knowledge and the nature of their messages exchanged to date.

As Morris and Shin also pointed out, the communication protocol and channel between the agents are relevant to such cost-benefit calculations. Alex's estimate of the reliability of the communication channel to Beth should increase with every confirmation message he successfully receives from her. Moreover, if it is common knowledge that their communication channel has high reliability, then their subjective probabilities regarding a successful outcome may be high enough, conditional on even a single confirmation. Although there are scenarios in which such common knowledge is not a good assumption (Alex is backpacking in the Amazon with an iPhone or is walking in Manhattan with a BlackBerry), high-reliability communication protocols and channels—and the common knowledge thereof—can serve to substantively improve the chances of coordination.

Of course, the successful confirmation of the meeting is not the only coordination problem that Alex and Beth must resolve. Harvard Square is a large place and, even with the best of intentions, two people can easily slip by each other unnoticed. Nevertheless, there are several more narrowly circumscribed places that stand out because they are intimately and uniquely associated with it: the Harvard Bookstore, the newsstand at the intersection of Massachusetts Avenue and JFK Street, the four entrances to Harvard Yard.

There are at least two more potential focal points, bringing the total to eight. If the eight points are sufficiently far apart and Alex and Beth pick different points, subsequently searching the alternatives in some sequence, they can still fail to meet in spite of having solved the problems of credible confirmation. If, on the other hand, Alex knows that Beth will pick the newsstand as the meeting place—perhaps because she has mentioned it to him in the past—and if Beth also knows that Alex knows this and he knows that she knows that he knows, then the two still have good odds of meeting up at the appointed time. Once again, a finite almost-common knowledge hierarchy of interactive beliefs (level 3 in this case) takes the place of the full common knowledge normally required for the successful realization of the jointly optimal outcome in the coordination game.

Not all coordination problems are created equal, however, and each is resolved according to background rules and epistemic preconditions that are specific to the problem statement. This contingency of coordinative processes on epistemic preconditions is an opportunity for empirical inquiry (although it may frustrate a priori game-theoretic modeling of coordination). To the extent that coordinatability is a good proxy for a network's cohesion (being the degree to which the agents in a network can successfully coordinate on the achievement of outcomes that are valuable to the network as a whole), and given that the epistemic preconditions for coordination are dependent both on the specific group of agents trying to coordinate and on what they are trying to coordinate, we should be able to make inferences about coordinatability by measuring interactive epistemic states and make inferences about network cohesion from the (inferred) coordinatability of a network, given specific domains in which coordination is desirable.

Cliques, Central Agents, and Coordinata. The epistemic approach to network cohesion also unpacks questions regarding specific network and subnetwork structures and topologies and their effects on social capital. "Cliques" and "hub-and-spoke" networks, which feature central agents that are densely connected to a large number of agents that are sparsely connected, are obvious candidates for an epistemic analysis, representing basic building blocks for the analysis of network structure.

Whatever makes a clique—a fully connected subgraph of a network—a clique in the vernacular sense of a set of people who are "in the know" about a mutually salient issue as evidenced by their ability to coordinate their actions for joint gains, must necessarily lean on some enhanced ability of clique members to coordinate and co-mobilize. This implies that members know more about each other's state of knowledge and state of knowledge about each other's knowledge than do nonclique members. Recognizing these logical links allows us to ask the question: "Are fully connected subgraphs of friendship-interaction-collaboration networks better at achieving co-mobilization and coordination by virtue of sharing higher-level (interactive) epistemic states?"

Central agents "know and are known by" others in their network, but that is hardly the entire epistemic story of their network advantage. In the epistemic plane, one can focus on the role of a multiply connected agent (the leader, the DA, the broker) as a *network mobilizer* or a *network coordinator*.

A network mobilizer has valid insight into (1) the structure of the network, (2) others' perceptions of that structure, and (3) the set of mobilization rules (R) and thresholds (S) that are "mutual knowledge" among various subnetworks comprising the network, as illustrated in Figure 3.2. In the figure, the mobilizer's knowledge (mobilization rules and thresholds for network agents) is shown above the semicircle that intersects agent A, and the network structure is shown below. Agent A understands how to mobilize sparsely connected groups to act cohesively by making the "right introductions"—those that decrease barriers to mobilization for the greatest number of agents in the network. (A mobilization barrier is the difference between the minimum number of others that must mobilize for an agent to mobilize and the actual number of others the agent knows will mobilize if he does.) Agent A will also

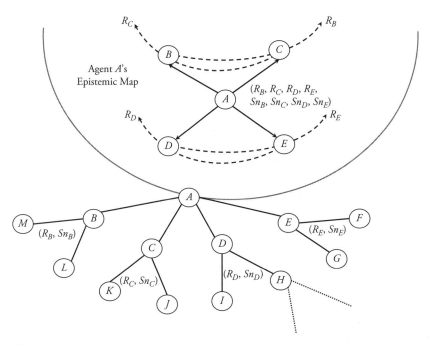

FIGURE 3.2 Mobilizer (Agent A): Epinet of Enabling Epistemic States

understand the precise nature of the "co-mobilization rules" of specific other agents whose connectedness makes them good mobilizers in turn.

A network coordinator, as illustrated in Figure 3.3, knows enough about what other agents know and about what they know that others (including the coordinator) know to make predictions about which of several possible focal points of relevant coordination games are salient to coordination of the network as a whole. Once again, the coordinator's (i.e., agent A's) epistemic state in the figure is shown above the semicircle, and the structure of the network is shown below.

Armed with a suitable instrument for measuring higher-level epistemic agreement and disagreement among network agents, we can ask, "Does centrality confer on the central agent(s) the kind of epistemic advantages that are sufficient conditions for mobilizing and coordinating networks, and, if so, under what conditions?" We do not, as is typically done, simply assume that centrality confers these advantages, and infer an agent's social capital directly from his/her network position.

Coordinata are propositions (such as proposition P in Figure 3.3) that refer to objects and events that are salient to the network as a whole and

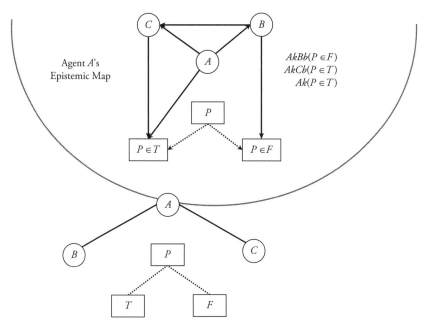

FIGURE 3.3 Coordinator (Agent A): Epinet of Enabling Epistemic States

thereby serve as focal points for its members in coordination games. Epinets explicitly model coordinata as nodes in the epistemic network (along with agents) having edges that represent the *believes* or *knows* relation. Thus, as described in Chapter 2, if *A knows B knows P* (or *AkBkP*), for example, then there exists an arc that spans agents *A*, *B*, and proposition *P*. This allows us to specify the propositions that matter to the coordinatability and mobilizability of a network, to specify the epistemic preconditions for coordination, and to measure the degree of departure of the epistemic network from these preconditions in much the same way that the modeling of human agents specifies choice functions and decision rules under assumptions of rationality, and then measures systematic departures from rationality.

Unlike traditional game-theoretic analyses, epinets operate at the level of propositions rather than events. They require the modeler to make explicit the epistemic state space of the network (including all higher-order and interactive beliefs) as part of the modeling process rather than assume that the logical preconditions for Nash and correlated equilibria are already in place. By taking a syntactic view of the state space (rather than the semantic view of game-theoretic analyses), epinets also help to resolve ambiguities that can arise from different agents using different language systems to refer to the same raw feelings or qualia (e.g., Shin 1993).

The language system used to represent propositions in epinets is itself one of the variables that must be specified by the researcher—in advance of any further modeling. It is true that ambiguity still lurks concerning the ways in which words attach to objects and properties and in the ways in which sentences attach to events and states of affairs—even once a language system and a set of salient propositions are specified. But this ambiguity is no longer hidden by the (semantic) formalism that classically assumes that all agents have the same interpretation of "the same" event.

Understanding Social Networks via Epinets: A Study of Faculty Networks

If cohesion (of the kind that fosters coordinated collective action) is central to the accretion and use of social capital, and if the epistemic imagery of cohesion is to be an explanation-generating engine for social network processes, then it is essential that the empirical tools for probing the epistemic structure of networks be built, assembled, and sharpened to suitable degrees. In particular, take "cohesion" to mean "epistemic coherence" of level 1 beliefs (what you and I know or think to be true), level 2 beliefs (what I think you think regarding the truth value of some proposition P), and level 3 beliefs (what I think you think I think about the truth value of P). In this case, cohesion can be measured and made precise. For some proposition P whose truth value is independently known, Alice and Bob form a cohesive dyad where Alice knows P (which means that P is true by the definition of the *knows* operator), knows that Bob knows P, and knows that he knows she knows P; at the same time, Bob knows P, knows that Alice knows P, and knows that she knows he knows P.

Cohesiveness can be a matter of degree and is tracked by epistemic coherence. Alice may know P and know that Bob knows it, but she may not know that Bob knows she knows it and vice versa. This epistemic gap allows Alice and Bob to act cohesively in some situations but not in others: a difference in measured individual states that makes a difference to predicted joint action. We show that epistemic coherence of this kind underscores the behaviors that we might expect of cohesive network structures by enabling networked agents to co-mobilize, coordinate, and thereby cooperate and collaborate successfully in specific domains. In this way, we show that epistemic coherence should be developed into a full-fledged instrument for performing *network spectroscopy*.

Faculty Networks. We developed a questionnaire to measure both the social network and associated epinets related to "issues"—represented by propositions with well-defined truth values—that are relevant to coordination and co-mobilization of the networked agents surveyed. Using this instrument, we constructed faculty interaction, collaboration, and friendship networks in a disciplinary department of a North American management school (twelve of fifteen faculty participated; eleven provided usable responses), and we measured the betweenness, degree, and eigenvector centrality of each faculty member in each network.[1] The results in Figure 3.4, which graph respondents' level 1 beliefs about alters in the interaction, collaboration, and friendship networks, provide an image of these networks in a language that is familiar to social network researchers.

We then added an epistemic twist to the standard network-mapping process, asking each respondent to answer a set of questions regarding his or her level 2 knowledge (what s/he thinks his/her alters think about their tie), and level 3 knowledge (what s/he thinks his/her alters think s/he thinks about their tie). These results are shown in Figure 3.5, in which the epinet's edges link faculty possessing interactive knowledge at levels 2 and 3 (i.e., NC^2 and NC^3). The epinets indicate that different members of the network have level 2 and level 3 beliefs about the network structure that are often different from true level 1 beliefs and different from each other: what Abe thinks the network of friendship, interaction, and collaboration ties "is" can be quite different from what he thinks Cam thinks it is, and both may think differently from what Abe thinks Cam thinks Abe thinks it is.

To the extent that a mobilizer or coordinator of the department should have valid views of other agents' image of the network in order to solve problems of coordination and co-mobilization, and to the extent that "valid" is taken to mean "logically coherent with the views of other agents in the network," these findings point to a lack of cohesion between what any one agent in the network knows (level 1) and what s/he believes others know (level 2) and what s/he believes others believe s/he knows (level 3).

Faculty-Relevant Propositions: The Substrate(s) of Epinets. To be precise about network coordinatability and mobilizability, we need to be specific about focal points in potential coordination games (and "issues" in mobilization scenarios). Networks do not coordinate in general or in a content-free fashion: they coordinate (or co-mobilize) around issues and events, which are

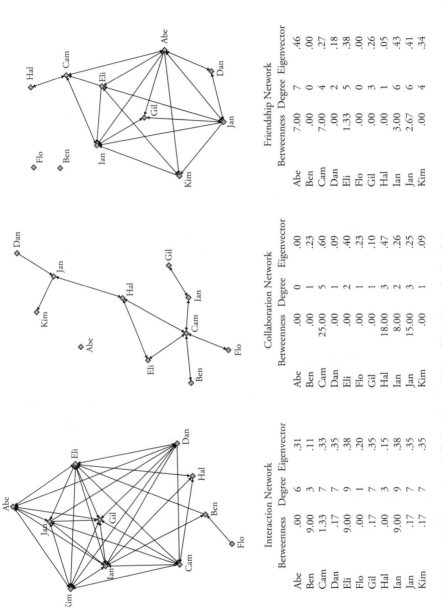

Interaction Network

	Betweenness	Degree	Eigenvector
Abe	.00	6	.31
Ben	9.00	3	.11
Cam	1.33	7	.33
Dan	.17	7	.35
Eli	9.00	9	.38
Flo	.00	1	.20
Gil	.17	7	.35
Hal	.00	3	.15
Ian	9.00	9	.38
Jan	.17	7	.35
Kim	.17	7	.35

Collaboration Network

	Betweenness	Degree	Eigenvector
Abe	.00	0	.00
Ben	.00	1	.23
Cam	25.00	5	.60
Dan	.00	1	.09
Eli	.00	2	.40
Flo	.00	1	.23
Gil	.00	1	.10
Hal	18.00	3	.47
Ian	8.00	2	.26
Jan	15.00	3	.25
Kim	.00	1	.09

Friendship Network

	Betweenness	Degree	Eigenvector
Abe	7.00	7	.46
Ben	.00	0	.00
Cam	7.00	4	.27
Dan	.00	2	.18
Eli	1.33	5	.38
Flo	.00	0	.00
Gil	.00	3	.26
Hal	.00	1	.05
Ian	3.00	6	.43
Jan	2.67	6	.41
Kim	.00	4	.34

FIGURE 3.4 Faculty Interaction, Collaboration, and Friendship Networks (Level 1)

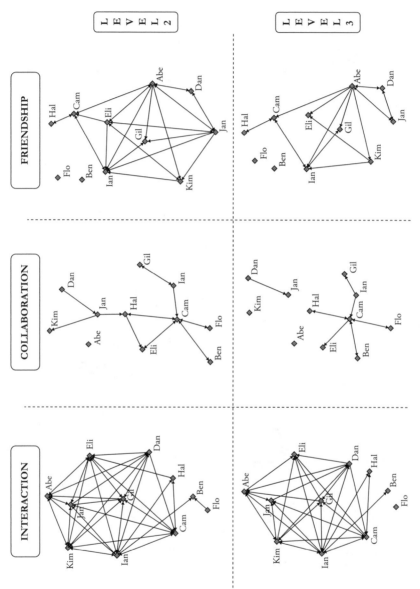

FIGURE 3.5 Faculty Interaction, Collaboration, and Friendship Networks (Levels 2 and 3)

represented via propositions that refer to them. We therefore asked our questionnaire respondents to indicate their state of knowledge regarding the truth value of propositions referring to certain issues of common and immediate concern, including changes to a PhD program run by the department, as well as their beliefs regarding other faculty members' beliefs regarding the truth value of these propositions, and their beliefs regarding other faculty members' beliefs regarding their own beliefs about the truth value of these propositions. The questions had unambiguous and uncontroversial "true/false" answers (corresponding to the truth values of the propositions in question), which could be independently verified by reference to existing documents.

Epinets for the five propositions (a through e) related to the PhD program are shown in Figures 3.6 through 3.8. Figure 3.6 lists the five propositions

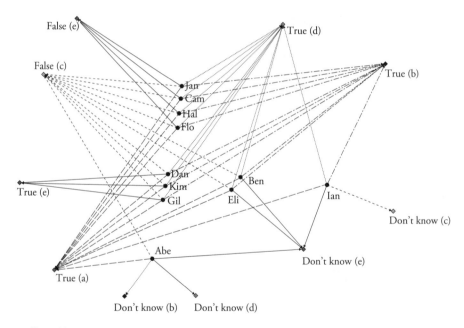

Propositions:
(a) A new proposed curriculum for the PhD program was articulated by . . . and circulated last month to department members: T or F?
(b) The proposed curriculum includes the microeconomics sequence required of graduate students in economics: T or F?
(c) The proposed curriculum requires no course work in sociology: T or F?
(d) The proposed curriculum includes graduate econometrics training in addition to department-specific research methods courses: T or F?
(e) The proposal was discussed by the school-wide PhD program committee and given a conditional endorsement: T or F?

FIGURE 3.6 Level 1 Epinet: PhD Program Propositions (a)–(e)

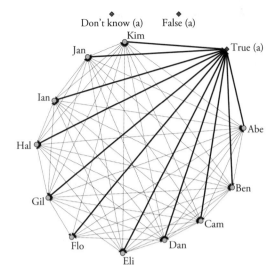

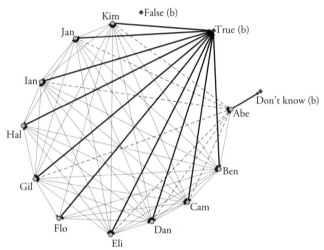

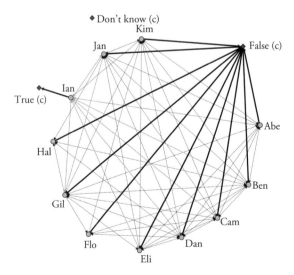

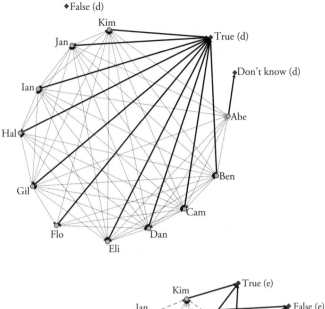

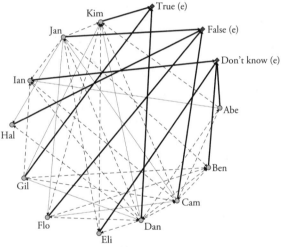

FIGURE 3.7 Level 2 Epinets: Propositions (a)–(e)

and presents the epinet for faculty members' level 1 beliefs regarding them. Figures 3.7 and 3.8 present the epinets for faculty members' level 2 beliefs (what each thinks his/her alters think about the issue) and level 3 beliefs (what each thinks his/her alters think s/he thinks about the issue) for each proposition separately. There are, again, significant discrepancies among the epistemic

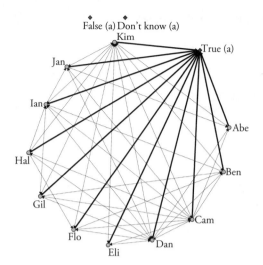

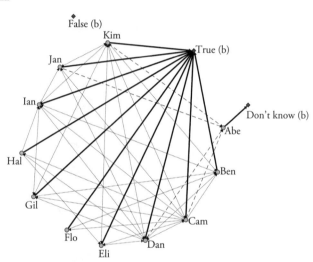

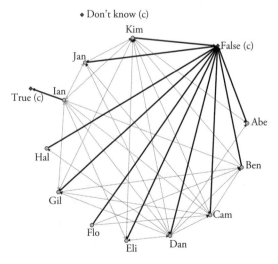

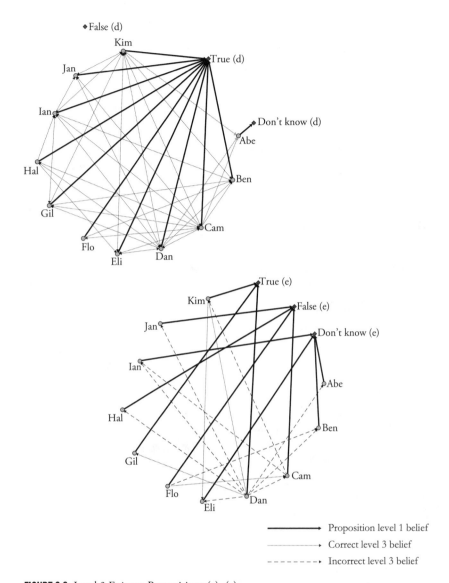

FIGURE 3.8 Level 3 Epinets: Propositions (a)–(e)

networks at different levels. Indeed, here we find substantial evidence of *inaccurate* level 2 and level 3 beliefs (i.e., *AkP* but *BkAkQ*). Although there are no inaccurate level 2 or level 3 beliefs regarding proposition a, there are inaccuracies regarding propositions b and d with respect to Abe who ~*kP*(*b*, *d*), but who others think knows *P*(*b*, *d*), and regarding proposition c with respect to and Ian who $kP(c) \in T$, but who others think knows $P(c) \in F$, as well as widespread inaccuracies in level 2 and level 3 beliefs regarding proposition e.

If we take coherent level 1 and level 2 beliefs to be a proxy for the instantiation of epistemic preconditions for successful mobilization of the network around an issue, and coherent level 1, level 2, and level 3 beliefs to be proxies for epistemic preconditions for the successful coordination of the network around focal points categorized by the events to which the propositions refer, we see that—even in a relatively densely connected network made up of agents who are expected to be sophisticated in terms of both network effects (several are social network theorists) and epistemic preconditions for equilibrium selection in coordination games (several are applied economists with backgrounds in game theory)—the structure of the network belies a level of epistemic cohesion that does not bode well for the coordinatability and mobilizability of the network as a whole.

Centrality, Cliques, and Coherence. The data were further analyzed to address two additional questions. First, to what extent does network centrality (measured using betweenness, degree, and eigenvector measures) confer advantages of (1) accurate level 2 mutual knowledge about other agents' beliefs, and (2) accurate level 3 almost-common knowledge about other agents' knowledge of a focal agent's own beliefs? To answer this question, we correlated our questionnaire respondents' network centrality with their level 2 and level 3 knowledge regarding the five propositions regarding the departmental PhD program noted previously.

Level 2 knowledge (NC^2) was measured for each faculty member, A, on an issue-by-issue basis as the number of other faculty members, B, for which $AkBkP$ & $BkAkP$ was true—that is, for which A and B correctly identified each other's responses (whether true or false). Level 3 knowledge (NC^3) was measured for each faculty member, A, as the number of other faculty members, B, for which $AkBkAkP$ & $BkAkBkP$ was true—that is, for which A and B knew that each had correctly identified the other's responses (again, whether true or false). This analysis examined commonly held assumptions about the role of central agents in mobilizing and coordinating social networks, for which accurate level 2 knowledge and level 3 knowledge are epistemic preconditions.

Our findings are shown in Table 3.1 for both level 2 and level 3 knowledge regimes regarding the five propositions (a through e) related to the PhD program. Central faculty in the collaboration network tend to exhibit higher

TABLE 3.1 Correlations of Network Centrality and Level 2 and Level 3 Knowledge, Propositions (a)-(e)

		Level 2 knowledge						Level 3 knowledge					
		a	b	c	d	e	Overall	a	b	c	d	e	Overall
Collaboration network	Betweenness	na	.21	−.13	.21	.40	.17	−.14	.06	−.25	.05	.21	−.01
	Degree	na	.38	−.09	.38	.44	.28	−.22	.18	−.21	.17	.12	.01
	Eigenvector	na	.45	−.03	.45	.54	.35	−.41	.12	−.30	.12	−.10	−.12
Friendship network	Betweenness	na	−.32	−.41	−.32	.51	−.13	.18	−.17	−.08	−.18	.11	−.03
	Degree	na	−.47	−.28	−.47	.14	−.27	.34	−.22	.01	−.26	.16	.01
	Eigenvector	na	−.40	−.34	−.40	−.02	−.29	.41	−.12	.03	−.15	.10	.05
Interaction network	Betweenness	na	.20	−.83	.20	.37	−.02	−.08	.14	−.40	.14	−.50	−.14
	Degree	na	.15	−.63	.15	−.07	−.10	.23	.22	−.22	.21	−.20	.05
	Eigenvector	na	−.07	−.27	−.07	−.35	−.19	.54	.25	.17	.23	.23	.29

accuracy of level 2 beliefs (they are more likely to know what other faculty believe) but not of level 3 beliefs (they are not more likely to know what other faculty believe they know). Overall, there is little association between faculty members' network centrality and the accuracy of their higher-level beliefs in any of the networks. As well as pointing to a method for studying the epistemic structure of various kinds of networks, these findings suggest that an agent's network centrality may not be, as is widely held, a good proxy for his/her degree of being "in the know" if we are careful enough to define "in the know" as level 2 or level 3 interactive knowledge.

Our second question was to what extent do the cliques of the interaction, friendship, and collaboration networks also comprise "social pockets" of coherent levels 1, 2, and 3 knowledge. To answer this question, we examined clique coherence by identifying all of the cliques comprising the interaction, friendship, and collaboration networks (i.e., fully connected subgraphs of the respective networks)[2] and comparing the coherence of intra-clique and network-wide knowledge for each. We measured a clique's knowledge coherence, on a proposition-by-proposition basis, as the proportion of dyads sharing common knowledge at level 2 and level 3 (i.e., NC^2 and NC^3) with respect to each of the propositions related to the PhD program.

More formally, we computed coherence as $t_{(NCn)}/(k \times (k-1)/2$, where $t_{(NCn)}$ is the number of dyads sharing knowledge at level n, and k is the number of vertices in the subnetwork. A value of 1 (or 100 percent) indicates that the clique corresponds to a mutual knowledge neighborhood (for NC^2) or to a common knowledge neighborhood (for NC^3). Thus, a 100 percent match represents a state of the world in which each clique member agrees on the proposition, knows this fact (level 2), and knows that each other clique member knows this fact (level 3).

Table 3.2 lists the cliques making up each network, gives their level 2 and level 3 coherence for each proposition, and compares each one to the overall network. Both the cliques and the network as a whole generally showed high mutual knowledge (NC^2) for issues a through d but not e. As a result, with several exceptions (e.g., the Abe-Dan-Jan friendship clique), the cliques were *not* more "in the know" in terms of level 2 knowledge and only the Dan-Gil-Kim interaction clique outperformed the overall network on all five propositions. Indeed, with 97 percent level 2 coherence across the five propositions, this clique corresponded to a mutual knowledge neighborhood in the epistemic network.

Level 3 coherence is far weaker, although several of the interaction network cliques did achieve moderate level 3 coherence and outperformed the network as a whole. The Dan-Gil-Kim clique, in particular, had 87 percent level 3 coherence across the five propositions, but this level corresponded only weakly to an almost-common knowledge neighborhood in the epistemic network. Nevertheless, this clique was remarkable for several reasons. First, it comprised peripheral faculty. Second, although their coherence on issue e was relatively high, their shared beliefs were incorrect. Had their beliefs served as a set of focal points for this clique's members, they would have coordinated on the *wrong* signal. These findings suggest a further caution in interpreting network-level topological features—cliques in this case—as being too strongly indicative of networked agents' proclivity to act in a synergistic fashion either to co-mobilize or to coordinate.

Taken together, the findings suggest that network-topological and structural features *alone* should not be taken as universal predictors of network cohesion or as variables that predict an informational advantage accruing to centrality. Neither clique membership nor agent centrality may confer the informational advantages that *should* accrue to the central and the tightly connected. If such an advantage is critical to the brokerage and closure that constitute social capital, then a different, augmented view of the epistemic conditions of social capital formation and maintenance is required. The network researcher's "tool kit," accordingly, should be expanded to include measures of the epistemic states of networked agents (individual, collective, and interactive), and the "networker's tool kit" should be expanded to include operators and operations that function at the level of epinets and not just at the level of ties among agents.

Interpretation, Misattribution, and Oblivion

We have thus far constructed and untangled epinets anchored by propositions that refer clearly to events or objects, that have well-defined truth values that can be independently ascertained by reference to an independent source (such as a memorandum that serves as distributed knowledge), and about which networked agents have simple beliefs (true, false, true with probability p). In such cases, we showed how the degree of coherence of interactive belief hierarchies can be used to assess the degree of cohesion of the network and the coordinatability and co-mobilizability of its members.

The epinet approach to describing relationships and interactions among human agents linked by various kinds of ties is also useful when describing situations (1) in which various subnetworks coalesce around propositions that have ill-defined truth values that may depend on interpretations shared by different subnetworks regarding the referents of these propositions or the definitions of their subjects and objects; and (2) in which some or many of the agents in the network are oblivious to certain propositions or to the state of affairs to which they refer.

Such situations can pose problems for formalistic approaches to describing interactions, which specify either complete "event spaces" whose constitution is common knowledge among agents in the network, or propositions that unambiguously refer to such events and therefore have easily ascertainable truth values and can be combined and recombined using first-order logic. These situations can also cause trouble for empirical approaches, which employ questionnaires that impart knowledge to the respondents whose knowledge they are in fact meant to measure—asking agent A about proposition P makes it impossible to determine whether or not agent A is in fact ignorant of the truth value of the proposition or, rather, oblivious of the possibility that the proposition is true.

TABLE 3.2 Clique versus Network Belief Coherence, Propositions (a)–(e)

	Clique members	Knowledge		Cohesion for proposition a	b	c	d	e	Overall	Clique vs. network cohesion for proposition a	b	c	d	e	Overall
All network members		Level 2	$t_{(NCn)}$	90	68	64	67	10	299						
			%	82%	62%	58%	61%	99%	54%						
		Level 3	$t_{(NCn)}$	50	41	27	42	3	163						
			%	45%	37%	25%	38%	3%	30%						
Collaboration network	Cam-Eli-Hal	Level 2	$t_{(NCn)}$	5	4	2	4	0	15						
			%	83%	67%	33%	67%	0%	50%	2%	5%	−25%	6%	−9%	−4%
		Level 3	$t_{(NCn)}$	4	3	0	4	0	11						
			%	67%	50%	0%	67%	0%	37%	21%	13%	−25%	28%	−3%	7%
Friendship network	Abe-Eli-Ian-Kim	Level 2	$t_{(NCn)}$	19	11	12	11	1	54						
			%	95%	55%	60%	55%	5%	54%	13%	−7%	2%	−6%	−4%	0%
		Level 3	$t_{(NCn)}$	9	7	5	7	0	28						
			%	45%	35%	25%	35%	0%	28%	0%	−2%	0%	−3%	−3%	−2%
	Abe-Cam-Eli-Ian	Level 2	$t_{(NCn)}$	11	5	6	5	1	28						
			%	92%	42%	50%	42%	8%	47%	10%	−20%	−8%	−19%	−1%	−8%
		Level 3	$t_{(NCn)}$	3	2	0	2	0	7						
			%	25%	17%	0%	17%	0%	12%	−20%	−21%	−25%	−22%	−3%	−18%
	Abe-Gil-Ian-Jan	Level 2	$t_{(NCn)}$	12	6	6	6	1	31						
			%	100%	50%	50%	50%	8%	52%	18%	−12%	−8%	−11%	−1%	−3%
		Level 3	$t_{(NCn)}$	4	3	0	3	0	10						
			%	33%	25%	0%	25%	0%	17%	−12%	−12%	−25%	−13%	−3%	−13%
	Abe-Dan-Jan	Level 2	$t_{(NCn)}$	6	2	6	2	0	16						
			%	100%	33%	100%	33%	0%	53%	18%	−28%	42%	−28%	−9%	−1%
		Level 3	$t_{(NCn)}$	4	2	3	2	0	11						
			%	67%	33%	50%	33%	0%	37%	21%	−4%	25%	−5%	−3%	7%

Interaction network														
Cam-Dan-Eli-Gil-Ian-Jan-Kim	Level 2	$t_{(NCn)}$	41	41	30	41	5	158						
		%	98%	98%	71%	98%	12%	75%	16%	36%	13%	37%	3%	21%
	Level 3	$t_{(NCn)}$	29	28	18	28	2	105						
		%	69%	67%	43%	67%	5%	50%	24%	29%	18%	28%	2%	20%
Cam-Eli-Hal-Ian	Level 2	$t_{(NCn)}$	9	8	2	8	0	27						
		%	75%	67%	17%	67%	0%	45%	-7%	5%	-42%	6%	-9%	-9%
	Level 3	$t_{(NCn)}$	6	5	0	6	0	17						
		%	50%	42%	0%	50%	0%	28%	5%	4%	-25%	12%	-3%	-1%
Abe-Dan-Eli-Gil-Ian-Jan-Kim	Level 2	$t_{(NCn)}$	41	29	30	29	5	134						
		%	98%	69%	71%	69%	12%	64%	16%	7%	13%	8%	3%	9%
	Level 3	$t_{(NCn)}$	24	20	15	20	2	81						
		%	57%	48%	36%	48%	5%	39%	12%	10%	11%	9%	2%	9%
Ben-Eli-Ian	Level 2	$t_{(NCn)}$	4	4	1	4	0	13						
		%	67%	67%	17%	67%	0%	43%	-15%	5%	-42%	6%	-9%	-11%
	Level 3	$t_{(NCn)}$	1	1	0	1	0	3						
		%	17%	17%	0%	17%	0%	10%	-29%	-21%	-25%	-22%	-3%	-20%
Dan-Gil-Kim	Level 2	$t_{(NCn)}$	6	6	6	6	5	29						
		%	100%	100%	100%	100%	83%	97%	18%	38%	42%	39%	74%	42%
	Level 3	$t_{(NCn)}$	6	6	6	6	2	26						
		%	100%	100%	100%	100%	33%	87%	55%	63%	75%	62%	31%	57%

NOTE: $t_{(NCn)}$ is the number of dyads sharing knowledge at the indicated level, and % indicates the percentage of all dyads sharing knowledge.

These problems are inherent to the research programs in question: they are wired into the analytical fabric on which researchers predicate their activities. This means that any disciplined attempt to deal with them in a coherent framework must relax at least some of the constraints of the paradigms in which they have originated. This is precisely what epinets allow us to do. In particular, by relaxing conditions of agent-level informational omniscience and perfect recall as precursors to any model of interactions with interdependent outcomes, we can build epistemic portraits of interactions among agents and model the structure and dynamics of the resulting network at the level of epistemic moves—actions that change the network's informational landscape (a topic of Chapter 5). At the same time, the notions of "awareness" (knowing that you know something) and "oblivion" (not knowing that you do not know something) make it possible for us to posit individual and collective interactive epistemic states that are more accommodating to intuition and realistic descriptors of what agents in a network actually know and believe.

In particular, we introduce a syntactic state space comprising propositions over which agents can have an expanded set of epistemic states—including "interpretations" of a proposition, almost-common knowledge of various degrees, oblivion, and "oblivious knowledge" (an agent knows P but does not know, at time T, that she knows it, perhaps because she has temporarily forgotten P and it is therefore not immediately salient to her). This allows us to describe an expanded set of epistemic moves and maneuvers that networked agents can perform to change the informational and epistemic state of the network as a whole.

Consider Figure 3.9. Alice (A) and Bob (B) each have their own interpretation of an epistemically simple proposition, P, and each believes the other "knows" his/her and not the other's interpretation. If P is (as in our empirical study) the proposition *A new PhD program structure has been put forth by x*, Alice *knows* that *there is a proposal on the table to be considered, discussed, and modified*, and Bob *knows* that *there is a proposal on the table to be ratified by time T*. Alice also believes that Bob knows that *there is a proposal on the table to be considered, discussed, and modified*, and Bob believes that Alice knows that *there is a proposal on the table to be ratified by time T*.

Moreover, there is a proposition, Q, that relates to a request for comments regarding the proposal, of which Bob is oblivious (does not know it and does not know he does not know it because the department chair accidently left

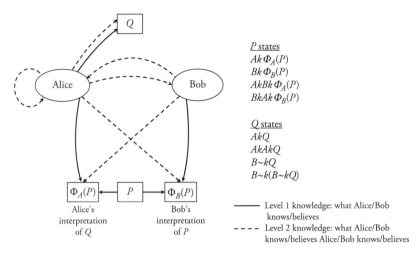

$\underline{P\,states}$
$Ak\,\Phi_A(P)$
$Bk\,\Phi_B(P)$
$AkBk\,\Phi_A(P)$
$BkAk\,\Phi_B(P)$

$\underline{Q\,states}$
AkQ
$AkAkQ$
$B{\sim}kQ$
$B{\sim}k(B{\sim}kQ)$

$\Phi_A(P)$ — Alice's interpretation of Q

P

$\Phi_B(P)$ — Bob's interpretation of P

——— Level 1 knowledge: what Alice/Bob knows/believes

– – – Level 2 knowledge: what Alice/Bob knows/believes Alice/Bob knows/believes

FIGURE 3.9 Complex Epistemic States

him off the "cc" list on the e-mail making the request). Q might lend inferential support to Alice's interpretation of P and lend differential inferential support to her interpretation as against Bob's interpretation, but it need not do so: even if Bob *knew* Q, he might still believe that his own interpretation of P is the correct one, depending on his view of an informal request for comments and of the degree to which these comments are binding or otherwise on those who make them.

An epistemic game theorist might be inclined to cut through the inferential and interpretative quagmires of natural language and simply create a contracted state space of events (*proposal ratified by time T, proposal not ratified by time T*), ascribe personal probabilities of these events to Alice and Bob, impose coherence conditions on these probabilities (they should sum up to 1), and have Alice and Bob conditionalize their posterior expectations of that event on new information that emerges from the group communication process surrounding the proposal. This modeling strategy, however, hides the degree to which natural language predicates like "ratify" are subject to interpretation (e.g., How binding? How irreversible?), and an expansion of the state space is required to accommodate various eventualities arising from differences in interpretation. More important, this accommodation also hides the nuanced epistemic space changes that accompany the dialogical games surrounding a complex proposal, which a syntactic representation (based on propositions and interpretations) reveals.

A Case of Misattribution: The "Paradigm War" in Organizational Studies. The use of "interpretations" in the expanded epistemic state space of networked agents is critical in the mapping of more complicated dialogical games, such as those played by researchers and scholars in the context of journal articles that ostensibly instantiate a communicative community. One particularly telling example arises from an episode of trans-disciplinary dialogue in organizational studies that has come to be referred to as the "paradigm war" (Pfeffer 1993, 1995; Van Maanen 1995a, 1995b). In this episode, researchers with different conceptual and methodological commitments attempted to debate the epistemological foundations of "the field," which comprises phenomena and problem statements drawn from many different spheres of managerial and organizational practice (Moldoveanu 2009).

The dialogical game that ensued featured a set of interactive beliefs and knowledge structures that attributed certain commitments to various "camps" (Moldoveanu and Baum 2002). These attributions were based on appropriation of terms and definitions (realism, constructivism, relativism, dogmatism) from the literatures of epistemology and philosophy of science and on the use of these distinctions and concepts to attribute certain epistemological stances and commitments to one another. The attributions can be modeled in an epinet (see Figure 3.10) as a set of propositions that "look" epistemically simple (i.e., admitting simply defined truth values) but are in fact complex, theory-laden interpretations of definitions supplied by a field of study (the philosophy of science) that is itself an evolving dialogical game with radically different norms of justification, inference, and dialogical practice.

The camps represented in the paradigm war were loosely formed around focal groups of researchers committed to data gathering and analysis (qualitative/quantitative) and justification and explanation (hypothetico-deductivists/inductivists; formal modeling/informal modeling), which harness existing epistemological stances (realism/constructivism) as justification for these practices. However, the discussants' understanding of the epistemological foundations of their own work bore only a loose resemblance to the use of these terms in the philosophy of science literature, which made it important to consider the consequences of interpretations and misinterpretations as well as those of attributions and misattributions in the ensuing dialogical game.

Researchers from the realist camp, it turned out, ended up portraying realism (loosely, a commitment to the terms of a theory or model as representing

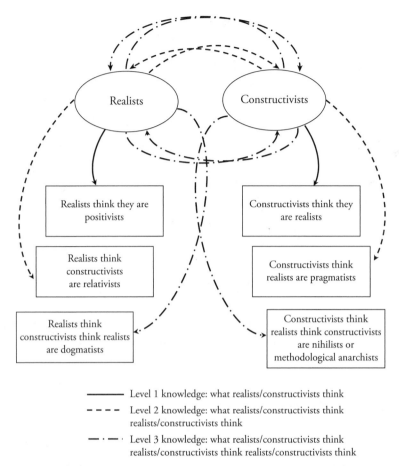

Realists

Constructivists

Realists think they are
positivists

Constructivists think they
are realists

Realists think
constructivists
are relativists

Constructivists think
realists are pragmatists

Realists think
constructivists think realists
are dogmatists

Constructivists think
realists think constructivists
are nihilists or
methodological anarchists

——————— Level 1 knowledge: what realists/constructivists think

– – – – Level 2 knowledge: what realists/constructivists think
realists/constructivists think

— · — · Level 3 knowledge: what realists/constructivists think
realists/constructivists think realists/constructivists think

FIGURE 3.10 "Paradigm Wars" Interactive Belief Hierarchy
SOURCE: Adapted from Moldoveanu and Baum, 2002.

real objects and events and to the link between the truth value of hypotheses
and the realness of the terms of the model from which hypotheses are derived as theorems) as closely resembling positivism (a commitment to models
that contain only quantities and qualities that are directly perceptible by the
senses). This led researchers in the "constructivist camp" to claim an epistemological high ground on the basis of a set of logical problems that had arisen
in regard to positivism as a theory of knowledge and of a view of themselves
as being more realistic in their modeling assumptions (where the common
language term "realistic" had been falsely conflated with "realism" as an epistemological commitment).

Researchers in the realist camp, in turn, focused on the insistence of constructivists that a representation is an emergent phenomenon resulting from an interaction of an observer (the researcher) and a subject (the topic of research) in order to claim that constructivism is a form of relativism (which makes the truth value of any hypothesis or explanation relative to the researcher's conceptual and perceptual frame of reference). The realists used this claim to charge the constructivists with a form of incoherence (always a pejorative in academia) that they perceived to be at the core of all relativist stances (because to the extent that relativism relies on the tenet *All truth values assigned to descriptive sentences are relative*, that tenet must itself be either relative if it is to be meaningful at all or false otherwise).

Interpretation matters in each of these instances: to understand the structure and dynamics of the dialogical game unfolding among researchers of different methodological persuasions, we must parse not only the propositions that researchers use to refer to their own and each other's commitments but the content of these propositions as well—the precise set of associations, references, and truth conditions that researchers use to make sense of these propositions.

It is also not the case that such dialogical games are *epi*-phenomenal, that they do not make a difference in the behavior of the researchers as agents in a network (in this case the larger network of researchers studying organizations). To the contrary, the models of self and other that emerge serve as coordinata (focal points in coordination games) for subnetworks of researchers who vote on tenure and promotion cases that welcome new networked agents or deny them entry, and who use these dialogically emergent identities to plan and organize conferences, give advice to granting agencies on research funding, and discuss matters of strategic and operational importance with executives. Thus, interpretation—and the complex epistemic states that arise from interpretative processes—matters as more than just idle talk (or journal article writing) in ways that are inextricably linked to the nature and function of the interpretations they produce.

The Case of Status: Between Oblivion and Glory. Epinets centrally feature propositions that carry meaning made up of both denotation and connotation, and they can therefore express both judgments of value and judgments of fact. As a result, they can be used to texture what we currently understand by status—yet another important feature of social networks. Many social network analyses invoke status as an *explanans* or an independent variable that measures an essential property of a social arrangement (e.g., Benjamin and Podolny 1999).

Status-based explanations of network effects have the basic structure of positive feedback explanations more generally: the haves get more overtime, with repeated interactions, than the have-nots get, and the disparity continuously increases. This explanatory mechanism owes its form largely to the centrality measures used to quantify status (e.g., Bonacich centrality (Bonacich 1987)), which explicitly weight the connectedness of an agent by the connectedness of the other agents to whom she is linked. Changing one's status, by this definition, is a costly and risky process, as it involves either forming ties to well-connected network agents (who may have little or no incentive to respond to overtures from unknowns) or modifying the centrality measures of these agents relative to those of the agents to whom one is connected (which is often not a controllable process).

Despite the apparent resistance of an agent's status to change that can be causally attributed to his/her actions, there are often fashions, fads, and paradigms that emerge, grow, and fade out in established industries that are not necessarily disrupted by demand shocks or technological change. The status of the image-creating agents representing them tracks their ebbs and flows. Such changes seem difficult to explain based only on tie formation and decay mechanisms operating on a network topology. One can, after all, have qualitatively different degrees of status (ranging from knownness to glory), and one may be known for attributes that are "good" and so desirable, or "bad" and to be avoided. *Being known for X* is easily represented in epinets but not so easily in models that simply specify the presence and strength of inter-agent ties.

Status depends in part on a property for which the agent has acquired and retained his/her status. If status is "fame," for instance, then a critical property of that fame (aside from the network positions of the agents to whom one is famous) is *what, precisely one is famous for*—that is, the *P*-ness of the famous agent. A California vineyard that makes Chardonnay may be famous for the "oakyness" of its vintages and accordingly competes with other "oaky" California Chardonnays that make up its reference or comparison class. Should next year's vintage turn out "buttery," however, the vineyard will likely be charged with an error, which may affect its status among other Chardonnay vintners to a greater or lesser degree. Should the error persist, the reference or comparison class for the vintner will also likely change and perhaps become Burgundy Chardonnays, which are famed for being buttery.

There is a link between one's *degree of fame* and what one *is famous for*. This link can be manipulated by a network agent to effect endogenous change in his network status by playing with the semantic structure of P. Suppose that A is f_{AP} famous for P and f_{AQ} famous for Q and that the subsets g_{AP} and g_{AQ} of G are disjoint. Then A is $(f_{AP} + f_{AQ})$ famous for the composite property P and Q. A, however, can only *socially* aggregate his fame constituencies if he can successfully justify the *semantic* aggregation of the individual properties P and Q—that is, if he can show that the composite property P *and* Q is meaningfully different from P and from Q. To do this, A could show how his *P-ness* matters to the agents that make up g_{AQ} and how his *Q-ness* matters to the agents that make up g_{AP}. Ideally, A would show that his *Q-ness* is causally essential to his *P-ness* and vice versa.

A common example is a high-status automaker (e.g., BMW, Porsche) entering the sport utility vehicle (SUV) market with high-performance products (e.g., X5, Cayenne) based on power plants and transmissions developed for its sedans and coupes. In the process, the automaker restructures the image of SUV consumers and thus gleans from its entrenched position and image a reputation in the new market for all-terrain performance that helps it sell more vehicles with advanced transmission technology (e.g., AWD) in the sedan and coupe markets.

More formally, epinets can be used to reveal the propositional and value-laden structure of the *status* of an agent in a network, as follows.

Reach of Agent A. The fraction f or subset g of all agents in the network who are epistemically connected to A—that is, whose epistemic states change in response to a signal emitted by A. A stock analyst's estimate of the true market value of Apple, for instance, may change the epistemic states of some investors regarding that value, depending on their degree of confidence in the analyst's estimate. Changes in A's epistemic states do not necessarily lead to *isomorphic* changes in the epistemic states of agents in her reach.

For instance, if B is in the reach of A, BkP, and B discovers that AkP, then B might change his epistemic state from kP to $k(\sim P)$. If B has reason to believe that A is self-deceived or a deceiver (as may be the case with our stock analyst), he is still in A's epistemic reach, even though the change in A's epistemic state is obviously negatively correlated with the intended epistemic import of B's announcement. Reach, then, is a weak epistemic link in that it does not guarantee an epistemic state change in the recipient of a signal that is perfectly correlated with the epistemic state of the transmitter of the signal, or the epistemic state of the transmitter that is consistent with the signal being accurate.

Clout of Agent A. The fraction f or subset g of agents in network G that change epistemic state from $\sim Kp$ to Kp because of the discovery that AKp, or from Kp to $K(\sim p)$ because of the discovery that $Ak(\sim p)$—that is, for whom it is true that $K(AKp) \rightarrow BKp$ & $K(AK(\sim p)) \rightarrow BK(\sim p)$. A weatherman's announcement of tomorrow's forecast, for instance, changes the epistemic states of those tuning into the announcement: it changes their estimates of the truth value of propositions such as *It will rain tomorrow*. Clout reaches further than "reach" in the quantification of the epistemic influence of a network agent. It captures the network epistemic effects of opinion leaders and experts whose signals have high degrees of *credibility* (or, alternatively, who enjoy the greatest level of *confidence* of those in their reach) and therefore whose experiences can provide warrants for propositional beliefs held by network agents to be true.

Knownness of Agent A. The fraction f or subset g of agents in G who know of A: BKA—that is, who know $P = (I\ know\ or\ am\ acquainted\ with\ A)$. A's knownness captures the *name recognition* of A in G. Philipp Kohlschreiber, for example, may have a high knownness among dedicated tennis fans, while Juan Martín del Potro may be highly known to both tennis fans and sports fans more generally as the winner of the 2009 U.S. Open tennis championships. Note that clout need not imply knownness: a stock analyst working for an investment bank of repute may not herself be *known* in the investor community, but the credibility of her pronouncements is safeguarded by the reputation of the bank that employs her. Knownness may also be associated with more complicated propositional structures and, in particular, with value-laden propositions. A may be known for being a mass murderer or a highly successful high-technology entrepreneur. In this case, the knowledge by acquaintance ("that is A") at the core of knownness may be replaced by a more specific association of A with some property X for which A is known.

To distinguish between this more specific collective epistemic state and knownness, we need a more textured concept, which follows.

Fame (Infamy) of Agent A. The fraction f or subset g of agents in G who know that A has positive property P, $BK(P_i)$ (negative property N, $BK(N_i)$).

Fame (infamy) is equivalent to *knownness for P* (*knownness for N*). Thus, we refer to a successful serial entrepreneur as famous in the sense that she is known for being a successful serial entrepreneur, and we refer to an organized crime boss as *in*famous in the sense that he is known for being an organized crime boss. The *P*-ness (*N*-ness) of *A* is the key feature distinguishing knownness from fame or infamy—epistemic states that are dependent on *semantic* properties of *P*: minimally, positivity and negativity.

Renown of Agent A. The fraction *f* of agents in *G* who know *A*, know all of the agents who know *A* (and know that these agents know *A*): *BKA* & *BK*({*L*}: *LKA*), where {*L*} is the set of agents (with cardinality). Renown is a higher-order epistemic state that characterizes the relationship between an agent *A* and a network *G*. The actor Brad Pitt may be *known for being known*, even if those who know him for being known do not *know him for something* (i.e., even if they have not seen any of his movies). Pitt's second-level knownness—his renown—therefore need not be correlated with any specific judgment of fact or value about him. It is simply the case that he enjoys not only name recognition but also recognition for and of the fact that he enjoys it. As in the case of knownness, we need a more textured epistemic property to capture the notion of being known for being known for a particular quality or attribute.

Glory (Notoriety) of Agent A. The fraction *f* (or subset *g*) of agents in *G* who know all of the agents that know that *A* has positive property *P* (negative property *N*): *jK*(*l*: *lK*(*PA*)) (*jK*(*l*: *lK*(*NA*))). Glory (infamy), then, is *renown for P(N)*.

The network epistemic states just presented can be combined to understand in a precise way an agent's status. Bill Gates, Microsoft cofounder and chairman, for instance, is known to a large subset *g* of the North American population (the network *G*); he is famous for (*P* = *starting up Microsoft*) to a subset *h* of *g*; he is infamous for (*N* = *trying to corner the desktop software market*) to a subset *j* of *g* (which may or may not be a proper subset of *h*); he is renown to a large subset *k* of *g* who know about all of those who know of him; he is glorious for (*P* = *starting up Microsoft*) to a subset *l* of *h* who know about those that make up *h*; and he is notorious to a subset *m* of *j* for (*N* = *trying to corner the desktop software market*). He has *clout* with regard to software industry–related issues with a large number of (sometimes uninformed and unsophisticated) investors and technology analysts in the software and electronics sectors, and he has *clout* with a smaller number of software and computer technology executives (with whom he has credibility and of whom he knows that he has credibility with them). Together, these network-epistemic variables can be used to characterize the "status footprint" of an agent and to specify in detail the epistemic relationships and influences that the agent is part of or capable of entering and exerting, respectively.

Measurement Implications. These new concepts and distinctions enable us to take an epistemically textured view of measures of network influence that have in the past been related only to the topology of ties and the position of an agent in the network—that is, centrality measures (Wasserman and Faust 1994; Jackson 2005). In particular, they allow us to distinguish among the differences that differences in agent centrality make in their influence in the network.

Degree centrality measures the proportion of agents in the network to whom an agent is connected. It is therefore a measure of "connectedness." But how "connected" a person is depends to a large extent on what exactly is meant by a connection. At the very least, a meaningful tie should have something to do with "knowing and being known," which in turn, can be unpacked into knownness and renown. One's connectedness in a network is a meaningful (partial) measure of one's influence provided that those connections contribute to one's knowledge of other agents and knownness of other agents, as well as contribute to one's knownness for being known in the network. Human agents engage in many interactions that do not confer on them the knownness property—they remain indistinguishable strangers to one another. It is therefore useful to qualify simple degree centrality measures with the more textured epistemic language of status and influence to articulate more precisely *which* differences in degree centrality make a difference in the influence of a network agent.

Closeness centrality is a measure of the accessibility of the network to an agent in a situation in which network distance significantly attenuates interpersonal connection: Alice is far closer (affectively or informationally) to her friends than to her friends' friends' friends (provided she does not know her friends' friends or her friends' friends' friends directly), and her proximity to people from whom she is separated by two or more degrees decays rapidly as a function of the number of degrees of separation.

One way to unpack accessibility as meaningful to Alice's influence in the network is to consider the *reach* and *clout* that she has there—the degree to which she can communicate with and change the minds of various network agents. Reach may be a function of Alice's closeness measure—think of rumor mills. However, it need not be—think of expert networks selectively tuned into certain network agents via e-mail alerts and filters, or professional groups selectively focused on particular areas of study and practice, with only agents having overcome barriers to entry such as training and certification "cleared" to communicate freely with other members of the same group.

In each case, clout adds further resolving power to closeness as an influence measure by specifying the epistemic import that an agent's signals have for the epistemic states of other agents in the same network. Clout is an epistemic certifier for signals emanating from the agents who have it. As in the case of reach, an agent's clout may or may not directly correlate with her closeness centrality: acknowledged experts in a field of knowledge or a professional practice may have clout in their network by virtue of their track record of professional or research practice (publication record, citedness, word-of-mouth fame acquired through participation in conferences).

Betweenness centrality measures the (mathematical) probability that the shortest path connecting any two agents in a fully connected network passes through a particular agent. It is an intuitive measure of the informational advantage that an agent gains by virtue of his/her connectedness: being "in the know" in a situation in which information functions as "social currency" should be correlated with being "along the greatest proportion of trajectories" in the network connecting one agent to another. However, as with other centrality measures, the causal import of betweenness centrality to the network advantage of a high-centrality agent depends on the precise definition of the connecting ties that define the network in the first place. We have argued that the epistemic dimension of a tie—the set of individual and interactive beliefs of the two connected agents—is critically important in the definition of that tie.

Ties based on coherent interactive hierarchies of higher-level beliefs are bound to be more "conductive" of relevant information than ties based on superficial interactions (no matter how frequent) that are not characterized by such coherence. Moreover, an agent's clout is in itself a key indicator of the degree to which information transmitted by that agent to any other agent is evaluated as valid and worthy of further communication. In Chapter 4, we introduce the concept of superconductive geodesics and paths through a social network based on the (modal and subjunctive) epistemic state of *trust* (in agents' integrity and competence). These distinctions should help to qualify and refine inferences about an agent's "network advantage" made on the basis of purely topological features such as his/her betweenness centrality.

Eigenvector centrality measures the degree to which an agent is connected to agents who are themselves well connected. Thus, eigenvector-central agents are connected to the well-connected. This measure is recursive: one can also be well connected to those who are well connected to the well-connected and so forth.[3] "Connected" is conflated with "influential" in a way that can be greatly helped by notions such as renown, fame, glory, and clout. To the extent that "connection to the well-connected" confers on the so connected the kind of epistemic influence (clout) that is desired for true influence to be inferred, it is useful as an explanatory variable for an agent's network position.

However, one can achieve "instant" clout—and therefore influence—in a network on the basis of a well-broadcast discovery that makes the subject famous (in our sense) overnight (for example, the "discovery" of cold fusion by Pons and Fleischmann in the late 1990s), and make the subject just as instantly notorious (for example, the forgetfulness and oblivion in the aftermath of failures of other laboratories to reliably repeat Pons and Fleischmann's studies). When we measure the topological and structural features of an agent's position in a network as proxies for his/her influence, we run the risk of measuring either too little or too much (not *any* and not *all* ties and connections matter to what we are after) or of inferring too much (certain ties matter only against the background of certain distributions of information and certain collective and interactive epistemic states of the networked agents). Understanding the epistemic preconditions for influence and connectedness provides an adaptively useful set of filters on the variables we heed when "measuring networks."

Summary

We have shown how epinets can be used to describe the zones and regions of coherence, agreement, and cohesion that undergird social structures and social networks. Also, we have shown how coherent epistemic states can safeguard inferences about network coordinatability and mobilizability and help us predict who will co-mobilize and coordinate and who will act as mobilizers and coordinators. We have moreover shown how to use epinets in empirical settings to test for the degree to which networked s agents are coordinatable or co-mobilizable, and to analyze the epistemic conditions that enable an agent to function as a mobilizer or coordinator of his or her network. Using the syntactical approach to epistemic state spaces, we have demonstrated how subtle linguistic phenomena like conversational implicature, interpretation, and attribution can be unpacked and analyzed in the conceptual space that epinets create.

We further extended the notion of an epinet to show how a networked agent's status, renown, fame, and glory can be textured and refined by using the epistemic states of the agents comprising the network as important qualifiers. The epinet representation thus tracks the outcome of each exchange of information among agents in the network to the agents' resulting epistemic states, which in turn makes it possible either to build more descriptively accurate models of the dynamics of the interaction—"epistemic moves" (which we explore in Chapter 5)—or to measure the network using more accurate and realistic instruments.

Chapter 4

"I Think You Think I Think You're Lying"

Trust, Secrecy, Covertness, and Authentication in Social Networks

We use epinets to unpack and analyze the epistemic structure of trust. We follow the approach of mapping the microstructure of the "epistemic glue" of social interactions and relations and ask, "What must someone think or know about what another thinks or knows when there is a trust relationship between them?" We propose and empirically examine a model of trust as a form of confidence in the competence and integrity of another person, wherein the trustful knows that the trusted knows a fact if that fact is true, and says it if s/he knows it. This unpacking allows us to explore the dark side of the phenomenon of trust—how it can be broken without appearing to be broken—as well as the interplay between breaches of trust in integrity and trust in competence.

Trust matters: "No single variable . . . so thoroughly influences interpersonal and group behavior . . ." (Golembiewski and McConkie 1975: 31); "Trust is indispensable in social relationships" (Lewis and Weigert 1985: 968); "Trust, in economic exchanges, can be a source of competitive advantage" (Barney and Hansen 1994: 188). The idea that trust is critical to economic activity has a sociological lineage dating back to the early writings of Max Weber (1992) and a lineage in political thought dating back at least to Alexis de Tocqueville (2000: 142), who wrote:"The art of association then becomes . . . the mother of action, studied and applied by all."

Blau (1964: 64) identified trust as "essential for stable social relationships," and Durkheim (1933: 28) wrote implicitly of trust when he spoke of the need for a "series of secondary groups," interposed between the state and the individual, that are "near enough to the individuals to attract them strongly in their sphere of action and drag them, in this way, into the general torrent of social life." Fukuyama (1995) conceived of "spontaneous sociability" arising from mutual trust as a foundation of economic prosperity, arguing that trust is the means by which culture influences economic behavior, and that "high-trust" and "low-trust" cultures exhibit fundamentally different economic development paths.

These various ideas capture different and sometimes overlapping aspects of trust, as we will see. Our focus here is on the specific epistemic structures that constitute trustful-trusting relationships. In other words, we ask the question "What must agents know or believe about what those whom they trust know or believe in order for their relationship to be one of trust?" By unpacking and analyzing the epistemic glue specific to trust, we accomplish three things: (1) we build models of trust that allow us to look closely at its "dark side": apparent and real breaches of trust and their authentic and inauthentic repairs; (2) we unpack "dense" social structures such as "circles of trust" and superconductive informational conduits in terms of the epistemic glue that holds them together; and (3) we represent and model moves and strategies that agents may use to manipulate trust-based relationships in a network and thereby influence and change the network's trust topology.

Trust as *Explanans* and *Explanandum*

Throughout these analyses, trust appears implicitly as an *explanans* of subsequent social behavior rather than an *explanandum* in need of further elucidation. This situation has motivated several attempts to unpack trust—as a behavioral disposition, as a congruity of mutual expectations, as a special kind of relationship. Each attempt is informative but also unsatisfactory in one or more ways.

Trust as a Behavioral Disposition. Trust can be defined as the instantiation of cooperative behavior in the prisoner's dilemma game or one of its variants (Lewis and Weigert 1985). Such a definition relies on a view of trust either as an individual disposition to behave in a particular way or as an individual behavior pattern. It leaves out the interpersonal aspect of trust as a relation between the trusting and the trusted (Barber 1983) as well as the cognitive component, which stresses the mutual expectations of the trusted and the trustful (Gambetta 1988). In the same tradition, trust is also defined in negative terms as the absence of high-net-benefit opportunistic behavior. Williamson's argument (1975, 1985), for example, is that economic transactions are structured to eliminate opportunistic behavior in the transactors. Trust appears as a consequence of the absence of opportunistic behavior when there are no penalties for engaging in it.

Behaviorist definitions make no reference to the underlying beliefs of the trusting and the trusted about each other or about the situation at hand. Trust must therefore be inferred ex post from observation of past behavior. Rendering trust a function of past observed behavior alone also rules out investigation of subtler aspects of trust-based interactions, such as forgiveness for certain apparent or real breaches of trust and mutual forbearance in noisy interactional regimes, which limits the precision of the resulting trust model. When a firm chooses one form of relational contracting over another, we may assume that the rejected form was decided against because of some failure of trust between the firms, but we cannot predict the contract that they will enter into by reference to the beliefs, expectations, and modes of inference that they use.

Moreover, when behavioral researchers refer to the "probability" of an agent taking a particular action, they refer to the disposition or objective probability of that agent doing so, rather than the subjective probability that colors the perception of his/her observers. Thus, an individual's trustworthiness becomes the only relevant variable, making it difficult to analyze situations in which trust is preserved in the face of seemingly guileful behavior or it breaks down in spite of apparently principled behavior. Such situations are relevant to the dynamics of trust, however, because the interpersonal interpretation process that leads to the buildup and breakdown of trust is grounded not only in direct behavioral observation but also in theories, beliefs, and interpersonal assumptions that influence what constitutes the relevant observations (Kramer 1999).

Trust as an Interpersonal Entity. The interpersonal dimension of trust is emphasized by researchers who focus on the relationship between trustfulness and trustworthiness (Barber 1983) and by those who focus on comprehensive measures of trust in a relationship (Butler 1991; Mayer, Davis, and Schoorman 1995). Interpersonal approaches to trust are better at picking out more nuanced constructs, such as benevolence, that are specific to the trusting-trustful relationship. On this relational basis alone, however, we cannot distinguish between insightful benevolence from someone who knows her benevolence can be taken advantage of but nevertheless chooses to extend it, and credulous benevolence from someone who does not know that she is being taken advantage of, in which case benevolence is more likely to actually be gullibility.

To unpack trust at this level, we must be precise about what agents know and how they know what they know. Interactive reasoning offers a tool for probing such differences. The insightfully benevolent agent knows that the other agent knows that he can be taken advantage of, whereas the gullibly benevolent agent possesses no such interactive knowledge.

For example, Axelrod (1984) recounts the story of a series of prisoner's dilemma games between a Russian male diplomat and an American female diplomat played under "noisy" conditions in which the observation of a defection of one player by another could have been due either to an error on the part of the reporting procedure or to that player's intention to defect. The American diplomat came out significantly ahead and explained that she defected more frequently than she would have had there been no noise in the game because she thought the Russian diplomat, on the basis of his cultural stereotypes about the cooperativeness of women, would attribute most of her defections to reporting errors rather than to intent. The Russian diplomat confirmed that he thought of American women as less inclined to defect than American men and had therefore attributed his opponent's defections to reporting errors.

Trust as a Cognitive-Rational Entity: Congruity of Mutual Expectations of Competence. Friedland (1990) posited the desirability of trustworthy behavior on rational grounds alone: In a game in which each player has a choice between cooperative and uncooperative behavior and the perspective of an indefinite number of future interactions, strategies that started out cooperatively and then retaliated responsively and proportionately for uncooperative behavior were likely to bring greater payoffs than either strategies that were uncooperative from the beginning (exemplifying completely untrusting players) or strategies that were cooperative and unresponsive to uncooperative behavior (exemplifying players who trusted blindly).

Hill (1990) argued that, since transaction costs shape the form of economic exchange and since the lack of trust between two transactors increases transaction costs, a reputation for trustworthiness is economically valuable for an agent who does not know ex ante who his potential business partners might be. Trustworthy behavior builds an individual's reputation for trustworthy behavior, increasing the expected value of that individual to his prospective partners.

Such cognitive-rational congruity views of trust rest on implicit assumptions about agents' beliefs about each other's beliefs. Suppose that Ada trusts

Bart to carry out a particular action because she believes him to be a rational person who values his reputation and does not want to damage it by shirking his obligations. Implicitly, Ada assumes that Bart indeed cares about his reputation and that Bart believes that she sees his actions as a signal of his trustworthiness. If Bart is rational but believes his actions are only imperfectly observable by Ada, then he might still rationally act opportunistically and take advantage of her. If Ada knows this as well, then she will rationally *not* trust Bart.

In a trustful-trusting relationship, it is not enough that agents trust one another, however; each must also trust the other to trust her, trust him trust her to trust him, and so forth. Ada's rational trust of Bart rests on her beliefs about Bart's beliefs regarding the situation at hand. In turn, Bart, if he is rational, must consider whether or not his actions will have the desired signaling value. If he believes that Ada is ill disposed toward him and negatively attributes his behavior "no matter what he does," then Bart may not act cooperatively. If Ada knows this and believes that Bart believes that she is ill disposed toward him, she will not expect him to act cooperatively.

These higher-level beliefs are critical to the joint realization of successful cooperative outcomes among rational agents because, given the usual payoff structure of competition-cooperation decisions (highest payoff for matched cooperative actions, lowest payoff for mismatched actions, medium payoff for matched competitive actions), then each agent must believe that the other knows the payoffs in order for cooperation to be individually rational.

Trust as a Cognitive-Moral Entity: Congruity of Mutual Expectations of Integrity. The moral approach to trust posits norms as guarantors of cooperative behavior because they are ethically justified: "Trust is the expectation by one person, group, or firm of ethically justifiable behavior—that is, morally correct decisions and actions based on ethical principles of analysis—by another person, group, or firm in a joint endeavor or economic exchange" (Hosmer 1995: 399). Granovetter (1985) grounds trust in the expectation that would-be exchange partners will conform to shared norms and obligations, and he cites with approval Arrow's (1974) idea that economic interactions are grounded in a "generalized morality" that is implicitly agreed on by members of a society. It is rational to act morally and moral to act rationally—the argument goes—and it proceeds to define morality as a commitment to a body of shared norms of behavior. However, an implicit epistemic backbone safeguards valid inference here, which is that it is also rational to assume that everyone else is rational and therefore to believe all will also act morally by virtue of being rational.

To deepen our understanding of trust, we make its epistemic backbone explicit, by asking, "What do interacting individuals have to believe about each other's beliefs in order to engage in the mutually beneficial behavior that is thought to exemplify a 'high-trust' relationship?" and "What is the difference between an 'attributed' norm and a 'shared' norm?" An attributed norm is one that Anja believes that Bruce shares when in fact Bruce may or may not share it. Thus, Anja may be wrong about the attributions she makes about Bruce. A shared norm, in contrast, is one that Anja and Bruce each subscribe to and correctly believe that the other subscribes to as well, that the other believes that s/he subscribes to, and so on.

Even so, ambiguities remain that can only be resolved by further epistemic analysis. It is difficult for any observer of an action to identify unambiguously the norm or maxim to which an action conforms (Moldoveanu and Stevenson 1998). The very same action taken by an agent may be unjustifiable in one moral system (deontological, say) yet be justifiable in another (utilitarian, say).

Observers' interpretation of each others' actions matter. Whether or not Anja believes that Bruce is acting in conformity to a particular norm (N) and not to some other norm (M) is critical to her decision to trust him, having observed his behavior. In turn, Bruce's belief that Anja believes he is acting in accordance with N (rather than M) is critical to his interpretation of her retaliatory behavior as a breach of trust in its own right or as a rightful retaliation for Anja's transgression, by her actions, of M. Finally, Anja's belief that *Bruce believed Anja believed that he was acting according to N rather than M* is accordingly critical to her subsequent conciliatory strategy and reinterpretation of Bruce's behavior. A detailed consideration of the epistemic states of agents, and of the interactive epistemology of their predicaments, can usefully inform the way we study rule- and norm-based behavior that is mediated by trust.

Interactive Epistemic States and Trust

Interactive epistemic states form a basis for analyzing the logic of trust, whether a moral or rational basis is used as an interpretive schema for trustworthiness. They are also a basis for distinguishing between these bases. Expecting that trustworthy behavior is in the best interest of an agent's would-be partner and expecting that the would-be partner shares the specific trust-based ethic of the agent are two plausible grounds for expecting the would-be partner to be trustworthy. Either can work as an explanation of trust, but each works in different ways. As a result, if Alice trusts Bob on *rational* grounds, and Bob trusts Alice on *moral* grounds, the resulting interaction can produce coordinative failure and mutual recrimination.

In the case of a "misunderstanding," Alice may simply try to adjust the incentives of the coordination game or her signaling strategy, but Bob may make a radical negative attribution about Alice's moral character. Breaches of trust—and their repair—can highlight much about the basis on which trust is extended or rescinded and, indeed, about the very nature of trust in a relationship.

To disambiguate this explanatory conundrum, we distinguish between "trust in integrity," corresponding roughly to the moral view of trust, and "trust in competence," corresponding roughly to the rational view of trust, and we argue that the conjoint condition—trust in integrity *and* trust in competence—explains a wide range of trust phenomena. We define trust in competence as a state of epistemic certainty or knowledge held by one agent that another knows a proposition if that proposition is true (and relevant to the agents' interaction); we define trust in integrity as a state of epistemic confidence that an agent would assert what s/he knows to be true in a situation when that mattered. We analyze different combinations of trust in integrity and trust in competence, and examine the differences these combinations make.

Conceiving of trust in competence and trust in integrity as epistemic states of networked agents makes it possible for researchers to study trust explicitly by asking agents questions like "What do you believe?" or "What do you think *X* believes?" rather than implicitly and circularly by asking questions like "Whom do you trust?" It also makes it possible to study trust predictively (by inferring trusting-trustful behavior from response patterns) rather than post-dictively (by inferring these patterns from past behavior).

Because of the precise language in which trust phenomena are represented, however, we must pay special attention to the propositions we focus on; after all, we do not expect a trusted alter to either know or state *anything* that is true or to know everything there is to know about the trustful *ego*.

We therefore define a range of applicability for our trust model by focusing on the propositions that are *relevant* to each agent. To do so, building on the analysis in Chapter 3, we focus on propositions that are important to the co-mobilization and coordination of two or more agents in a network.

We show that what matters in a wide range of contexts is what agents think about what other agents think and about what other agents think they think about a situation. We accordingly posit that trust in integrity and trust in competence should be concomitant to a more coherent set of level 2 (*I think you think*) and level 3 (*I think you think I think*) beliefs, as agents who trust one another are more likely to exhibit coherent interactive belief hierarchies wherein what ego thinks alter thinks matches what alter thinks, and what ego thinks alter thinks ego thinks matches what ego thinks.

We model the knowledge and belief systems involved in the phenomenology of trust and argue that trust in a social network can be understood as a set of interactive beliefs that the trustful and the trusted share about each other's propensity to register and report relevant and truthful information to one another. Prototypical of such relevant information are propositions that represent the backbone of coordinative, communicative, and collaborative activities. What matters to coordination and co-mobilization in a wide range of contexts is the coherence of agents' thinking about other agents' thinking (level 2 beliefs) and agents' thinking about what others think they think (level 3 beliefs) about issues that are important to the interaction.

We argue that trust in competence and trust in integrity safeguard coordination and cooperation among networked agents, and therefore that they should correlate with coherent hierarchies of higher-level beliefs, which are required for successful coordination and co-mobilization. We marshal evidence that is consistent with this argument.

After motivating our approach to representing trust, we extend our epistemic description language (EDL) to describing knowledge states of agents in a social network (their "epistemic states") and show how trust can be defined as an epistemic structure that depends on agents' level 2 and level 3 beliefs. Extending the EDL in this way enables us to analyze trust as a modal epistemic state in which agents have coherent beliefs about other agents' proclivity to know the truth (trust in competence) and to speak it (trust in integrity). We show how trust structures form the backbone of epistemically coherent subnetworks, and we use this language and the associated theory of trust to empirically investigate the interactive structure of trust among agents comprising a large intra-organizational network.

Finally, we extend our analysis to show how social networks can be analyzed in terms of "trust neighborhoods," "trust corridors," and "trust conduits" that form a network's preferred conduits for sensitive information. We contribute a method of conceptualizing trust that allows researchers to detect and measure its presence and degree predictively (by measuring what agents think and what they think other agents think or know) rather than descriptively (by observing instances of trusting-trustful behavior). We also create a path for linking trust directly with the ability and tendency of agents in a network to mobilize and coordinate—important precursors for cooperation and collaboration.

Trust as an Interactive Epistemic State

We now turn to the development of an epistemically precise characterization of trust. Our characterization uses modal epistemic structures such as the one described in Chapter 2 to define confidence. Thus, trust can be understood as a form of confidence. We decompose it into two separate entities, trust in integrity (agents' propensity to say no more and no less than what is true) and trust in competence (agents' propensity to know no more and no less than what is true):

Trust in Integrity (Strong Form) (T_I). "A knows that iff B knew P, B would assert P": $Ak(BkP \leftrightarrow BaP)$, where BaP denotes B acts on P or B asserts P, and P is a proposition relevant to the interaction between A and B. If A trusts B's integrity, then A knows that *iff B knows the truth, then B will assert the truth*. In this form, (1) B's knowledge of P is sufficient to guarantee to A that B will say P and (2) if P is false, then B will not say it; that is, B speaks the truth and nothing but the truth.

This definition of trust generates the following interactive belief hierarchy between A and B: Suppose that $P = B$ *does not trust A*. Assume that this proposition is known to B, unknown to A, and (evidently) relevant to the interaction between A and B. If it is true that A trusts B, then A knows that iff B knows that P is true, then B will assert it and therefore will inform A of his mistrust. Because of the biconditional (iff) nature of the relationship between knowledge and expression, A can infer from the fact that B does not say "I don't trust you" the fact that B actually trusts A. The argument is symmetric for A. Thus, trust in integrity as we have defined it generates an interactive belief hierarchy between the parties to the trusting relationship.

Our definition of trust in integrity (T_I) sidesteps two complications. The first is that B must be *aware* that he knows P in order to say P given that he knows it—that is, BK^2P. The second is that the biconditional ($\leftrightarrow$) relating B's knowing P to his asserting P is plausibly relaxed to the simple conditional, such that B will assert what he knows but will not necessarily know all that he asserts. These complications can be repaired, respectively, by the following relaxations of T_I.

Trust in Integrity (Weak Form 1) (T_{Iwf1}). "A knows that iff B were level 2 aware of P, then B would assert P": $Ak(Bk^2P \leftrightarrow BaP)$. This weak form of trust in integrity requires that B's awareness of P be independently ascertained by A: A's knowledge of B's knowledge of P is not sufficient to warrant A's knowledge that B will assert P. Thus, if B has reason to know P and A knows it and weak-form-trusts B, then B's failure to bring up P is forgivable in the sense that A can continue to trust B in the weak sense, provided that A considers it possible that B temporarily overlooked or forgot P. This weaker form of trust incorporates imperfect recall, which has an important explanatory function in some interactive analyses of games (Aumann 2001).

Trust in Integrity (Weak Form 2) (T_{Iwf2}). "A knows that if B knew P, B would say P or act as if P is true": $Ak(BkP \rightarrow BaP)$, where BaP denotes B *acts on P or B asserts P*. If A trusts B's integrity in this weak sense, then A knows that *if B knows the truth, then B will assert the truth,* but not necessarily that *all* B would assert is the truth. B, in other words, is "trusted" by A to assert the truth but not to assert "nothing but the truth."

The second part of our definition of trust refers to trust in competence. A may trust B's intentions but not necessarily B's ability to deliver, perform, or make good on them. In the way we have defined trust, A expects B to say only what B knows to be true but not to know what is true. Thus, we extend our definition of trust as follows.

Trust in Competence (T_C). "A knows that iff P were true, B would know P": $Ak(P \in T \leftrightarrow BkP)$. If A trusts in the competence of B, then A trusts that B is a faithful register of true propositions and not a register of false propositions—that is, that B registers "the whole truth."

Now we are in a position to characterize trust as the combination of trust in integrity and trust in competence. In its strong form, trust combines the strong form of trust in integrity (which we mean unless we signal otherwise) with trust in competence.

Trust Tout Court (T). "*A* trusts in both the competence and the integrity of *B*": $ATB \rightarrow (AT_I B \ \& \ AT_C B)$. If *ATB*, then *A* knows that *B* would assert the truth, the whole truth, and nothing but the truth.

Weaker forms of trust can be created by combining the trust-in-competence condition with the weaker forms of the trust-in-integrity condition, permitting us to create "trust hierarchies" and, rather than declare that trust exists or does not within a relationship, to become far more precise regarding the kind of trust that exists between two or more agents. Moreover, for any or all of a collection of agents *A*, *B*, and *C*, the relation *T* has the following properties.

Binariness B. $\forall$ *A, B*: *ATB* or ~*ATB*. "For any *A* and *B*, *A* either trusts or does not trust *B*."

Proof. We focus first on T_I. Suppose that $AT_I B$ and ~$AT_I B$—that is, $Ak(BkP \leftrightarrow BaP)$ & $Ak(BkP \leftrightarrow \sim BaP)$. But this contradicts the binariness property of the *k* relation (*a*). The same argument applies for T_C and therefore for the conjunction $T = T_I \ \& \ T_C$.

Transitivity T. $\forall$ *A, B, C*: *ATB* & *BTC* → *ATC*. "For any *A, B, C*, if *A* trusts *B* and *B* trusts *C*, then *A* trusts *C*."

Proof. If $AT_I B$, then $Ak(BkP \leftrightarrow BaP)$. If $BT_I C$, then $Bk(CkP \leftrightarrow CaP)$. Let $P = CkR \leftrightarrow CaR$ for some *R*. Clearly, *BkP* and, ex hypothesis, *BaP*. Because *A* knows that *B* will only say what *B* knows (to be true) and knows to be true only those sentences that are in fact true, *AkP* and therefore $AT_I C$. Now let $Q = R \in T \leftrightarrow CkR$. Clearly, *BkQ* and, given $AT_I B$, $Ak(Q \in T)$. Therefore, $AT_C C$ and therefore $AT_C C$ and $AT_I C$—that is, *ATC*.

Does the fact that *A* trusts *B* entail the fact that *B* trusts *A*? The answer is no, and the proof is by counterexample. Suppose that *A* trusts *B* to assert *the truth, the whole truth, and nothing but the truth* but that *B* does not trust *A* to do so. Let *P* represent the proposition *B does not trust A to assert the truth, the whole truth, and nothing but the truth.* Ex hypothesis, *P* is true. Since *A* trusts *B*, *B* will assert *P*, and *A* will know *P* and therefore will know that *B* does not trust *A*. So, if *A* trusts *B* and *B* does not trust *A*, then our definition requires *A* to know that *B* does not trust *A*. However, in order for *A* not to trust *B* as a result of this knowledge, it is necessary to make *A*'s trust in *B* conditional on her knowledge of *B*'s trust in her, which does not necessarily have to be the case: *A* may trust *B* because of the "kind of person *A* believes *B* is" rather than because of a set of expectations about *B*'s behavior given a set of incentives and a purely self-maximizing disposition.

Indeed, if we introduce a self-maximizing interpretation for the foundation of trust (a mutual expectation of cooperative behavior in situations with payoffs captured by the prisoner's dilemma game played between self-interested individuals (e.g., Axelrod 1997)), then it is the case that *A* cannot trust *B* coherently while knowing that *B* does not trust *A*. The proof is simple and follows directly from applying the definition of trust to the epistemic state space of the prisoner's dilemma game.

Epinets, Trust, and Coordination: A Study of Senior Management Networks

Our definition of trust is clearly too broad if it is applied to all propositions that are possibly true: *A* cannot reasonably know or expect that *B* knows and asserts all true sentences. The range of admissible propositions, then, should be restricted (just as in our definition of knowledge) to propositions that are *relevant* to the interaction between *A* and *B*. Coherence of higher-order beliefs among networked agents is a condition for successful coordination and mobilization; propositions that are the focal points of coordination and mobilization scenarios are thus particularly interesting to our model of trust: these are the propositions that are likely "relevant" to both *A* and *B*.

Interactive belief hierarchies are interesting even if we do not go "all the way to common knowledge" and focus on level 2 and level 3 beliefs, as we illustrated in Chapter 2. In spite of the fact that full common knowledge cannot be achieved through non-face-to-face communication (as in Rubinstein's (1989) e-mail game), most human agents *infer* common knowledge from level 2 knowledge when it comes to confirming a meeting by e-mail: they do not *confirm confirmations* or *confirm confirmations of the confirmations*, but nonetheless wait for confirmation before assuming that a meeting will take place at the proposed time and place.

Nov and Rafaeli (2009) showed that, in organizational contexts, individuals attach a premium to mutual knowledge (although mistakenly referring to it as common knowledge) relative to shared knowledge. This highlights the value individuals place on the interactive component of interactive belief hierarchies in coordination-intensive activities. Culture, whether social or organizational, may thus, as Kreps (1990) and Chwe (2000) explained, represent an interactively coherent body of shared beliefs: these may be either common knowledge or almost-common knowledge among the group's members.

Therefore, it seems reasonable, as we argued in Chapter 3, to focus on the coherence of interactive beliefs—"Does what I believe match what you believe I believe?" "Does what I believe you believe I believe match what I believe?"— as indicative of the mobilizability and coordinatability of networked agents and so indicative of a significant element of the value of network closure (as defined in the social networks literature rather than in the epistemic sense advanced in Chapter 2). If almost-common knowledge crucially serves to enable coordination on interdependent activities, and if we assume that individuals are more likely to engage in coordinated action with others whom they trust than with others whom they do not trust, then we should be able to observe a link between trust and coherence of interactive beliefs. If trust engenders hierarchies of coherent level 2 and level 3 beliefs, then we should observe a high correlation between coherent belief hierarchies and trust. Moreover, the correlation may be stronger than that between the coherence of belief hierarchies and, for instance, the centrality of linked agents or the number of shared ties among agents' alters within the network, measured by their constraint.

It is often assumed that network centrality brings with it an enhanced ability to mobilize or coordinate the network. However, as the analysis of the faculty networks presented in Chapter 3 illustrated, this need not be the case. Whatever the source of this enhanced ability, the arguments we advance indicate that it must possess an epistemic component, as mobilization and coordination are network processes that rest on level 2 and level 3 almost-common-knowledge conditions: Mobilizing agents must have accurate information about what other agents know, whereas coordinating agents must have accurate information both about what other agents know and about what other agents know they know.

Density of relationships, too, is widely held to influence the knowledge distribution and thus the mobilizability and coordinatability of a network. Chwe (1999, 2000), for example, took cliques (fully connected subnetworks) to be synonymous with pockets of local common knowledge. But, again, they need not be, as was also shown by the analysis of the faculty networks in Chapter 3. Indeed, one may communicate with several others who are all communicating with each other (i.e., one may be part of a clique), yet the mobilizability of each agent may not come to be common knowledge among clique members. Nor, as we have shown, is full-common knowledge necessary in many mobilization scenarios; rather, mutual knowledge of co-mobilization is sufficient.

Our epistemic definition of trust allows us to investigate trust relationships empirically and noncircularly: empirically by uncovering what agents believe about each other's propensity and know and speak the truth to each other; noncircularly by using the definitions of trust in competence and trust in integrity to probe the epistemic and logical structures of trust without ever asking, "Whom do you trust?"

Senior Management Networks. To examine these insights empirically, we collected network and epistemic data from senior managers of a large multi-divisional, multiregional Canadian telecommunications firm. The data were collected in two phases. The first phase gathered network and biographical data via an online survey. Respondents were invited to participate through a personalized e-mail linking to the survey, which asked them to identify their significant work relationships without restriction on number.

To ensure accuracy (e.g., consistency in spelling; distinguishing people with similar or identical names), when a colleague's name was entered in the survey, it was checked against a database containing the names and titles of all firm employees, and a list of suggested names and titles was presented to respondent from which s/he could select the desired individual. The respondent was then asked to rate the strength of each relationship from 1 (very weak) to 5 (very strong). In addition to work relationships, each respondent indicated his/her geographic location, divisional affiliation, and gender.

Of the 633 managers invited to participate in the survey, 593 (93.7 percent) completed it. The high response rate was the result of strong top management support and individualized e-mail reminders from the researchers.[1] We used these network data to compute each respondent's betweenness centrality, which measures the extent to which a respondent lies on the shortest paths between others in the network,[2] and constraint, which measures the cohesiveness of the respondent's relationships.[3] A respondent's network is constraining to the extent that it is directly or indirectly concentrated in a single contact; more constraint implies fewer bridging ties spanning structural holes.

The second phase of data collection took place during a series of voluntary workshops to which the 593 individuals who completed the initial survey were invited to receive feedback on their networks. Each attendee received a second personalized survey to complete. To assess level 1 beliefs, the survey asked respondents to indicate what they believed their firm's success depended on most: "innovation," "focus," or "marketing."[4] Respondents answered the same question for each alter (to a maximum of 10) with whom they had earlier rated their relationship strength as either 4 or 5 (on the 5-point scale).

We focused on propositions about drivers of the firm's success because they are relevant to both the successful coordination and the co-mobilization of the respondents: they can be thought of as focal points in a game in which managers try to coordinate their actions around a set of accepted goals. To the extent that these goals are common or almost-common knowledge, they form an important part of the "culture" of the organization (Kreps 1990).

Next, respondents rated, on a scale from 1 (definitely not) to 7 (definitely), the strength of their level 2 belief that they knew what each alter believed was the main driver of the firm's success, and their level 3 belief that each alter also knew how they had responded.

Finally, to assess trust in competence and trust in integrity, the respondents were asked to rate, on a 7-point scale, whether they could count on each alter "to be 'in the know' and to communicate what s/he knows."[5] A total of 302 responses were received from workshop attendees, of which 296 were usable for the analysis. Combining the network and epistemic survey data yielded 608 significant work relationships among the survey respondents, of which 113 were reciprocated at the required cut-off level (≥4 on a 5-point scale of relationship strength) for both respondents.[6]

Centrality, Trust, and Coherence. Table 4.1 presents descriptive statistics and bivariate correlations among the study variables for the sample of 608 significant work relationships. Of particular interest are correlations among respondent i's trust in competence and trust in integrity of alter j; level 2 and level 3 beliefs regarding alter j; knowledge of alter j's level 1 belief about the basis of the firm's success (variable ij matched; coded 1 if correct and 0 otherwise); and measures of respondent i's betweenness centrality and constraint. The correlations are strong and positive among the strength of trust and level 2 and level 3 beliefs, as well as for knowledge of alters' level 1 beliefs regarding the basis of firm success. Betweenness centrality and constraint are weakly correlated with these variables, however, and with one exception not significantly different from zero.

TABLE 4.1 Descriptive Statistics and Correlations for All Relationships

	Variable	Mean	S.D.	Min	Max	1	2	3	4	5	6	7	8	9	10	11	12	13	14
1	i Trust level	5.82	1.23	1	7	1.00													
2	i Level 2 belief strength	5.30	1.26	1	7	.40	1.00												
3	i Level 3 belief strength	5.35	1.29	1	7	.40	.66	1.00											
4	ij Matched	.59	.49	0	1	.17	.25	.17	1.00										
5	i Betweenness	.0017	.0019	.0000	.0127	-.01	.08	-.05	.06	1.00									
6	j Betweenness	.0016	.0018	.0000	.0127	.01	.03	.00	-.01	-.02	1.00								
7	i Constraint	.093	.056	.017	.439	-.01	-.04	.01	.04	-.53	.05	1.00							
8	j Constraint	.100	.059	.017	.656	-.03	-.01	.00	.06	.01	-.53	.01	1.00						
9	ij Same location	.61	.49	0	1	.12	.07	.13	.00	-.10	-.07	.04	.06	1.00					
10	ij Same division	.61	.49	0	1	.05	.02	.12	.08	-.14	-.05	.10	.08	.04	1.00				
11	ij Same gender	.69	.46	0	1	.06	.11	.12	-.04	-.14	-.03	.12	-.01	.11	.01	1.00			
12	i Male	.68	.47	0	1	.08	.12	.06	-.03	-.16	.01	.10	-.03	.14	-.10	.38	1.00		
13	i Tenure	12.00	9.67	1	35	.02	.09	.08	.01	-.06	.01	.07	.06	-.02	-.11	.03	-.04	1.00	
14	j Male	.73	.44	0	1	.02	.10	.11	.02	-.08	-.04	.06	.09	.11	.00	.23	.26	-.02	1.00
15	j Tenure	12.13	9.70	1	35	.07	.04	.03	.02	-.10	.01	.10	-.05	.01	.03	.05	-.02	.29	.01

SOURCE: Moldoveanu and Baum: "I Think You Think I Think You're Lying": Interactive Epistemology of Trust in Social Networks. *Management Science* 57(2), 2011, pp. 393–412. Copyright 2011, Institute for Operations Research and the Management Sciences, 7240 Parkway Drive, Suite 300, Hanover, MD 21076 USA. Reprinted with permission.

NOTE: $N = 608$; correlations > .08 significant at $p < .05$.

Table 4.2 reports ordinary least squares (OLS) regression estimates for a set of multivariate models of trust.[7] These models estimate each variable's independent association with trust, net of a set of control variables that may materially affect respondents' trust in alters, including respondent and alter gender and tenure with the firm; whether the respondent and alter are the same gender; and whether the respondent and alter work in the same location and/or company division. It is important to control for these respondent and alter characteristics because our theoretical variables, including the specific level 2 and level 3 beliefs we studied, may be correlated with other general and more specific types of information that the respondents may possess about each other.

The multivariate regression estimates confirm the correlational analysis. Net of the control variables, coefficients for both level 2 and level 3 beliefs are significant and positive, while the network variables are not. Notably, common work location and alter tenure are also positively related to respondents' trust in competence and trust in integrity of alters.

Table 4.3 reports multivariate logit regression models estimating whether or not respondents' were correct regarding alter j's level 1 beliefs about the basis of the firm's success (ij matched). These models estimate the independent associations of respondents' trust in alter j; level 2 and level 3 beliefs about alter j; and network positions, with respondents' correct identification of alter j's level 1 beliefs, controlling for respondent and respondent and alter demographic characteristics.[8] In the models, coefficients for both trust and level 2 beliefs are significant and positive, while coefficients for level 3 beliefs are not.

Notably, in the full model, consistent with the idea that network centrality and density influence knowledge distribution (e.g., Coleman 1988, 1990; Burt 1992), respondents whose network positions are more central and constrained are more likely to be knowledgeable about their alters' level 1 beliefs. Common work division is also positively related to knowledge of alters' beliefs, which is sensible in light of the beliefs assessed.

Reciprocated Ties. So far, we have examined significant work relationships regardless of whether or not they are reciprocated. We now turn to the 113 relationships that are reciprocated to present a more fine-grained, dyadic analysis of the effects of trust and belief strength.

Table 4.4 presents descriptive statistics and bivariate correlations among the variables for the sample of reciprocated relationships. Of particular

TABLE 4.2 Ordinary Least Squares Regression Models of Trust

	Coef.	(S.E.)	Coef.	(S.E.)	Coef.	(S.E.)	Coef.	(S.E.)	Coef.	(S.E.)
DV: *i Trust level*										
ij Same location	.25	(.10)**	.26	(.10)**	.26	(.10)**	.26	(.10)**	.18	(.09)*
ij Same division	.16	(.10)†	.17	(.10)*	.17	(.10)*	.18	(.10)*	.05	(.09)
ij Same gender	.03	(.12)	.03	(.12)	.03	(.12)	.03	(.12)	-.02	(.10)
i Male	.17	(.12)†	.19	(.12)†	.17	(.12)†	.18	(.12)†	.10	(.11)
i Tenure	.00	(.01)	.00	(.01)	.00	(.01)	.00	(.01)	.00	(.00)
j Male	-.03	(.12)	-.02	(.12)	-.02	(.12)	-.01	(.12)	-.12	(.10)
j Tenure	.01	(.01)†	.01	(.01)†	.01	(.01)†	.01	(.01)†	.01	(.00)*
i Betweenness			23.88	(27.31)			22.54	(31.65)	-1.70	(27.88)
j Betweenness			2.65	(27.91)			-10.80	(33.06)	-12.23	(28.88)
i Constraint					-.51	(.91)	-.11	(1.05)	-.25	(.92)
j Constraint					-.59	(.86)	-.79	(1.01)	-.73	(.88)
i Level 2 belief strength									.23	(.05)***
i Level 3 belief strength									.21	(.05)***
Constant	5.38	(.16)***	5.30	(.19)***	5.46	(.19)***	5.40	(.25)***	3.46	(.28)***
Model VIF	1.12		1.11		1.11		1.24		1.34	
F statistic	2.10*		1.71†		1.71†		1.45		11.96***	
Adj R^2	.01		.01		.01		.01		.19	

SOURCE: Moldoveanu and Baum: "I Think You Think I Think You're Lying": Interactive Epistemology of Trust in Social Networks. *Management Science* 57(2), 2011, pp. 393–412. Copyright 2011, Institute for Operations Research and the Management Sciences, 7240 Parkway Drive, Suite 300, Hanover, MD 21076 USA. Reprinted with permission.

NOTE: *N* = 608.

†$p < .10$; *$p < .05$; **$p < .01$; ***$p < .001$.

TABLE 4.3 Logit Regression Models of Knowledge of Alters' Level 1 Beliefs

	Coef.	(S.E.)	Coef.	(S.E.)	Coef.	(S.E.)	Coef.	(S.E.)	Coef.	(S.E.)	Coef.	(S.E.)	Coef.	(S.E.)
DV: ij Matched														
ij Same location	.01	(.17)	.03	(.17)	-.01	(.17)	.03	(.17)	-.06	(.18)	-.09	(.18)	-.07	(.18)
ij Same division	.34	(.17)*	.39	(.17)**	.31	(.17)*	.37	(.18)*	.33	(.18)*	.27	(.18)†	.30	(.18)*
ij Same gender	-.22	(.20)	-.20	(.20)	-.23	(.20)	-.22	(.20)	-.23	(.20)	-.27	(.21)†	-.30	(.21)†
i Male	-.04	(.20)	.01	(.20)	-.05	(.20)	.01	(.20)	-.05	(.21)	-.04	(.21)	-.14	(.21)
i Tenure	.00	(.01)	.00	(.01)	.00	(.01)	.00	(.01)	.00	(.01)	.00	(.01)	.00	(.01)
j Male	.16	(.20)	.17	(.20)	.13	(.20)	.14	(.20)	.16	(.20)	.10	(.21)	.08	(.21)
j Tenure	.00	(.01)	.00	(.01)	.00	(.01)	.00	(.01)	.00	(.01)	.00	(.01)	.00	(.01)
i Betweenness			91.12	(48.83)*			153.52	(59.07)**	150.60	(59.90)**	153.69	(60.26)**	121.56	(60.00)*
j Betweenness			-8.12	(46.69)			24.78	(56.69)	27.33	(57.26)	24.11	(57.24)	15.97	(57.71)
i Constraint					3.34	(1.58)*	3.99	(1.97)*	4.19	(2.00)*	4.22	(2.00)*	4.24	(2.02)*
j Constraint					1.90	(1.54)	2.25	(1.89)	2.47	(1.88)†	2.40	(1.85)	2.36	(1.86)
i Trust level									.32	(.07)***	.22	(.08)**	.16	(.08)*
i Level 2 belief strength											.21	(.07)**	.38	(.10)***
i Level 3 belief strength													.00	(.09)
Constant	.19	(.27)	-.08	(.32)	-.05	(.31)	-.76	(.44)*	-2.52	(.60)***	-2.93	(.63)***	-3.28	(.65)***
VIF	1.12		1.11		1.11		1.24		1.23		1.25		1.35	
Log likelihood	-409.60		-407.74		-408.43		-404.61		-394.06***		-389.21***		-381.44***	

SOURCE: Moldoveanu and Baum: "I Think You Think I Think You're Lying": Interactive Epistemology of Trust in Social Networks. *Management Science* 57(2), 2011, pp. 393–412. Copyright 2011, Institute for Operations Research and the Management Sciences, 7240 Parkway Drive, Suite 300, Hanover, MD 21076 USA. Reprinted with permission.

NOTE: $N = 608$.

†$p < .10$; *$p < .05$; **$p < .01$; ***$p < .001$.

TABLE 4.4 Descriptive Statistics and Correlations for Reciprocal Relationships

	Variable	Mean	S.D.	Min	Max	1	2	3	4	5	6	7	8	9	10	11	12	13	14	15	16
1	ij Trust level	6.10	1.14	1	7	1.00															
2	ij Level 2 belief strength	5.44	1.30	1	7	.39	1.00														
3	ij Level 3 belief strength	5.58	1.07	3	7	.28	.43	1.00													
4	ji Trust level	6.12	1.15	1	7	.30	.13	.17	1.00												
5	ji Level 2 belief strength	5.50	1.28	1	7	.13	-.07	.18	.37	1.00											
6	ji Level 3 belief strength	5.62	1.06	3	7	.15	.17	.17	.26	.44	1.00										
7	i Betweenness	.0015	.0017	.0000	.0102	-.07	.02	-.12	-.13	-.27	-.32	1.00									
8	j Betweenness	.0015	.0017	.0000	.0102	-.17	-.29	-.38	-.08	.11	-.09	.12	1.00								
9	i Constraint	.102	.056	.017	.439	-.02	-.09	-.11	-.03	.18	.10	-.54	.09	1.00							
10	j Constraint	.100	.055	.017	.439	-.03	.20	.13	-.03	-.13	-.12	.07	-.55	.03	1.00						
11	ij Same location	.62	.49	0	1	.29	.20	.31	.29	.20	.34	-.16	-.10	-.01	-.04	1.00					
12	ij Same division	.64	.48	0	1	-.03	.09	.07	-.04	.09	.09	-.14	-.08	.20	.17	.05	1.00				
13	ij Same gender	.76	.43	0	1	-.06	.02	.19	-.07	.01	.21	-.37	-.30	.04	.02	.12	-.03	1.00			
14	i Male	.73	.45	0	1	.05	.18	.11	-.02	-.01	.02	-.18	-.21	.07	-.03	.13	-.09	.31	1.00		
15	i Tenure	12.04	9.85	1	35	-.03	.11	.01	.18	.07	.10	-.18	-.20	.11	.18	.09	-.08	.18	-.02	1.00	
16	j Male	.73	.44	0	1	-.02	.00	.07	.06	.12	.09	-.15	-.17	-.03	.04	.11	-.12	.27	.39	.06	1.00
17	j Tenure	12.16	9.85	1	35	.19	.06	.10	-.04	.10	.01	-.18	-.16	.14	.13	.08	-.09	.17	.06	.38	-.03

SOURCE: Moldoveanu and Baum: "I Think You Think I Think You're Lying": Interactive Epistemology of Trust in Social Networks. *Management Science* 57(2), 2011, pp. 393–412. Copyright 2011, Institute for Operations Research and the Management Sciences, 7240 Parkway Drive, Suite 300, Hanover, MD 21076 USA. Reprinted with permission.

NOTE: $N = 113$; correlations $> .17$ significant at $p < .05$.

interest are respondents' trust in competence and trust in integrity of, and level 2 and level 3 beliefs about, each other and their network characteristics. As before, the correlations are strong and positive for respondents' trust in and level 2 and level 3 beliefs about alters. The correlation between respondents' trust in each other is also strong and positive. The correlations between respondents' level 2 and level 3 beliefs and their trust in each other are positive, although more weakly and significant only in the case of level 3 beliefs. Three of four correlations among respondents' level 2 and level 3 beliefs are positive and significant as well.

Among the network measures, a respondent's constraint is positively correlated with his/her own level 2 belief strength, consistent with the idea that the density of relationships promotes interpersonal cohesion and formation of norms (Coleman 1988, 1990). More strikingly, however, a respondent's strength of trust in, and level 2 and level 3 beliefs about, alter j are negatively and significantly correlated with alter j's betweenness centrality. These negative correlations resonate with the idea that network centrality fosters a competitive orientation among agents as they attempt to take advantage of opportunities for information brokerage and control to increase their autonomy and others' dependence on them (Burt 1992; Moldoveanu, Baum, and Rowley 2003).

Table 4.5 presents a multivariate analysis of trust in the reciprocated relationships. Because errors are likely to be correlated across equations estimating the trust of respondent i on alter j and of alter j on respondent i using the same data, we estimated these equations using a seemingly unrelated regression (SUR) model, which allows correlated errors between equations (Greene 2000). The multivariate analysis again confirms the correlation analysis. Consistent with those in Table 4.3, estimates based on reciprocated relationships indicate that the respondents' level 2 beliefs about alters are positively associated with their trust in them, while their level 3 beliefs are not. Estimates also show that respondents' independently reported trust in each other is positively related.

Moreover, respondents' network constraint is positively correlated with their level 2 belief strength. The estimates additionally indicate that respondents' trust in alters is negatively related to alter betweenness and positively related to alter constraint. Again, these findings are consistent with the idea that dense relationships promote interpersonal cohesion and norms of

TABLE 4.5 SUR Estimates of Trust in Reciprocal Relationships

Variable	Coef.	(S.E.)	Coef.	(S.E.)	Coef.	(S.E.)	Coef.	(S.E.)	Coef.	(S.E.)
DV: ij Trust level										
ij Same location	.70	(.21)***	.67	(.20)***	.69	(.21)***	.35	(.20)*	.30	(.20)†
ij Same division	-.10	(.21)	-.19	(.21)	-.07	(.22)	-.05	(.21)	-.11	(.20)
ij Same gender	-.32	(.25)	-.49	(.26)*	-.32	(.25)	-.28	(.26)	-.21	(.25)
i Male	.10	(.25)	.03	(.25)	.11	(.25)	.06	(.24)	-.14	(.23)
i Tenure	.01	(.01)	.02	(.01)†	.01	(.01)	.03	(.01)**	.03	(.01)**
j Male	-.06	(.25)	-.11	(.25)	-.06	(.25)	-.14	(.24)	-.03	(.23)
j Tenure	-.03	(.01)**	-.02	(.01)*	-.03	(.01)**	-.03	(.01)**	-.03	(.01)**
i Betweenness			-49.07	(64.01)			21.72	(75.78)	-1.75	(72.18)
j Betweenness			-135.44	(61.67)*			-161.16	(73.66)*	-120.45	(73.39)*
i Constraint					.59	(1.85)	.60	(2.14)	1.13	(2.01)
j Constraint					.37	(1.88)	2.77	(2.19)	3.58	(2.07)*
ji Trust level							.46	(.09)***	.39	(.09)***
ij Level 2 belief strength									.29	(.08)***
ij Level 3 belief strength									.01	(.10)
ji Level 2 belief strength									-.01	(.09)
ji Level 3 belief strength									-.05	(.10)
Constant	5.79	(.33)***	6.43	(.46)***	5.86	(.38)***	3.74	(.81)***	3.01	(1.02)**
R^2	.14		.18		.14		.21		.32	
χ^2	18.91**		25.01**		19.07*		57.64***		74.96***	

DV: *ji Trust level*

	(1)	(2)	(3)	(4)	(5)	(6)
ij Same location	.69 (.21)***	.66 (.21)***	.68 (.21)***	.62 (.21)**	.32 (.21)†	.24 (.21)
ij Same division	-.11 (.21)	-.20 (.21)	-.09 (.22)	-.14 (.22)	-.09 (.21)	-.14 (.20)
ij Same gender	-.34 (.26)†	-.51 (.27)*	-.35 (.26)†	-.58 (.27)*	-.32 (.27)	-.30 (.26)
i Male	-.10 (.25)	-.16 (.25)	-.10 (.25)	-.15 (.25)	-.15 (.24)	-.04 (.24)
i Tenure	-.02 (.01)*	-.02 (.01)*	-.03 (.01)**	-.02 (.01)*	-.03 (.01)**	-.03 (.01)**
j Male	.15 (.25)	.11 (.25)	.15 (.25)	.10 (.25)	.14 (.24)	-.01 (.23)
j Tenure	.01 (.01)	.02 (.01)†	.01 (.01)	.02 (.01)†	.03 (.01)**	.03 (.01)**
i Betweenness		-103.68 (64.94)†		-135.80 (78.71)*	-126.71 (76.36)*	-127.49 (76.35)*
j Betweenness		-62.32 (62.57)		-82.07 (77.08)	-42.07 (76.82)	-18.20 (73.87)
i Constraint			2.36 (1.87)	4.07 (2.24)*	3.91 (2.17)*	3.27 (2.06)†
j Constraint			.77 (1.89)	1.59 (2.29)	.07 (2.25)	.57 (2.16)
ij Trust level					.47 (.09)***	.42 (.09)***
ij Level 2 belief strength						-.06 (.09)
ij Level 3 belief strength						.00 (.11)
ji Level 2 belief strength						.26 (.09)**
ji Level 3 belief strength						.04 (.11)
Constant	5.86 (.33)***	6.46 (.47)***	5.94 (.38)***	6.90 (.58)***	3.63 (.84)***	2.75 (1.06)**
R^2	.14	.17	.15	.18	.19	.29
χ^2	18.61**	22.53**	20.84*	24.47**	53.68***	67.30**

SOURCE: Moldoveanu and Baum: "I Think You Think I Think You're Lying": Interactive Epistemology of Trust in Social Networks. *Management Science* 57(2), 2011, pp. 393–412. Copyright 2011, Institute for Operations Research and the Management Sciences, 7240 Parkway Drive, Suite 300, Hanover, MD 21076 USA. Reprinted with permission.

NOTE: $N = 113$.

†$p < .10$; *$p < .05$; **$p < .01$; ***$p < .001$.

cooperation (Coleman 1988, 1990), while central network positions create opportunities and incentives for information brokerage and control (Burt 1992; Moldoveanu, Baum, and Rowley 2003). Among the control variables, it is notable, and somewhat ironic, that more senior respondents expressed more trust in alters while simultaneously being less trusted.

Taken together, the results of the foregoing analysis corroborate the idea that trust is associated with deeper hierarchies of coherent level 2 and level 3 beliefs. The analysis reveals not only a strong covariation among respondents' level 2 and level 3 beliefs about alters and their trust in competence and trust in integrity of alters; it also reveals a strong covariation of their knowledge of alters' level 1 beliefs. In contrast, while respondents' betweenness centrality and constraint are positively associated with their knowledge of alter j's level 1 beliefs, they are either unrelated or negatively related with their trust in alters. Thus, within the large telecommunications firm examined here, centrality is not necessarily indicative of relative informedness (especially when higher-level knowledge is included in what counts as information) and the enhanced ability to mobilize or coordinate the network that accompanies it; nor is agent constraint necessarily indicative of common knowledge. Moreover, when high constraint in networks results from dense connections among agents (rather than connections through a single individual, as in a hierarchy), it ought to be positively related to trust (Burt 1992). Although constraint derives primarily from density in our empirical setting, this is generally not what we find. The epinet model thus does a better job of explaining trust—and predicting it ex ante—than do intuitive and widely accepted structural models.

How Trust Partitions and Propagates Information in Social Networks

Trust and security are vital to information diffusion, verification, and authentication in social networks and to a precise explanation of the network position advantage that accrues to certain agents. The effective brokerage of information across a structural hole is dependent on the trustworthiness of the broker to both the transmitter and the recipient of that information. Thus, if trust safeguards coordination and co-mobilization, it is reasonable to assume that it also safeguards coordination-intensive tasks such as truthful communication and therefore the spread of useful and veridical information within a network.

Communicating critical information is a coordination-intensive task because it takes place in the background of shared assumptions and orientations whose commonality is important to the accurate receipt of the information in question: "The CEO told me we are moving away from vertical markets" may be highly useful information to someone who knows the context of the conversation in which it emerged and quite useless information to someone who does not know it. In this section, we show how the description language we have introduced can be used to model the flow and authentication of information in a social network, and we pave the way to empirical analyses of informational dynamics in networks.

Trust Partitions. Epinets allow us to state how and why trust and security matter by making it possible to state sufficient epistemic conditions for the knowledge that trusting, trusted, secure, and authenticated networked agents fulfill. In particular, we define the following.

Trust Neighborhood ($N_{Ti}(G)$, $N_{Tb}(G)$*).* A fully linked subnetwork of G (clique) that shares trust in mutual competence and integrity (weak form). A trust neighborhood is a good model for a network of close ties where agents can rely on one another for truthful and truth-like knowledge sharing, conditional on awareness: if an agent is aware of P (knows it and knows she knows it), then she will share P with others. Thus, in a trust neighborhood communication is truthful but what is being communicated may not be "the whole truth." Trust neighborhoods can represent referral cliques, often used to get the "inside story" on people and organizations that have a history of interactions within an industry.

A referral clique is a clique of agents in which information flows are "trustworthy" in the technical senses of trust introduced earlier. Within a trust neighborhood (a "circle of trust"), sensitive information is likely to flow more reliably and accurately than it does outside of it. Our epistemic representation of trust allows us to map the trust neighborhoods within a network precisely and therefore to make predictions about the reliable spread of accurate information within the broader network of contacts.

Security Neighborhood ($N_{S}(G)$*).* A fully linked subnetwork of G (clique) that shares trust in mutual competence and integrity (strong form). Security neighborhoods are high-trust cliques. They may be good representations for networks of field operatives in law enforcement—where authentication of communicated information is crucially important to the payoff for each agent—or for conspiratorial networks—such as a subgroup of directors trying to oust the company's CEO. The reason for calling such a network a security neighborhood is that it has (common) knowledge of itself *as* a trust neighborhood and thus possesses an important authentication mechanism for communication, which trust neighborhoods based on weak-form trust do not possess.

If A and B belong to the same trust neighborhood, then C (a third party unknown to A but known to B) can interject herself in the communication between A and B and contribute information to them. If the fact that C is part of the trust neighborhood is not itself common knowledge, then the information that C contributes is not authenticated in the sense that it is not possible for A to decide whether or not to trust information coming from C without consulting B. If, on the other hand, A and B are part of a security neighborhood, then C will immediately be recognized as an outsider. Common knowledge of clique membership is a key element in authentication, which is itself important in subnetworks concerned with infiltration from the outside. A key property of a security neighborhood is thus that it necessarily has common knowledge of the fact that it is a security neighborhood as well as common knowledge of any fact that is relevant to it:

Proposition. A security neighborhood is a common knowledge neighborhood.

Proof. Consider a dyad (A, B) where ATB and BTA, both in the strong sense. For any P, it is the case that $Ak(P = true \leftrightarrow BaP)$ and $Bk(P = true \leftrightarrow BaP)$. For instance, let $P = ATB$. Since P is true and $Ak(P = true \leftrightarrow BaP)$, $Ba(ATB)$ is true. Now, suppose that P is true but there is some level of almost-common knowledge, n, at which it is not the case that $(AkBk)^n P$—that is, $\sim(AkBk)^n P$. Then, at the almost-common knowledge level, $n - 1$, it cannot be the case that $(AkBk)^{n-1} P$. To see this, let P^{n-1} represent the proposition $(AkBk)^{n-1} P$, which is true and, together with ATB, implies $(AkBk)^n P$. Therefore, if P is true, ATB and BTA, P is common knowledge.

Trust and Information Pathways. If "trust matters"—and if it matters crucially for the way in which an agent conveys information to an alter—then classifying network ties in terms of the degree of trust that the linked agents share should allow us to make progress in understanding the dynamics of critical information in a network. Concatenating trustful-trusting relationships, we can define the most likely, the fastest, or the most reliable paths by which relevant and truthful information flows in a social network.

Trust Conduit from Agent A *to Agent* J. Path *A-B-C . . . J* from *A* to *J*, passing through agents *B . . . I* such that *A* trusts *B*, *B* trusts *C*, *C* trusts *D . . . I* trusts *J*. Trust conduits can enable reliable knowledge flows in networks: information that comes from *A* is trusted by *B*, information that comes from *B* is trusted by *C*, and so forth, such that information flows credibly along a trust conduit. Trust conduits can represent knowledge pipes in organizations and markets, and thus they enable us to study the dynamics of new information propagation. They can also be used to effect a useful distinction between facts and rumors: facts are bits of information that have propagated along a trust conduit; rumors are bits of information that have not. Since facts can be used to check rumors, trust conduits not only enable speedy propagation of useful relevant information but also afford checks and constraints on rumor propagation. Rumors should thus die out more rapidly in networks seeded with many trust conduits than in those lacking them.

Trust Corridor. Because trust is generally not symmetric (particularly in its weak forms), we define a trust corridor as a two-way trust conduit. A trust corridor is useful for representing reliable bidirectional knowledge flows within a network, thus increasing the degrees of freedom associated with any particular flow. If reliable knowledge can flow in both directions in a knowledge pipeline, rumor verification can proceed more efficiently, as any one of the agents along the path of the corridor can use both upstream and downstream agents for verification.

Trust corridors may be a good representation for *expert networks* made up of agents who can verify relevant rumors that come to the attention of any one of them. They can thus be seen both to accelerate the reliable transmission of facts and to impede the promulgation of unverified or unverifiable rumors within a network. Figure 4.1 illustrates the trust neighborhood, conduit, and corridor concepts graphically. Figure 4.2 maps out these epistemic regimes for the telecommunications firm we studied. If trust safeguards effective communication of reliable and accurate information, then we expect relevant bits of information to propagate relatively faster and more efficiently within trust neighborhoods and along trust and security conduits.

Special network relationships are required for the propagation of "sensitive" information—information that senders wish to be assured will reach only and all intended recipients. In such situations, agents' knowledge of the

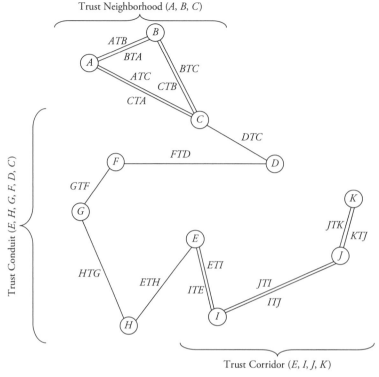

FIGURE 4.1 Trust Regimes
SOURCE: Moldoveanu and Baum: "I Think You Think I Think You're Lying": Interactive Epistemology of Trust in Social Networks. *Management Science* 57(2), 2011, pp. 393–412. Copyright 2011, Institute for Operations Research and the Management Sciences, 7240 Parkway Drive, Suite 300, Hanover, MD 21076 USA. Reprinted with permission.

integrity of the trust conduit they access is required for the conduit to function as an information channel. The conditions for such "superconductive" conduits can be made more precise through the use of epinets in the following ways.

Security Conduit from Agent A *to Agent* J. Path *A-B-C . . . J*, from *A* to *J* passing through agents *B . . . I* such that *A* trusts *B*, *B* trusts *C*, *C* trusts *D . . . I* trusts *J* and the conduit is common knowledge among (*A . . . J*). This feature renders such conduits robust against infiltration, as each user of the communication channel embodied in the conduit can be authenticated by any of the agents comprising it. Security conduits can be understood as authenticated knowledge pipes representative of operative agent networks (e.g., secret agent networks) in which rapid authentication of incoming messages can be

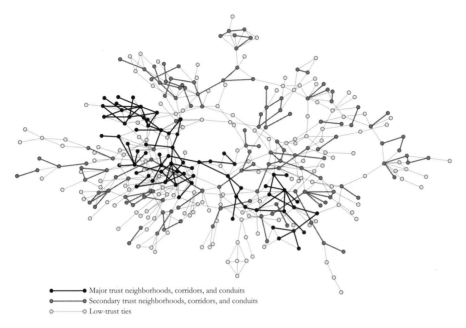

Major trust neighborhoods, corridors, and conduits
Secondary trust neighborhoods, corridors, and conduits
Low-trust ties

FIGURE 4.2 Trust Regimes within a Large Telecommunications Company
SOURCE: Moldoveanu and Baum: "I Think You Think I Think You're Lying": Interactive Epistemology of Trust in Social Networks. *Management Science* 57(2), 2011, pp. 393–412. Copyright 2011, Institute for Operations Research and the Management Sciences, 7240 Parkway Drive, Suite 300, Hanover, MD 21076 USA. Reprinted with permission.

performed quickly using agents' (common) knowledge of each others' conduit membership.

Security Corridor. A security corridor is a two-way security conduit that represents subnetworks in which (1) rumor verification can be more rapid than in one-way knowledge-conducting structures, and (2) the probability of undesired "infiltration" is low because of the authentication mechanism available to "strong-form" trust-based subnetworks. Security corridors may also represent authenticated expert networks that are characteristic, for instance, of robust social referral networks, which cannot easily be infiltrated and can be used for both fast rumor verification and the robust circulation of reliable knowledge.

Taken together, the epistemic building blocks we have introduced allow researchers to study not only the impact of trust on coordination and mobilization but also the impact of trust and trust-related structures (neighborhoods, conduits, corridors; security neighborhoods, corridors, conduits) on the propagation of information within a network. Seen through this lens, trust appears to provide a mechanism for the *informational superconductivity* of social networks and offers an explanation for the differential propagation of information in organizations and markets. Trust ties are informational super-conductors, and the subepinets that characterize trust and security neighbor-hoods can be thought of as resonant cavities in which sensitive information reverberates.

However, trust-mediated structures may exhibit epistemic quirks, or counterintuitive effects, that can be investigated using the precise description of epistemic states that epinets afford. We can, in particular, make predictions about the relative conductance of a trust conduit and the effects of perceptions about the relevance of a piece of information on that information's dynamics. Suppose that Alina communicates "in confidence" a secret piece of information, S, to Belinda, whom she trusts and therefore believes that S is safeguarded by this trust. Belinda immediately lets Claire, whom Belinda trusts, in on S. Claire proceeds in a similar fashion, and within days S becomes shared knowledge within the organization (even though very few know that others know it).

Has Belinda broken Alina's trust? And if so, *where*? The epistemic definition of trust we introduced suggests a simple answer: Belinda broke Alina's trust when she did not tell Alina that she told Claire S, because the proposition *I told Claire S* is relevant and true and Belinda knows it to be relevant and true. However, if Belinda trusts Claire, then she can justify not telling Alina that now Claire knows S by reasoning that because Claire will keep the information to herself, S will not get any further within the organization, which is something that Alina would not consider relevant. Of course, if Claire reasons the same way about Belinda, S will freely propagate and *become* relevant as a result of the very way in which Belinda has defined relevance. This example highlights both the importance of trust conduits in the propagation of "secrets" and the potentially insidious local effects of trust in promoting the very kinds of behavior that it seems designed to preclude.

Trust can be built, but it can also be broken and, with it, the network epistemic structures that are held together by trust ties. Because we have defined trust noncircularly (in terms of epistemic states and subjective beliefs that can be tested), it should be possible, using the representational tool of epinets, to investigate breaches of trust (intentional and otherwise) and identify specific consequences of trust-making and trust-breaking moves to the resilience of social networks.

Trust and the Fragility and Robustness of Social Networks

Recent interest in the characterization and optimization of network robustness (e.g., Callaway et al. 2000; Albert and Barabási 2002; Paul et al. 2006) has focused on the survivability of certain topological and structural features of a network (connectedness, diameter, characteristic path length) in the face of "attacks" that either sever ties among networked agents or remove from the network one or more agents that are topologically significant (e.g., "hubs" in center-periphery networks). Such analyses have proceeded in a more or less "mechanical" fashion by deriving the evolution of networks in the face of various random and probabilistic attacks, but they have not considered the relationship between certain kinds of attacks and certain ties, or the relative disruptiveness of various attacks on different network structures.

To make clear what we have in mind, suppose that you are a "social terrorist" who wishes to maximally disrupt the smooth functioning of a group, organization, or institution and are aware of the importance of trust-based ties to network integrity and of network trust and security neighborhoods to the reliability and speed of information propagation within the organization. With this knowledge, you can design strategies to disrupt the precise set of trust-based ties that safeguard passage of information between two subnetworks that are connected only by one or a few "trust brokers." These strategies can be targeted at undermining either trust in integrity or trust in competence through the introduction of noise and distortion in individual or group communications that make it difficult to ascertain the degree to which trust was broken or kept in any given interaction.

Alternatively, understanding the importance of common knowledge or common beliefs regarding the secureness of a security conduit or corridor, you can systematically introduce noise or doubt in the higher-level epinets that safeguard security or trust in order to undermine the integrity and cohesiveness of these trust-mediated structures. This can be done through communications that break up cohesive cliques and trust circles or that weaken the confidence of members of such subnetworks in the veracity or reliability of the information being communicated.

Based on such considerations, breaches and repairs of trust can illuminate the relative fragility and robustness of social networks in new ways. Because trust (in integrity and in competence) is defined as a relationship between agents' epistemic states, epinets enable us to study not only its effects on higher-level epistemic states and on the flow of information in networks, but also the dynamics of *trust-making* and *trust-breaking* phenomena. The Marquis de La Rochefoucauld pointed out in *Maxims* (1912) that it is impossible to distinguish a person who behaves in a trustworthy fashion because "that is the kind of person that he is" and a person who behaves trustworthily for a (potentially very long) period of time in order to advantageously exploit the trust that he has slowly and meticulously built up.

For example, A's trust in B creates opportunities for B to take advantage of A. In such a case, it is B's consistent and long-running refusal to take such opportunities in situations in which doing so has negligible costs that gives the trust relationship its unusual force. Once again, the importance of counterfactual and subjunctive epistemic states reveals itself: "If B wants to take advantage of me—A may reason—she *can*"; the fact that she does not functions as a certifier for the ongoing trust that A places in B.

Trust is a delicate relationship because it takes only one counterexample to the general-form statement "If P were true, then B would assert P or act as if P is true" to refute the proposition and thus undermine the trust that A has in B, while it takes an infinite—and therefore infeasible—number of confirmations to prove it. It may be objected that this account of trust is too simple because it leaves out phenomena such as contrition and generosity, which are valuable under noisy conditions (Axelrod 1997). Considering the effects of epistemic structures in such cases is beyond what we attempt to accomplish here, but it is clear that higher-level epistemic states are relevant to a comprehensive investigation of these phenomena.

For instance, if A has reason to believe that B construes their interaction environment as noisy, then A can exploit the fact that B is likely to interpret A's trust-breaking actions as noise. If B does not know this, then he is more likely to forgive A than if he knows that A has exploited the camouflaging properties of noise, in which case B may react even more punitively than he would in a noise-free environment in order to punish A's (double) breach of trust.

Such observations make it possible for us to offer an *endogenous* account of structural hole formation (Burt 1992), insofar as we understand structural holes as "trust holes" (of integrity, competence, or both). Suppose that A trusts both the integrity (strong form) and competence of B and B trusts both the integrity and competence of C. Then A trusts the integrity and competence of C (in the strong sense) and the subnetwork A-B-C constitutes a security neighborhood. Now suppose that, per La Rochefoucauld, B has worked on obtaining A's trust over time with the intention of breaking it at an opportune moment and that the opportune moment is the possibility of creating a trust hole between A and C that only B can bridge.

The key to B's realization of his intention is the recognition that the *knowledge* operator ("knows P," or kP) depends on the relevance of what is known to the aims of the knower(s). Thus, if C knows P (*Cedar needles are green*) but P is not relevant to A (an investment banker who has never seen a cedar tree), then the fact that C does not assert P cannot constitute a breach of A's trust of C; otherwise, the trust relationship condition would be too strong because it would require the parties to constantly assert propositions that are true but irrelevant. *Relevance* is thus a condition that can be made as precise as the rest of the analysis so far.

Relevance. P is relevant to C, for instance, iff C's knowledge of P will cause C to change her planned course of action in a particular case.

Armed with this analysis, B, our putative "insider" and trust breaker, can now exploit small and potentially transient asymmetries of information or insight in order to break off A's trust in C and therefore *create* the A-C trust hole that only B can bridge. In particular, to create the hole B sets up a situation in which (1) C knows P but believes that P is not relevant to A; (2) P is relevant to A; (3) A knows C knows P; and (4) C does not assert P, which is deemed by A to contradict the proposition *If P is true, A will assert P*, which underlies her trust in C.

Using this blueprint for the undermining of trust, B can look for situations that allow him to exploit asymmetries of *understanding* between A and C, wherein A and C attach different degrees of relevance to the same proposition, P, which both nonetheless consider true. On finding such a proposition, B must then ascertain that A knows that C knows P and must rely on the mismatch in ascribed degrees of relevance to cause the breach of trust.

For instance: telecommunications industries (such as WiFi, a protocol for wireless local area networking based on the *IEEE 802.11(a)* standard, and WiMax, based on the *IEEE 802.16(d–e)* standards) rely on large, established chip manufacturers like Intel for system developer ecosystems that embed their chips into products. A system manufacturer with private information about a chip's limitations can cultivate, say, Intel's trust by informing it of those limitations and of new market opportunities. And it can undermine Intel's trust in its other partners (such as software developers that target their applications to a chip's specific capabilities) by communicating information that it privately knows (e.g., from other suppliers) to be relevant to Intel but that it also knows will not be conveyed to Intel by its other partners in a timely fashion (because of their less intense interaction with Intel and time constraints). Thus, relative differences in interaction intensity can be used to seed breaches of trust based on asymmetries of understanding as well as information.

More broadly, the kind of epistemic network analysis that we have been engaging in can be employed to model the relative *fragility* and *robustness* of (trusting) relationships. In particular, *network fragility* correlates with the degree to which noisy interaction environments are more likely to engender breaches of trust that result in the dissolution of ties. Conversely, *network robustness* correlates with the degree to which noisy interaction environments are unlikely to produce breaches of trust that result in the dissolution of network ties.

We have seen that noise in interpretation of an agent's behavior by his/her alters creates the possibility for breaches of trust that are shielded by justifications ex post such as "I did not know it would hurt you." However, our definition of trust provides for distinguishing trust in competence from trust in integrity and therefore distinguishing "You should have known it" from "You should have said so" rejoinders. We are, as a result, able to investigate the reparability of breaches of trust in competence and trust in integrity separately, and to investigate whether different forms of breach—in the presence of different kinds of noise—are more or less likely to fracture a tie and compromise a network.

To the extent that trust neighborhoods form the *coordinative backbone* of a social network—the agent subnetwork most likely to coordinate its actions and co-mobilize purposefully—and to the extent that this coordinative backbone is critical to the functioning and usefulness of the network as a whole—the survivability of the network in its entirety depends on the resilience of the trust-based ties that constitute its "circles of trust"—its trust and security neighborhoods. The question "How fragile is network X?" then, can be made more precise by focusing on the specific trust and security neighborhoods that it comprises and asking (1) "How dependent is the existence of these neighborhoods on the specific ties they contain?" and (2) "How fragile are the ties on which these neighborhoods critically depend in the face of attacks meant to undermine the trust that buttresses them (in its various forms)?" Network robustness analysis turns, in this case, on (1) the epistemic structure of a network's coordinative backbone (its trust and security neighborhoods) and (2) the relative susceptibility of the network ties to attacks that may occur from either inside or outside.

One illuminating way to appreciate the fragility of a network's trust and security neighborhood is to consider the labors of our "social terrorist" as she attempts to unravel the "social fabric" that holds a network together on the basis of understanding (1) the epistemic structure of trust-based ties, (2) the topology of the relevant trust-linked subnetworks, and (3) the importance of trust-based subnetworks to the functioning and integrity of the network as a whole. She can proceed as follows.

Undoing Trust-Based Ties. Suppose that dyadic trust takes the logical form we have set forth for trust in integrity or trust in competence. Trust turns, in this view, on the subjunctive belief held by A that B would both know what is relevant and would assert it (to A). Knowing this, our terrorist can provide A with evidence that will lead A to believe either that B does not know something that A knows to be true and relevant—undermining A's trust in B's competence—or provide A with evidence that will lead A to believe that B has not communicated a fact that B knows to be true and relevant—undermining A's trust in B's integrity.

Based on her understanding, our social terrorist realizes that a key variable in this situation is A's own knowledge of what is true and relevant. If what is relevant changes quickly, then the truth value of various propositions spelling out relevant facts changes quickly as well since knowledge should "track" facts. If communications between A and B are less frequent than changes in what is relevant (or relevant propositions change their truth value), then our terrorist can undermine A's trust in B's competence by providing A with relevant information at a higher frequency, creating situations where A already knows what is true—and that A therefore believes B should know (but does not). Our terrorist can, of course, do this in the guise and camouflage of "being helpful" to A—which in fact she (partially) is. This strategy does not cast a shadow explicitly on A's trust in B's integrity unless A has reason to believe, at some point, that B knows something that is true and relevant and has not communicated it to A.

Knowing this, our terrorist can set up similar high-frequency communications with B, inform B of what is true and relevant (perhaps just *after* having informed A), and communicate to A that she has *already* conveyed this information to B. If the frequency of interactions between A and B is not high enough to track the changes in B's epistemic states that A has been informed of, then situations will arise in which *delays* in B's acknowledging or relaying to A the information received from our terrorist will function as evidence undermining A's trust in B's integrity. Our terrorist accomplishes this by *not* informing B that she has already informed A of the change in what is true or relevant, thus leaving B in a fog regarding the timing of the terrorist's relay of information to A. Our terrorist uses the *timing* of communications, and uncertainties about *who knew what and when*, to undercut A's trust in B.

Timing is one form of colored noise that our terrorist can introduce to undermine relational trust. It is well known that noise can "undo" cooperative outcomes more generally as a result of the camouflaging properties that the introduction of exogenous and potentially irrelevant information affords (Axelrod 1997). In the case of trust, however, noise need not be exogenous to the epistemic states of A and B. Rather, our social terrorist can introduce noise in communications between A and B by introducing and respecting new *distinctions* that *confuse A* regarding what B knows and says. For instance, to a network theorist, speaking of *the centrality of agent X in network N* is imprecise because there are many different forms of centrality: an agent with high betweenness centrality, for instance, may have altogether different powers of influence from those of an agent with a high degree or eigenvector centrality.

If A and B use a low-resolution language to communicate (for instance, they speak of centrality *tout court*), then our social terrorist can undermine A's trust in B's competence by training A to make distinctions that B does not (e.g., between degree and betweenness centrality) and then using the resulting asymmetry in *understanding* between A and B to weaken the credence that A places in B's propensity to know and speak the truth about what is relevant. In a situation in which, say, increasing the betweenness centrality of an agent results in a decrease in his/her degree centrality, our social terrorist can use a statement such as "His centrality has increased," uttered by B, to demonstrate to A that B in fact does not know (or has not said) what is true about what is relevant, because what is relevant has changed. Distinctions, then, judiciously made and enforced, can create asymmetries of understanding that undermine the subjunctive beliefs in competence and integrity that ground trust.

Unraveling Trust and Security Neighborhoods and Corridors. Armed with techniques for undoing trust-based ties, our social terrorist can further apply herself to unraveling trust and security neighborhoods, conduits, and corridors. If these topological structures are "superconductive" in the sense defined earlier, then they are the primary carriers of reliable and accurate information across a network. Moreover, their superconductive properties aid our terrorist in discovering them. The discovery process is far easier for trust neighborhoods than for security neighborhoods because in the former the agents lack common knowledge of which of them make up the neighborhood. Since the only way to access information flows in a trust neighborhood is to become a member of it, and it is easier to fool one person than to fool many people at the same time, our terrorist focuses her infiltration strategies on trust neighborhoods rather than on security neighborhoods.

Armed with knowledge of the trust neighborhood's topology, our social terrorist can perform the usual analysis of "tie redundancy" and select the ties that are minimally redundant—such as bridging ties between multiply connected subnetworks, which function as "trust bridges." The ability of a trust neighborhood to survive tie-level attacks, then, is closely connected to the redundancy of ties among any of the agents in the network. The prospect of a social terrorist, in this case, offers an alternative explanation for the importance of "closure," which is quite distinct from the "mutual monitoring" function argued for previously (e.g., Coleman 1988; Burt and Knez 1995; Krackhardt 1999): robust networks survive, in this view, because they are less susceptible to malicious attacks aimed at undoing trust-based dyadic ties.

Undermining the Relational Fabric of Networks. To the extent that the effective functioning of a subnetwork depends on the integrity of trust and security neighborhoods and corridors, its survivability is critically linked to that of its associated trust-based structures. Not all subnetworks are equally dependent on a trust backbone, of course. Knowing this, our social terrorist can identify the parts of the network that are most dependent on the integrity of a trust backbone, and she can concentrate her efforts on them. But how does she discern the various subnetworks on the basis of their relative dependence on a trust backbone?

If, as we argue, the value of networks is critically dependent on cooperative and collaborative outcomes, and to the extent that these outcomes rely on coordinated action, and, furthermore, if trust correlates with the cohesion of higher-level epistemic states required for coordination, then our social terrorist can concentrate on the subnetworks that face the most challenging coordination problems. They are likely to be the ones that experience quickly changing environments that require rapid, reliable, and accurate communication of complicated, noise-susceptible knowledge structures. Under such conditions, our social terrorist can inflict "maximum damage" with the least effort—provided that she has targeted the right ties in the trust backbone of the coordination-sensitive (sub-)network.

Summary

We have argued in this chapter for an interactive, epistemic definition of trust and for the importance of trust, so defined, to cooperative behavior in social networks. Trust is a complex epistemic quantity that can be measured noncircularly once it has been specified in terms of agent-level states of belief and knowledge. Its impact on the propensity of social networks to co-mobilize and coordinate can be predicted. Various epistemic structures and information flow regimes that arise in social networks can be understood using the basic building blocks of trust in competence and trust in integrity.

We have shown how trust can be defined in terms of the epistemic states of networked agents, how that definition can be used to measure it, and how epistemically defined trust relationships can function as safeguards of network coordination and information flow. Because trust is defined precisely in terms of agent-level epistemic states, it is possible to both measure it noncircularly using standard empirical methods and to manipulate agent-level epistemic states and observe how doing so affects it.

The proposed definition also makes it possible to measure the effect of trust on the propagation of information, knowledge, and beliefs within a network and thus achieve a more textured understanding of the mechanisms by which bridging a structural hole bestows its advantages; moreover, our definition allows us to model the effects of agent actions that make, break, and repair trust by considering the specific changes in the epistemic states of the networked agents that these actions produce.

Chapter 5

"I Know You Think She Thinks I Trust You—But I Don't"

Moves, Tactics, and Strategies Defined and Played in Epinets

We extend the use of epinets to the characterization of dynamic network processes. We use them in two distinct ways: first, as instruments for specifying changes in the epistemic states of linked or interacting agents and, second, as a tool kit for representing strategic interactions. Using epinets to represent interactions among epistemically linked agents allows us to resolve ambiguities inherent in game-theoretic approaches and to explicitly model subtle phenomena such as mind games, dialogical games, and information brokerage games.

We have thus far dealt with the structure of epinets: who knows what, who knows whom, what is known to be known by whom, and so on. We have examined network-level phenomena such as brokerage and closure through an epistemic lens, affording insight into the individual, collective, and interactive belief and knowledge structures that enable cohesion, co-mobilization, and coordination. We also have extended the epinet concept to show how an agent's status can be textured and refined using the epistemic states of networked agents as important qualifiers. As noted, trust is tricky: it requires the deployment of a special kind of epistemic logic that relies on subjunctive propositional forms to characterize a trust-based relationship in a noncircular way.

Our project required that we make some nontrivial departures from the lexicon of epistemic game theory: we replaced "semantic" state spaces comprising events (collections of states of the world) in favor of "syntactic" state spaces comprising truth-functional propositions and their interpretations. We relinquished often-deployed assumptions of completeness and commonality of the resulting propositional state spaces in order to accommodate intuitive epistemic states such as ignorance and oblivion. In doing so, we gained an epistemic modeling language for network phenomena that tracks the subjective experience and intuition of networked agents. This made it possible to "measure" epinets via tools such as questionnaires and surveys; at the same time, it made it possible for us to build and test models of the correlates of different degrees of epistemic cohesion and sharedness and of trust within a network.

It is true that the resulting models do not have the well-behaved "equilibrium" features of game-theoretic models or the simplicity of structure-disturbance-action-performance explanations of standard social network analyses; however, they do lay bare the hidden epistemic content of a network, which in many cases is what makes its inner world turn. *What, however, about the dynamics of epinets?*

From Structure to Dynamics: Epinets as Trackers of Epistemic State Changes

We have inherited at least two different conceptions (along with associated imagery) of the informational dynamics of networks. One is the *strategic-agentic* view: human agents make decisions based on information they use to update their existing beliefs and on objectives they seek to maximize, conditional on the information they have and their own constraints of body, mind, time, and resources. Networks are quintessentially about interaction, and interaction is about interdependence. Thus, a theory of decisions with interdependent outcomes made by agents who are aware of these interdependencies is needed. And that is what game theory supplies, albeit, as we have argued, at a cost that we cannot afford: equilibrium, one of the key elements of game theory's explanatory engine, is predicated on a number of epistemic preconditions that are not good descriptors of "what humans do" with their minds; they are also not reasonable assumptions about rational agents whose positive and negative introspection is less than perfect.

A second conception is the *system-dynamic* view of information as flowing through a network that resembles a cellular telecommunications system (minus the humans), the World Wide Web, or the biochemical signaling pathways of a complex neurological, enzymatic, or immunological subsystem—coupled to the automatic, rule-based behavior of the networked agents, whose states change as a function of information regarding changes in the states of other agents with whom they are linked. This is a "passive" view of the informational dynamics of networks because information conveyance is not purposefully corrupted, it has no higher-order effects (such as the establishment of mutual and common knowledge) and it determines the behavior of the agents receiving it.

In spite of the (largely emergent) complexity of these models of network dynamics (Watts and Strogatz 1998; Albert and Barabási 2002), the interaction rules and agent-level (node-level) decision, action, and tie formation rules that govern their evolution are mechanical, simple, and often deterministic, which raises questions about the degree to which the resulting dynamics represent networks of human agents endowed with considerably more insight and intelligence—even if they are less reliable in the implementation of action plans. Network epistemics—the part of our modeling approach that relates to the nature, structure, and spread of information within a network—can significantly advance the degree to which modelers of social network dynamics can incorporate into their models "who-knows-what-and-whom-when" insights and data that can be used to tailor their models' governing assumptions.

In view of these options, we are in the predicament of navigating our modeling enterprise between the Scylla of the "unbounded rationality" of game-theoretic models to derive equilibrium results on the basis of what rational agents need to know to converge to an equilibrium set of strategies (albeit at the pain of assuming they know too much), and the Charybdis of the "mechanistic social action" used by network theorists to make predictions about the evolution of collective processes in social networks (albeit at the cost of assuming that human agents either know too little or can do too little with what they know).

The epinet approach facilitates this tricky passage. It broadens the set of epistemic conditions placed on networked agents ex ante by rational choice and game-theoretic approaches, and it allows us to incorporate subtle and important epistemic states as descriptors of what agents know—including confidence, trust, and oblivion—while at the same time permitting incomplete and incommensurate state spaces among individual agents. It allows the incorporation of inferential moves and logics that represent what agents can do with what they know more loyally than either the 'logically omniscient' approaches of game theory or the mechanized models of network dynamics.

More important, this approach allows the dynamic evolution of epistemic conditions within a network—from oblivion into knowledge and awareness, or from trust into its opposite (as we saw in Chapter 4)—as a function of individual agents' actions. Epinets allow us to track both the ways in which agents learn to change their behavior by virtue of new information and the ways in which they proactively shape the informational and epistemic landscape of the network as a whole.

In this chapter, we illuminate what happens to the traditional concerns of modelers of many different persuasions about describing, explaining, and predicting the *dynamics* of social interactions among networked agents. If the modeling language of epinets is to be truly useful as an explanation-generating engine and modeling tool, then it should serve as a source of both explanatory concepts akin to those of game theory (equilibrium, subgame perfection, learning) and predictions regarding network dynamics (topological structure, asymptotic evolution of centrality measures, probability of finding at least n agents that have at most k ties to other agents under certain assumptions). To show that this is possible, we break down the core discipline of using epinets to measure social networks, map out different information and epistemic regimes within them, and specify a range of epistemic moves and strategies that agents can use to bring change to the structure of their epinets.

Specifying and Measuring Epinets

Specifying an epinet entails articulating the agents that make up the network or subnetwork of interest along with the epinet's individual, collective, and interactive epistemic states. True to the primitives of the EDL introduced in Chapter 2 (e.g., Figure 2.1), this involves specifying not only agents but also the truth-bearing statements—the "propositions"—that constitute the basis for the epinet. Propositions admit different *interpretations* that may be specific to the epinet's agents. For instance, if $P = Agent\ A_1\ was\ at\ a\ lunch\ with\ 30\ other$ *people, seated at five tables at which [famous person X] was present*, one interpretation may be that A_1 *had lunch with X*; an alternative interpretation may be that A_1 *was in the same room with X*. These are both viable interpretations of P because they may be considered true if P is true, but it is not the case that P is considered true if they are true. They are partial or distorted representations of P.

To ascertain *differences* among interpretations, we can examine differences in their material and logical implications, as well as differences between these implications and the implications of P. For instance, *having had lunch with X* suggests a level of familiarity and access to X that may entail *being able to introduce A_2 to X* or *being able to ask a specific and personal favor of X*, which P may not necessarily entail and which is certainly not entailed by an interpretation of P as *having been in the same room with X for 90 minutes*.

The first step in specifying an epinet is determining an identifiable set of agents, an epistemic core (a set of relevant propositions that to various degrees are known, believed, known to be known and believed, and so on, by the agents), and a set of individual epistemic states. In the foregoing example, depicted in Figure 5.1, agents A_1 and A_3 know some interpretation of P and are aware of knowing that interpretation (they know they know it); A_2 is oblivious of both P and its different interpretations (she does not know it and does not know she does not know it); A_3 and A_n are both knowledgeable and aware of a different interpretation of P (they know and know they know); whereas A_4 knows the same interpretation of P that A_3 and A_n know, but is not aware of knowing it (perhaps because she has temporarily forgotten it).

A network or subnetwork defined by a set of high-density interactions or "close ties" may be characterized by an epistemic core (comprising propositions and their interpretations), and specification of agents and epistemic cores proceeds in a "bootstrapping fashion": adding a proposition adds more agents, who in turn add more propositions, up to the point where additional agents do not add additional elements to the epistemic core and where additional propositions added to the epistemic core do not add additional agents. Alternatively, one can specify boundaries on the epistemic core of a network (a technical field of knowledge) and add agents according to the rule *Who knows P?* where P is some element in that core; or one can ex ante specify the set of agents (membership in some professional organization, department, or

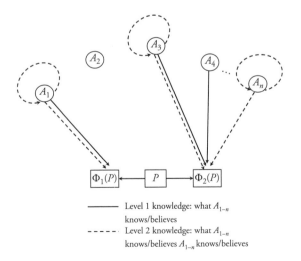

───── Level 1 knowledge: what A_{1-n}
      knows/believes
- - - - - Level 2 knowledge: what A_{1-n}
      knows/believes A_{1-n} knows/believes

FIGURE 5.1 Epinet of Networked Agents: Individual Epistemic States

field of activity) and construct the set of propositions that are constitutive of those agents' membership (related, for instance, to a set of common goals and principles).

Measuring Knowledge and Belief(s). "Measuring epinets" is well within the standard tool kit of networks researchers, but "measuring the epistemic cores" of the associated network is not. We can measure beliefs via questionnaires and surveys, provided that we take into account the possible effects of the phenomenon of "cheap talk," the demand characteristic of distorting private information, and the information impact of using a survey instrument. An agent cannot be oblivious of a proposition that appears as a question on a survey because the instrument has made him aware of it, regardless of whether or not he knows its truth value or the answer to the question.

We can also measure the set of propositions that the agents in an epinet know or believe by deploying standard belief elicitation protocols that have been used in decision analysis for many years, via bets on the truth value of particular propositions: "How much will you bet on a lottery that pays X if P is true and $0 otherwise?" elicits a number, Y, which can be used in conjunction with X to measure an agent's subjective degree of belief in the true value of P as $p(P) = X/(X + Y)$. Of course, here, too, agents' answers may not indicate true beliefs because "How much *would* you bet?" creates very different incentives from those created by "How much *will* you bet in *this* situation here and now?" Even when a "real" experiment can be conducted, the answer may vary as a function of the absolute values of X and Y and the subject's risk and uncertainty preferences. Specifying an epinet's epistemic core is, again, a bootstrapping process of *ascription* (Moldoveanu 2011) followed by experimentation: once a plausible epistemic structure is ascribed to the network, the hypotheses that emerge regarding what agents know can be tested.

Specifying Interactive Epistemic States. An epinet can be specified further by the addition of the *interactive* epistemic states of its agents vis-à-vis its epistemic core. Returning to our example as presented in Figure 5.2, A_1 knows that A_3 knows an interpretation of P that is different from his own (but the opposite is not the case), and A_3's interpretation of P is mutual knowledge (level 2 common knowledge [NC_2]) between A_3 and A_4. This allows the modeler to make conjectures regarding certain interactions that could take place among subsets of agents on the basis of existing interactive epistemic conditions in the network: since mutual knowledge of a salient proposition or interpreta-

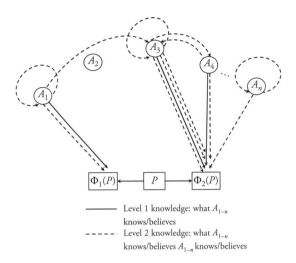

FIGURE 5.2 Epinet of Networked Agents: Interactive Epistemic States

tion enables co-mobilization in scenarios in which joint outcomes depend on the truth value of that proposition, we can look for co-mobilization possibilities among the agents who share mutual knowledge of a salient proposition.

Moreover, the epinet can be used as a "self-correction tool" for the modeler. If it becomes clear or plausible that A_4 knows that A_3 knows some interpretation of P, then we may not be able to consistently claim that A_3 is not aware of that interpretation. The ascription of epistemic states can thus be revised recursively to maintain the coherence of the overall model. (Of course, coherence of the *model* of an epinet is not the same as coherence of the *epistemic states of the agents being modeled*: we can coherently model *noncoherent* epistemic states of networked agents, but that requires a set of assumptions about the informational and computational endowments of the agents that make up the epinet—in this case, a situation in which A_4 acts as if she knows that A_3 knows their shared interpretation of P, but does not act as if she *knows* that interpretation, which is a very special condition indeed.)

Epistemic Trails and Conductivity

Unlike energy, mass, momentum (at nonrelativistic speeds) and money (in the absence of inflation), information is not conserved: one agent's passing of a bit of information to another agent does not cause the transmitter to *lose* that information. For this reason, information *flows* through networks are difficult to track in the same way that the flow of money and matter can be tracked (via tracking *local* changes created by a conservative exchange process). The modeling tool kit of epinets allows us to build real-time descriptions and predictive models of the information dynamics in teams, groups, organizations, or other collaboration and interaction networks.

Gossip, rumor mills, and information cascades are all processes by which social capital is exercised, amplified, extinguished, or wasted (Burt 2005). They can be used to study the echo of individual actions in groups or the bandwidth of the individual signals that are amplified by the informational rumor mills that interactions generate. What is needed to make the study of information propagation in networks as precise as that of strategic form games is a representation of information flows textured enough to make predictions about the nature, structure, and consequences of information-bearing signals passing through the network (in the form of gossip and rumor, for example).

Epinets track the flow of information among agents simply and intuitively via epistemic state changes among the agents in them. As proposition *P* propagates, the epistemic states of various agents vis-à-vis *P* change as *P* "makes the rounds": an agent oblivious of *P* before being informed of it may come to know or believe *P* after some relevant interactions. *P*'s dissemination thus produces an epistemic trail (or "wake") made up of changes in the epistemic states of networked agents vis-à-vis *P*.

An epistemic network may differentially conduct information-bearing signals passed among and between agents, and it is the function of trust ties (including conduits and corridors) to represent the information-carrying properties of social networks. Trust ties can be characterized (as in Chapter 4) using modal modifications of epistemic logic that yield subjunctive forms of the type *Alice trusts Bob if she knows that if Bob knew P he would communicate it to her* (trust in integrity) and/or *Alice trusts Bob if she knows that if proposition P were true he would know it* (trust in competence) or, combining the two forms, *Alice trusts Bob if she knows that were P true he would communicate it to her.*

Returning to our example, in Figure 5.3, a bidirectional trust link is introduced between agents A_1 and A_2 and between agents A_3 and A_4. Incorporating the trust links of these agent pairs completes the epinet. The inclusion of trust links and bridges allows us to predict the instantiation of preferential information flows within the network (who says what to whom and when) and the limits and boundaries of valid information flows.

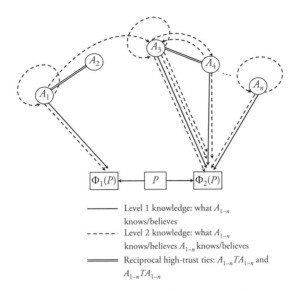

FIGURE 5.3 Epinet of Networked Agents: Trust and Epistemic Links

Epistemic Dynamics of Trust

Because we use propositions to model epistemic states of agents and networks, we can examine the structures induced by already existing epistemic structures by looking at the consequences and implications of the states' corresponding propositions. We saw an example of this in Chapter 4, where we showed that there are forms of trust that are transitive: A trusts C if A trusts B and B trusts C. The informational and social lubricant functions of trust can in turn be studied via epinets by mapping the epistemic structures that are *induced* by trust in relationships.

In Figure 5.4, the trust between agents A_1 and A_2 induces an epistemic structure in which each agent discloses fully to the other about proposition P, regarding which each has a different interpretation (stage 1), and about their private interpretations of it (stage 2). If P encodes a firm's pattern of sales performance over the past three quarters that generates one interpretation, *Sales have been relatively flat over the past eight quarters*, and another, *Sales have spiked rapidly over the past three quarters* (which are both valid), then the trust link between A_1 and A_2 induces a (new) information structure in which the partial truths of the two interpretations are pooled and become distributed (and common) knowledge, along with the information set (proposition P) on which the interpretations are based.

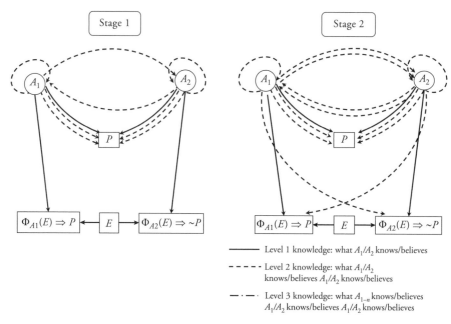

FIGURE 5.4   Epinet of Epistemic Links across a Trustful-Trusting Tie

The epistemic wake that information leaves in a network is dependent on the trustworthiness of the information's source. A pathological liar's alerting me to the two-faced nature of my boss may not convince me that she is two-faced, but I will not henceforth be oblivious to the possibility that the liar is right. Alice's telling Bob that he is about to be fired in a situation in which he was previously oblivious of the possibility changes Bob's epistemic state from oblivion to knowledge or belief regardless of whether or not he considers the information coming from Alice to be trustworthy (he can assign an arbitrarily small probability to the possibility referred to by the proposition *I will be fired within the next N days.*

Since epinets deal in propositions and interpretations rather than in events and states of the world, we can also track the specific *distortions* of information that intervene when information is communicated across networks. And we can make predictions about the relative speed, accuracy, secrecy, covertness, and reliability with which information in networks flows across certain links (such as trust and security). As a result, we can be both more precise in the rendition of informational effects in networks and more detailed in our conjectures regarding the network structures that are more apt to carry reliable, timely, and accurate information.

Modeling and Tracking Information Flows in Epinets: The Case of a CEO Ouster

The use of epinets to track the flow of information in a network via epistemic state changes among networked agents is illustrated in Figure 5.5. The agents are the top management team and the board of directors of a medium-sized public company. The epistemic core of the network is a proposition expressing a decision by the board to replace the CEO because of consistently poor revenue performance over the past ten quarters. The specific decision, initiated by one board member and ratified at an emergency board meeting (which did not include the CEO) at 8:00 A.M. on Day 1 (T_0 in the figure), was to replace the current CEO with an acting CEO (one of the board members) at a

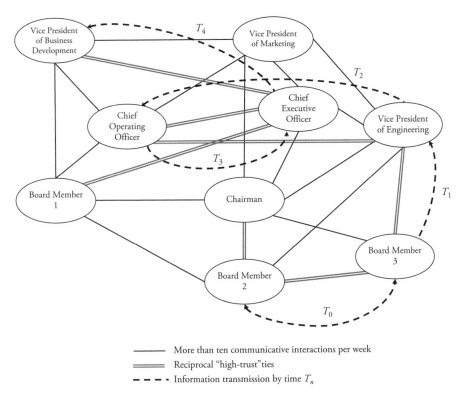

FIGURE 5.5 Information Propagation on an Epinet

subsequent meeting (which was to include the CEO) scheduled after the end of public market trading at 5:00 P.M. on Day 2.

The CEO was aware that the board of directors was concerned with the company's performance, but was oblivious to his own imminent departure. For reasons having to do with the maintenance of public market confidence and with potentially damaging actions that the outgoing CEO could take vis-à-vis sensitive client relationships, the board decided that news of the CEO's departure would be kept secret until the board meeting at which the change would be announced. However, it was also thought prudent, in view of recent unrest and ambiguity in the company's product development team, to communicate the news on a "confidential-do-not-repeat" basis to the vice president of engineering, who was instructed to maintain strict confidentiality as to the time and date of the executive changes and at the same time to convey to the development team that the board had full confidence in the company's ongoing viability and future health. The specific proposition regarding which the epistemic states of the agents were tracked was thus $P = $ *the CEO will be replaced by the board of directors at 5:00 P.M. on Day 2*.

Figure 5.5 shows the interaction network among the protagonists comprising the board of directors and the top management team (which can be thought of as either a collaboration network or an interaction network). Edges (single lines) indicate mean interaction frequencies greater than ten per week. These frequencies were estimated on the basis of interviews with six executives and board members regarding their patterns of mutual interactions and their estimates regarding patterns of alter interactions within the network. The figure also shows trust links within the network (double lines) representing bidirectional "high-trust" links between pairs of executives.

Trust relationships were evaluated on the basis of responses to a 360-degree feedback survey of the top management team (the results of which were made public) that addressed professional competence (trust in competence), information distortion and withholding (trust in integrity), and disposition toward the good of the company as a whole, as evidenced by behavior (trust in integrity). Discussions were also held with three board members regarding the specifics of information propagation among directors and between the board of directors and the top management team.

The specific decision regarding the removal of the CEO was initiated by board member B_3 and coordinated by board member B_2, who shared a "high-trust" link with B_3. It was agreed that the sensitive information would be passed to the vice president of engineering at 12:00 P.M. on Day 1 (T_1 in the figure), with the clear instruction that the specific time and date of the executive changes were not to be disclosed to anyone in the company under any circumstances. The vice president of engineering was also told that the conveyance of this information was on the basis of a closely held "circle of trust" comprising B_2, B_3, and himself, which implied that the resulting clique was a "security neighborhood" whose members shared common knowledge about clique membership and the trust connections that held the clique together.

The ensuing propagation of the sensitive information (specifically proposition P) is tracked in the figure, and was reconstructed through interviews with various members of the network (including the vice president of engineering and the vice president of business development) on Days 1 and 2 and after the critical announcement at the end of Day 2. The propagation of proposition P closely tracked the network's "superconductive" trust corridor. At 8:00 A.M. on Day 2 (T_2), the vice president of engineering conveyed the critical information to the company's chief operating officer, who, by 12:00 P.M. on Day 2 (T_3), had informed the soon-to-be-outgoing CEO. In turn, the CEO informed the vice president of business development of the board's impending action before 5:00 P.M. on Day 2 (T_4). Thus, by the time of the announced board meeting, most of the company's top management team and director-level managers knew about the impending change and its specifics.

The accounts given by the conveyors of the information are just as interesting as the specific topology of the information flows within the network. The vice president of engineering, for instance, insisted that the chief operating officer "looked as if he already knew" at the time their conversation took place and therefore saw the conveyance of the information not as imparting anything new but rather as establishing common knowledge of a proposition of which there was already distributed knowledge. There is an obvious tension between this account and the specific circumstances under which the vice president of engineering was informed of P; those circumstances were that no one else on the management team knew what was taken into confidence regarding P. This tension highlights a real contradiction, as the vice president of engineering either truly believed that the chief operating officer had come into possession of the critical information through other channels, which contradicts the trust that he had placed in the instructions received and the certification that he was the only recipient of this information, or he did not truly believe it, in which case he breached the trust that had been explicitly placed in his cooperation.

Note that the notion of a contradiction is specific to the propositional state space structure of epinets, which allows the rules of logic to be used to examine consistency conditions among the various propositions that form the core of an epinet. In contrast, semantic state spaces do not permit examination of such contradictions among various beliefs, which are, in that case, numerical degrees of belief assigned by agents (or ascribed by modelers to agents) to various collections of states of the world ("events").

Moves and Strategies in Epinets

We are now in a position to define moves and strategies on epinets. We use the same basic principle to create an analogue to the game-theoretic idea of a strategy or move, and we define a move on/in an epinet as an action undertaken by an agent that changes the epistemic states of one or more of the other agents in the same epistemic network. This definition is meant to track a strategy in a game, which is a choice made by an agent that changes the game's state space (the space of possible outcomes and associated payoffs). If Alice sacrifices her queen in a game of chess, for instance, the epinet corresponding to the game represents her move as a change in the epistemic states of Alice and Bob (her opponent) regarding both the fact of the sacrifice of the queen and its imputed implications.

Unlike the game-theoretic notion of a strategy, the epistemic network conception of a move is that it is specifically meant to track epistemic state changes. Alice's choice to defect on Bob in a repeated two-player version of the prisoner's dilemma game (a "strategy" in the game-theoretic rendition of the game) is a move in the epistemic network linking herself, Bob, and the set of propositions that encapsulate their representations of the possible outcomes of the game if and only if it changes the epistemic states of Alice and Bob relative to proposition P: *Alice defected*.

The differences between the two conceptions are several. First, the "epistemic state of the game" is a complex object made up of Alice, Bob, what Alice knows, what Bob knows, what Alice knows Bob knows, and so forth. Thus, Alice may know P (it is her intent to defect, and defection is the effect of her action), but Bob may not know this (he may think that Alice made an error because she does not understand the game or because there is a defect in the scorekeeping mechanism).

Moreover, a move that changes Alice's and Bob's first-order beliefs regarding P is different from one that changes their higher-level epistemic states regarding P. This stipulation makes it possible for the epinet modeler to track "all of the differences that make a difference" in the resulting interaction. If Bob knows P and knows that Alice knows P, he will likely have a very different view of Alice (and of the game) than he would if he did not know P and did not know that Alice knew P. Moreover, if Alice knows that Bob knows she knows P, she may take a very different approach to her subsequent interactions with him (perhaps trying to get him to believe that she has made an "honest mistake" or justifying her choice by other means) than she would if she either did not know Bob knew she knew P or if she knew that Bob did *not* know she knew P.

Moreover, the *trust* that Bob has in Alice (and vice versa) is causally relevant to how Bob interprets any *account* that Alice offers for her choice, just as the trust that Alice places in Bob is causally relevant to Alice's interpretation of Bob's acceptance of that account. Epinets expand the descriptive arsenal of game-theoretic approaches in ways that track agents capable of (at least finite) reasoning that uses first-order and epistemic logic, and moves on epinets are meant to allow modelers to track the choices that agents make at the level of epistemic state space expansions, contractions, and modifications.

We reserve the term "strategies" on epinets to refer to sequences of moves made by an epistemic agent that are designed to produce a particular effect. Thus, Alice's objective in the repeated prisoner's dilemma game she plays with Bob may be to "come out ahead" at the end of N moves, given that she knows that at the outset she enjoys Bob's trust. Her strategy in the game, in that case, is a coherent set of epistemic moves aimed at prolonging Bob's state of uncertainty regarding her intentions in the production of a series of outcomes that jointly corroborate proposition P: *Alice defected on move k*. These epistemic moves can range from those that cast doubt in Bob's mind about his ability to correctly interpret the structure of the game and to determine the truth value of P, to those meant to repair Bob's trust in Alice's integrity and competence notwithstanding the fact that he has made the correct inference regarding the truth value of P. Alice's strategy is the sequence of moves in the epinet that she chooses to make to maximize her overall objective.

Kinds of Moves. Moves on epinets have different epistemic effects, and it is useful to distinguish among them on the basis of these effects. Two classes seem particularly important. One class comprises *divisive* and *collusive* moves made at the level of the interactive epistemic structure of the network (what agents think other agents think), which impact the relational structure of the network at the level of agents. The second class comprises *distortive* and *clarifying* moves made at the level of the propositions that represent the network's epistemic core.

Divisive and Collusive Moves. Divisive moves foster asymmetries or imbalances in the agents' epistemic states and therefore weaken the epistemic network's potential for co-mobilization and coordination. They are moves that shift the epinet *away* from common knowledge of propositions relevant to networked agents at the level of interactive belief structures; moves that undermine the epistemic reach and clout of networked agents; and moves that undermine the epinet's trust and security structures.

Divisive moves can be easily illustrated in the context of a clique (Alice, Bob, and Charlie) that is also a trust neighborhood (Alice strong-form trusts Charlie, who strong-form trusts Bob, who strong-form trusts Alice, or *ATC & CTB & BTA*) and that initially shares common knowledge of a collective purpose and of a set of propositions that are relevant to its pursuit. Divisive moves (which Alice can make) are those that take the clique from a state of common knowledge of relevant propositions and a strong-form trust to a state of distributed or private knowledge and a breakdown of trust. Alice can, for instance, undermine the trust between Bob and Charlie by selectively timing her interactions and signals to each of them so as to weaken the belief each has about the propensity of the other to share relevant and valid information. Or she can undermine the commonality of the epistemic core of the group by selectively informing Charlie (Bob) of information that she withholds from Bob (Charlie) and that differentially facilitates her and Charlie's (Bob's) capacity to coordinate or co-mobilize over that of Bob and Charlie.

Divisive moves can furthermore be classified as auditable/inauditable and ex post deniable/undeniable according to their discoverability after they are made. Alice can deniably and inauditably provide selective information to Charlie (Bob) via communication channels that are memoryless (such as word of mouth), and she can make these channels plausibly deniable by avoiding any discoverable tracks they may leave such as invitations to one-on-one meetings; she can "bump into" Bob (Charlie) and impart the selective information without leaving a trace of the interaction.

Moreover, Alice can develop *covert* communication channels with Bob and Charlie by using previous experiences separately shared with each of them to *encode* information that she communicates to them, even when all members of the clique are present (the quintessential "common knowledge–establishing" event in game-theoretic analyses). She can, for instance, cultivate a common shared interest with Bob in Durrenmatt's plays and refer to Charlie's actions in the presence of both Charlie and Bob using passages and leitmotifs from those plays in a way that makes the coded message she is delivering ("This is a Fraulein Doctor expression") common knowledge among the three but leaves the uncoded part (*Charlie is trying to manipulate us*) *covert* to Charlie (who has not read Durrenmatt's *The Physicists*).

In this case of encrypted communication, Alice introduces a relevant proposition (*Charlie is trying to manipulate us*) of which Charlie is *oblivious*, in spite of the fact that he is aware of the precise substance of the (encrypted) signal that she has communicated to Bob. The communication is moreover covert vis-à-vis Charlie if he does not know that Alice has actually used an encrypted communication protocol that employs a private key (say, the proclivities of characters in a play that only the transmitter and receiver have read and that each knows the other to have read) to which only she and Bob have access.

Finally, the covertness of the communication is deniable ex post if, on "discovery" by Charlie that Alice has used an encrypted message to communicate to Bob about him in his presence, Alice can explain her choice of language by pointing to a feature of the code that leads Charlie to misinterpret her intent and the effect of her communication on Bob (for instance, that Charlie is like the character in question not in his manipulativeness but rather, for instance, in his sensitivity to situational details).

Collusive moves, in contrast, are moves that drive an epinet toward common knowledge of a common epistemic core; moves that extend the epistemic reach and clout of an agent within an epinet; and moves that establish, extend, and repair information propagation structures like trust and security neighborhoods, conduits, and corridors.

Consider a triad in a network of dense interactions—where the densest interactions link Frieda to Gail and Hal—which, in spite of the frequency of mutual interactions, is divided in the epistemic states of its members as to propositions regarding issues of common interest and is moreover *not* a trust neighborhood. A collusively minded epistemic agent, Frieda, can *move* to increase the coherence of the clique's distributed epistemic states (who knows all and only the propositions of common interest) and interactive epistemic states (who knows others know and others know she knows all and only the propositions of common interest) by (1) distributing the information she knows and knows Gail and Hal do not know (because of both ignorance and oblivion), (2) credibly signaling to Gail and Hal that she knows they know the information that she is sending them, and (3) signaling to Gail and Hal that she is sending them all and only the information that she knows (and is therefore oblivious of whatever information she is not sending).

Although there is no signaling move that is sufficient for the development of trust among clique members, Gail's collusive signaling move clearly facilitates trust in competence and trust in integrity through the diligence of her communicative protocol. To the extent that trust is extended to one whose signaling is directed to the evolution of a coherent set of epistemic states of the clique as a whole in spite of private incentives (e.g., looking informed when in fact one is not, which drives Frieda to signal that she knows more than she does and thereby decreases Hal's and Gail's ability to be maximally informative in their own signaling moves), Frieda's moves help to turn the triad into a trust neighborhood.

Distortive and Clarifying Moves. Distortive and clarifying moves are those that operate on the epistemic core of the network (i.e., propositions that are jointly and severally relevant to the agents in an epinet) rather than on its interactive structure. However, these moves often have indirect effects on the network's relational structures through their influence on the interactive belief structures that their deployment induces.

Distortive moves ambiguate, confuse, and otherwise distort the network's epistemic core. They come in different forms, depending on both the *intent* of the agent making them and the *effect* of that agent's making them at a particular time.

Lies are straightforward modifications of the truth value of a proposition known by the liar to be true (false). *P = Amy will arrive on the 7:00 P.M. British Airways flight from Heathrow Airport*—said *of* someone who will not arrive on that flight—is a lie in both intent and effect if it is uttered by someone who knows Amy will not arrive on that flight and if it induces a belief in the interlocutor that tracks the truth value of *P*—that is, if it causes the receiver to come to *know P* by hearing the liar utter it, or if it strengthens the receiver's belief in the truth of *P* by hearing the liar utter it. Lies can therefore differ with respect to their intent and effect in ways that depend on the trust structure of the link across which they are communicated: if Alice lies to Bob by uttering *P* and Bob knows that Alice is a liar, then the intent and effect of the lie do not track one another.

Lies can induce straightforward modifications of the trust structure of an epinet, depending on their verifiability. In the case of *P*—a sentence with an easily ascertainable truth value—the utterance of the lie can trigger a modification of the trust structure of the link, even though the inferential link from the ascertainment of the lie to a specific form of trust that was broken is not determined. On ascertaining that Alice has lied, Bob may modify his knowledge that she is competent (she would know *P* if *P* were true: trust in competence), or he may modify his knowledge that Alice is sincere (she would assert *P* if she knew it: trust in integrity), depending on other considerations.

Of course, lies need not induce breaches of trust in competence or integrity and can even strengthen trust in a relationship. White lies are those uttered by an agent who knows that the utterance will not induce a change in the epistemic state of the receiver vis-à-vis the content of the message. If, for instance, Alice and Bob have an understanding that they will try to forestall an attempt by Charlie to find Alice, Alice's stating *P* to Bob at a table at which Charlie is present is a white lie vis-à-vis Bob, provided that Bob knows Alice knows that *P* is false and that Alice knows Bob knows this (and that she is only saying it so that Charlie hears it and is misguided).

Whether or not an utterance conveys a lie depends on the interactive epistemic states of the transmitter and the receiver in ways that color and texture the perceived intent and effect of the communication. Pink lies are those that, though well intentioned, do not accomplish the "encryption" effect that white lies achieve: If Alice does *not* know that Bob knows she is purposefully lying in order to mislead Charlie, then Alice's intent in uttering *P* is a lot fuzzier than in the case in which she does know it. Moreover, if Bob in fact does *not* know that Alice is lying in order to mislead Charlie, then the effect may be that of a straightforward ("black") lie.

Palters are distortions of the propositional content of a message that are aimed at inducing a set of level 1 and higher epistemic states in the receiver that (1) are relevant to the truth value of a proposition *P* and (2) do not track *P*'s truth value. They may, for instance, be held to be true when *P* is true, but the opposite is not the case. Unlike lies, palters do not involve outright distortions of the truth value of *P* via relevant messages. The goal is to "color" the truth, not to change it outright.

Palters convey either more or less than *P* does and therefore represent departures from the implicit trust-related norm of saying (and knowing) "the truth, the whole truth, and nothing but the truth." *M = I had lunch with Barack Obama yesterday*, uttered by Kim to Jill, is a palter relative to Kim's knowledge that she had lunch at a table with five other people—none of whom was Obama but had been invited by him, along with twenty-five others, to lunch at five tables, one of which was occupied by Obama—because it induces an epistemic state in Jill that does not *track P*. Jill's interpretation of *M* may be that Kim is on terms with Obama that are cordial enough to warrant a lunch conversation, which is not similarly warranted by *P*.

Once again, palters differ with respect to both intent and consequence: *M* may be a palter in intent but may not be one in consequence provided that Kim has a "calibration mechanism" that filters Jill's utterances to compensate for "reading too much" into what she says. Also, the degree to which *M* is a palter in intent is, again, subject to what Jill knows about the way in which Kim processes signals coming from her: if Kim knows that Jill filters her signals to compensate for palters (especially in a public setting) and furthermore knows that Kim knows it, then the intent of the palter is not as nefarious as it would be if Kim and Jill did not possess this knowledge. The interactive epistemics of the situation therefore provide a natural "baseline" for adjudicating the palter's intent and effect.

Palters can function as "self-defining truths"—that is, they can work as performatives and not just as declarative or constitutive terms. *P = I have heard many people say she is having a hard time with the new curriculum design*, uttered by someone who (without knowledge of any facts) has been saying for some time, to anyone who will listen, that *there are troubles with the new curriculum design* is a palter in the sense that (1) it does not convey the full epistemic structure of the link of communications that has led to *P* being true, even though, (2) *P* is now true (in view of the speaker's tireless paltering efforts). This example highlights the degree to which it is not only the epistemic content of an epinet or only the epistemic *structure* of the epinet in which a message is transmitted, but also the epistemic dynamics of a message that can make a material difference in the epinet's ensuing structure and dynamics.

We use the term *bullshit*—a colloquialism that, following Frankfurt (2005), we attempt to rescue from lay and imprecise usage—to denote moves on an epinet that (1) attempt to change or modify the receiver's epistemic state relative to a proposition of common interest, in a situation where (2) the transmitter does not know anything about the proposition's truth value. Unlike liars and palters, bullshitters are either ignorant or oblivious of the truth value of relevant propositions. They are simply interested in changing the epistemic state of the receiver vis-à-vis one or more propositions of common interest. *P = We are doing very well with the new product design* uttered by a director in a division whose quarterly budget is predicated on the performance of the current product suite, in the absence of any data or facts that confirm or inform the assertion, is a typical example of bullshit.

The difference between bullshit and palters is easy enough to grasp definitionally but difficult to tease apart in practice without further information about the epistemic states of agents in the epinet. *P = We are doing well but not great*, uttered by a program director giving guidance to university faculty regarding enrollment, may represent a palter if the speaker *knows* the current year-over-year demand characteristic for program applicants, or it may be bullshit if the director in fact does not know it and is simply trying to come off well. This suggests that one can differentiate between bullshit and palters by designing questions ("How do you know?" "What is the basis for saying . . . ?") that help distinguish between the two classes of distortive moves in a particular setting. The resolving power of such questions, of course, depends on the degree to which the bullshitter/palter's answers are themselves intelligible to the questioner and on the extent to which they are auditable/verifiable.

Relative to our inventory of distortive moves, *clarifying moves* are easy enough to define as moves that drive the signals exchanged by epinet agents toward a content that tracks all and only the truth value of the epinet's epistemic core. We can distinguish here between two types of moves. *Sanctioning moves* seek to alter the trust neighborhoods and interactive epistemic states of a network as a function of the messages that various agents emit (e.g., publicly unmasking liars and thereby undermining their epistemic role within the network by undermining the trust that others in the epinet might have in their competence and integrity). *Substantive moves* have to do with auditing, filtering, and classifying the messages that are passed by one or more agents within the network without publicly undermining the agents' epistemic roles.

Sanctioning moves act on the epistemic structure of the network as a whole, while substantive moves operate on the propositional content of messages passed between agents. The former may thus be aptly considered escalations of the latter to the level of structural interventions on epinets. Among clarifying moves, we can also distinguish between *interrogatory moves*, which attempt to unpack the propositional structure and epistemic content of a message through a series of questions that may be guided by insight into potential breaches of trust, and *declarative moves*, which openly challenge and criticize particular utterances as fallacious, obfuscating, mendacious, or otherwise distortive. As before, both moves induce a set of interactive epistemic states vis-à-vis both the message passer (liar? bullshitter? palter?) and the mover (tendentious? fair?) that affect whether the utterance succeeds in achieving its purpose, notwithstanding the mover's intent.

Epistemic Stability, Robustness and Immunity: In Lieu of Equilibrium

Using epinets to model social interactions in general and social networks in particular requires us to update the standard explanatory tool kit of rational choice theory and its interdependent rational choice offspring (game theory) to account both for the propositional state spaces that epinets use and for the textured description of individual epistemic states (oblivion) and interactive epistemic states (almost-common knowledge, knowledge of someone else's oblivion) that we have introduced. Epinets allow us to track epistemic state changes of interacting and networked agents at a level of precision and empirical operationalizability that is not possible using standard state space models that assume agents at least know and understand their own state spaces and share state spaces of events and states of the world about which they have updatable beliefs.

Without common priors assumptions, game-theoretic analyses cannot "get off the ground," so to speak, without the modeler ascribing a common state space to the set of interacting agents. This may work well enough for games that are "prestructured"—as they are in certain auctions and laboratories—but not so well for those played out "in the wild." In such cases, the particular epistemic states—and belief hierarchies—of the networked agents must be tested, discovered, and elicited rather than imputed or ascribed.

The net result of this explanatory maneuver is that the tried and true explanatory trope of equilibrium—a set of strategies that are mutual best responses such that no agent has the incentive to unilaterally deviate from her/his own course of action—needs to be replaced by a set of explanatory concepts that track the more complex state space description afforded by the epinet approach. In particular, to the extent that equilibrium relies on a common set of priors and, at the very least, on a common state space for the "game" being played, it does not survive the discovery that different agents inhabit different epistemic state spaces and perhaps use radically different ways of interpreting a state space that is, in the semantic approach, "the same" at the level of events.

There is no way for an agent to update beliefs or knowledge of a state space that has components of which s/he is oblivious. Moreover, if the state space comprises propositions rather than the raw, unstructured qualia that constitute "events," and if different agents have different elementary languages in which they formulate their propositions, then obliviousness of the proposition-generating languages of other agents also precludes the use of standard equilibrium concepts to explain, predict, rationalize, or justify the outcome of an interaction or a set of interactions.

Within the epinet formalism, then, we must replace the standard notion of equilibrium with a more textured set of explanatory concepts that relate to an epinet's informational and epistemic regimes. In particular, we can describe general forms of "homeostasis" within an epinet using the following concepts.

Stability. The (epistemic) stability of an epinet relates to the degree to which sets of epistemic states (individual, collective, interactive) are time-invariant in situations in which the truth values of the propositions in the epinet's epistemic core do not change and the epinet's interactive epistemic structures (mutuality, commonality, distribution, trust, security) remain unchanged in the face of changes to the truth values of these propositions. Stable epinets, in other words, maintain their information transmission structure in the face of new information (e.g., trust conduits and corridors remain unchanged in response to changes in "the world," as do epistemic cliques that enable co-mobilization and coordination), and their epistemic cores do not change in the absence of new information.

Robustness. Robustness relates to the degree to which the epinet preserves its epistemic core in the face of unintentional errors of communication ("white noise") among networked agents and the degree to which the epinet's epistemic structures (mutuality, commonality, trust, security) remain unchanged as a result of unintentional, random errors of new information registration and communicative mishaps. Thus, it is a measure of the degree to which the stability of the epinet is "fault-tolerant," where "fault" is strictly taken to mean the random errors and unintended actions that convey information to networked agents.

Immunity. Immunity is a measure of the degree to which the epinet preserves its epistemic core in the face of intentional distortions, deletions, and misrepresentations of information (which can take the form of lies, paltering, and bullshit, as well as breaches of trust in the form of errors of omission) in situations in which the truth values of propositions in its epistemic core do not change. It is also a measure of the degree to which the epinet preserves its interactive epistemic structures (mutuality, commonality, trust, security) in the face of attacks by insiders or outsiders designed to undermine its integrity and stability.

Immunity, then, is a form of robustness to *intentional* attacks (Albert, Hawoong, and Barabási 2000). Central to the notion of epinet immunity is the degree to which trust and security neighborhoods, conduits, and corridors can *survive* "malware" in the form of attacks on the very structures that safeguard the passage of reliable, accurate, and timely information among its agents.

Taken together, stability, robustness, and immunity form a set of explanatory concepts that replace the standard notion of equilibrium in situations in which an epistemic network is a complex, evolving entity, an always-already-happening process of information transmission, reception, distortion, and correction. They are all "dynamic equilibrium" states that allow modelers to bridge the "passive signaling" imagery of standard social networks and the active choice-functional representation of standard game theory models, in the absence of a complete and shared "bird's-eye" view of all epistemic states of the agents in the network.

The reader will notice that we have stayed at the level of referring to stability, robustness, and immunity as "measures" without positing a specific formulation for each. In each case, a measure can be a probability of survival after a period of time or following a critical event, it can be a percentage of an epinet's links that remain intact after a threatening event, or it can be the degree to which specific epistemic states (almost-common knowledge about P) required for coordination or co-mobilization survive an attack or an error. Different interpretations may be useful for different epinets, which is why we have not pressed any one particular measure.

Summary

An epinet is an always-already-happening process of information transmission, reception, distortion, and correction or filtering—quite aside from being an identifiable structure whose topology can be analyzed at any given point in time. We have shown that flows of information can be tracked by epinets via epistemic state changes that they induce. We have accounted for the ways in which agents' choices and decisions shape information flows in an epinet by introducing the concepts of epistemic moves and strategies that are meant to capture purposeful interventions by networked agents on the epistemic landscape.

We have seen that the moves and strategies that epinets enable us to speak about require concepts of homeostasis that are different from game-theoretic equilibria, and we have sought to distinguish among different levels of an epinet's invariance to changes and challenges to its structure. Finally, we have defined stability, robustness, and immunity in ways that are both intuitive and amenable to translation in the language of epinets.

Chapter 6

"What You May Think We Think We Are Doing Here"

By Way of Conclusion

We consider the effects of our EDL through the very epistemic prism we have constructed, and we offer an interpretation of the epistemic analysis of networks and interactions as a set of brokering and closure-producing moves, where brokering happens across communities of researchers with different representational and methodological commitments (epistemic game theory, network sociology) and where closure acts at the level of a nascent group that is interested in the epistemic structure and dynamics of interactions and networks. We conclude with thoughts for future directions of research and development.

———————

The very idea of a language for modeling the epistemic states of individual agents to make forward predictions about the structure and dynamics of social networks and interactions cuts obliquely across models of inquiry in different disciplines.

Game theorists—and epistemic game theorists in particular—consider the data produced by competitive or cooperative interactions as instantiations of *equilibria* among the actionable strategies of the agents involved. The task of the modeler or the theorist is to reverse-engineer the epistemic conditions that provide sufficient grounds for agents to act rationally and therefore choose strategies that are in equilibrium. Notions of common knowledge, common priors, and the common assumption of rationality emerge as *explananda* for why agents' strategies are in equilibrium (which is assumed ex hypothesis).

The fact that equilibrium is assumed—rather than derived or predicted—makes the modeler's task both easier and more difficult: easier because it fixes a set of propositions about the right representation of a state of affairs (an outcome is the logical and material consequence of strategies that are in equilibrium); more difficult because logical problems with the representation (such as those related to agents' unawareness or to their logical sloth or lack of logical omniscience) become genuine challenges to the internal validity of the model (either to the assumption of equilibrium or to the epistemic assumptions necessary to ensure it).

Network theorists—who reside at the "empiricist" end of the rationalist-empiricist spectrum—prefer to make "realistic" measurements of variables (e.g., the nature and distribution of ties among agents, flows of information) that may be plausibly (or "realistically") linked, whether causally or functionally, to some future state of the network or the interaction. The breadth of the variable space considered, and the lack of a formal language for addressing agents' epistemic states and the impact of these states on information flows, makes propagating the resulting models forward in time a high-variance enterprise: the networker's modeling tool kit does not have the kind of logical depth that permits game theorists to "look forward" into the future of a set of interactions.

The EDL we have introduced offers an alternative that rectifies the difficulties inherent in both approaches. It uses a set of primitives (agents, propositions, epistemic states) that are intuitive and measurable via instruments such as questionnaires, surveys, or forced choices among gambles, and that jointly allow a sensitive rendition of networked agents' epistemic states. At the same time, it sets out logical and meta-logical procedures that allow us to perform logically deep forward modeling of the interactions among epistemic states, information flows, and agent-level actions—modeling that is sensitive to distinctions that the analytical apparatus of epistemic game theory does not allow.

Indeed, the "move" that we are advocating can itself be understood through the epistemic prism as an attempt to broker, in the following ways, a closure-inducing "bridge" across disciplinary ways of seeing and doing.

The EDL as an Act of Brokerage

This text is itself an act of brokerage among several disciplines—most markedly between at least two. The first comprises researchers concerned with epistemic game theory, interactive epistemology, and the formal representation of knowledge structures and their dynamics in groups and collections of human agents. This discipline is cohesive in the epistemic sense in that its members share a set of assumptions: (1) assumptions about how knowledge and information are represented: (a) through propositions structured by first-order logic that "refer" to objects and events along with their negations, conjunctions, and disjunctions, and (b) through degrees of belief that obey the axioms of probability theory; (2) assumptions about how knowledge and informational states evolve (e.g., Bayesian kinematics); (3) assumptions about how the beliefs of interacting human agents in turn interact with one another; and (4) assumptions about how agents calculate *equilibria* in games they may be construed as playing or their interactive equilibration of conjectures regarding other people's beliefs.

The cohesiveness of this disciplinary group inheres in the distributedness of representations (models) and procedures (rules, algorithms, heuristics) for manipulating them among group members. Equally important, each member knows that every other member is equipped with a common set of representational and procedural bits of knowledge and is prepared to use them in practice, and knows, moreover, that each member knows that every other member knows this. This epistemic structure enables communication among members on the basis of a common "code": each contributor to the dialogue that constitutes a "research program" uses a code and associated rules for putting words together in such a manner that they will be understood as intended. The use of the code is enabled by norms of communication and justification (provability from parsimonious axioms) that, once again, are distributed and common knowledge among group members and embodied in practicing members who come to recognize each other by "the way they think," for which the way they speak serves as a proxy.

The disciplinary group on the other side of the brokering bridge we are trying to engineer comprises researchers who study social networks. They commonly represent human groups as networks of agents and their relationships, and they seek to understand the behavior of groups as a function of the structure and dynamics of ties that bind group members through empirical investigations of the structure and dynamics of relational patterns. This disciplinary group is cohesive in that its members share ways of representing human groups.

One way is through network graphs wherein individuals are represented by "nodes" and wherein relations of friendship, collaboration, and interaction (among others) are represented as "edges" connecting these nodes. Another way is through variables of interest in the analysis of the structure and evolution of a network (the strength of the ties that make up the network, the centrality of an individual in her subnetwork, her strategies and tactics regarding tie formation and dissolution, and so on). The modeling tropes shared by this group are clustered around ways and means of describing patterns of relationality among human agents, and they form a distributed representational knowledge base that is more or less common knowledge among social network researchers.

The cohesiveness of this group is predicated not only on the distributedness and commonality of the declarative knowledge that corresponds to the domain of social network analysis but, just as important, on the distributed knowledge of this distributedness—the knowledge that every other member knows that this knowledge is distributed. And, as in the case of epistemic game theory and interactive epistemology, the resulting cohesiveness at the level of representations is only efficacious as a social adhesive if the members of the social network analysis group also share norms of discourse and justification—in this case, phenomenological plausibility, empirical testability and validity—that go hand in hand with the representational basis of the underlying discipline.

Brokers are frequently sources of "good ideas" in their own networks (Burt 2005), but "good ideas" do not just flow across brokering ties that bridge structural holes in *any way*. Rather, they must bridge structural holes in the in the *right way*, and the rightness of the *right way* depends on the epistemic structure of each of the otherwise disconnected subnetworks, comprising both what individual members know—declaratively and procedurally, implicitly and explicitly—and what each member knows that the others know.

The broker treads an epistemic landscape that has considerable interactive depth, and s/he succeeds (or fails) in large part as a function of his/her ability to identify and use the organized, intelligible, *common knowledge cores* of the interactive epistemic tangle that characterizes the fields s/he is attempting to bridge. This detailed understanding of the common knowledge cores of at least two distinct groups is integral to the broker's ability to speak the "native language" of each one.

The brokering we are attempting—in real time—relies on our signaling credibly to members of each disciplinary group that we speak their native tongue well enough to be considered worthy interlocutors. This does not merely entail the ability to cite relevant material in the social networks and interactive epistemology literatures and to form correct sentences in the technical syntax of each field. It means being able to employ the specialized codes and knowledge structures that are common or almost-common knowledge within each field in a way that heeds the discursive practices and the justification and validation norms of both.

An epistemic picture of the cohesiveness required for genuine brokerage emerges: it describes the minimal epistemic preconditions for successful coordination and cooperation among individual members of the subnetworks being connected. We are nearly there in terms of describing brokerage as the construction of an *epistemic bridge*. What is missing is how the broker creates marginal incentives for members of disjoint "communities of practice" to "tune in" to each other's codes, language systems, paradigmatic problems, and solution procedures. To this end, the broker must understand the canonical problems that in some sense "define the field," not just the specific language systems for representing phenomena that are indigenous to each subnetwork, and s/he must establish a basis for "gains from *epistemic* trade" by tailoring the communicative acts that establish a bridge between fields. So, then, what goes into engineering the right epistemic bridge between epistemic game theory and social network analysis?

Interactive epistemology and epistemic game theory, taken together, represent a disciplined attempt to speak precisely and coherently about human beliefs and conjectures in order to explain, predict, criticize, or rationalize human actions and interactions. For epistemic game theorists, formalization is a tool rather than an end in itself. This distinguishes them from logicians, who are more interested in creating a complete and consistent axiomatic system that solves certain technical problems without regard for descriptive accuracy or phenomenological plausibility. Social network theorists are also interested in representations and methods for testing models that use them to explain and predict patterns of human behavior and interaction. The degree of formality and choice of formalisms employed by the two theory groups differ, but they share at least some epistemic objectives relative to which the usefulness of brokerage can be determined.

Key decisions for us as "epistemic bridge builders" in this case are these: *what* to formalize, *how much* to formalize, and *when not* to formalize. Were social network theorists willing (and able) to follow the discussions unfolding in epistemic game theory, they would likely contribute novel problems, dilemmas, paradoxes, and predicaments of direct interest to epistemic game theorists as a result of their direct empirical analysis of real human groups, organizations, and institutions. In turn, they may contribute appropriate ways of representing epistemic states that can be transformed into novel empirical measurement and observation instruments. They could, for instance, use the more elaborate modeling language of epistemic game theory to measure new properties of the structure and dynamics of human networks—such as epinets of various kinds—and examine how epinets influence tie formation and decay, and network dynamics more generally.

Standard semantic models of epistemic rationality and the structure and dynamics of interactive beliefs are based on parsimonious formalizations of human agents' epistemic states ("states of the world," "events," "personal probabilities for events") that map onto representational tropes (such as the unit interval in real numbers), thus allowing analyses of more logically complex concepts such as exchangeability, conditionality, and equilibrium—often with other substantive assumptions such as independence, common priors, and logical omniscience (Aumann 1976, 1989). The logical depth of such analyses comes at the cost of reduced intelligibility of the formalism by outsiders who may be interested in epistemic phenomena. It also comes at the cost of a loss of representational power that empiricists would rather avoid.

The semantic approach also raises difficulties for the coherent representation of certain epistemic states, such as unawareness (which we termed "oblivion"), that are more or less "self-evidently" relevant to everyday human interaction (Dekel, Lipman, and Rustichini 1998). As we observed in Chapter 1, a syntactic view of epistemic states that focuses on *propositions* about events, rather than events themselves, as proper arguments of knowledge states can help resolve such difficulties.

Making propositions the "stuff" that epistemic states are made of raises the possibility that traditional game-theoretic concepts ("information partitions," "states of the world"), which do not translate easily into lay language or an alternative, less formal but still technical language, can be replaced by more intuitive concepts that function as templates for empirical analyses of the contents of networked agents' minds. A successful epistemic bridge between social network and epistemic game theorists, then, will feature just the right degree of formalization of just the right quantities and their properties to show traditional empiricists the benefit of appropriating the more nuanced distinctions enabled by formal languages; it will also show purveyors of more complex formalisms the benefit of widening their current set of distinctions to include insights from the field.

A second important question to ask as epistemic bridge builders relates to the empiricism of a research practice. Epistemic game theory has evolved as an a priori discipline, spawned by researchers who questioned the logical bases and preconditions for equilibria in games played among ideally rational agents (e.g., Aumann 1976; Brandenburger 1992). Empirical studies of what actual agents actually know about other actual agents with whom they interact—or *how* different ways of knowing produce different interdependent action regimes—have never been part of the field's activities or concerns. Social network analysis, in contrast, has never *not* been about empirical measurement of some property of a pattern of human relations. It may be that logicians are simply uninterested in the empirical analysis of epistemic structures and that empiricists are simply uninterested in logical analyses thereof (in which case, our effort is wasted).

It may also be that the sorts of questions epistemic game theorists want to answer are not addressed by social network theorists because, for example, there are no models that make the right distinctions or perhaps the sorts of novel questions about network epistemics that network theorists want to ask require understanding of a field that takes too much effort for uncertain returns. A successful epistemic bridge, then, will create a language that makes it possible for epistemic game theorists to tune into social network theorists' empirical analyses and for them to generate insights for social network theorists to conduct novel empirical research.

Seeding Closure. Our work is not only an attempt to build a bridge, however; it is an attempt to *seed* and *catalyze* closure. It endeavors to create a common representational basis for crystallizing a network of diverse researchers into a more or less interdisciplinary research group. Research groups are communities of communication and practice. Semiotically speaking, a research community is a set of human agents who write scholarly papers and give talks for and to each other.

A scholarly paper—in an age of technical and linguistic specialization—is a communicative act that uses a code to translate "everyday" or "folk" language into "technical" language. Mastering the dual acts of encoding and decoding is an effortful and "scaffolded" activity (Clark 1988). It corresponds to achieving the standing to speak in the forum of an academic journal or conference by learning the specialized language systems and communication norms that all participants hold in common, and it represents a barrier to entry to the field.

Scaffolding refers to the embedding of technical discourse within a fabric of discourse produced by other members of the same community, such that the "meaning" of various code words can remain implicit. "Beliefs," for instance, may be represented by probability weights associated with events or propositions about events, and may be governed by a logic of coherence and updating that is taken for granted by members of the research community.

This commonality of the "taken for granted" makes within-group communication both more reliable and more efficient: the meaning of technical jargon need not be communicated when it is transmitted and is also, in some sense, "secure" from eavesdropping by outsiders lacking similar training. This view of a professional or research network gives new meaning to the phrase "closure closes": it "closes up" the range of possible participants to any dialogue or communication, and it "closes off" participation by outsiders.

Building closure in a new community of communication that spans elements of two distinct disciplinary subnetworks entails creating shared and common knowledge structures that give meaning to network echoes of one's own written and spoken acts, even when they themselves remain implicit. Networks theorists are interested in making more precise distinctions that guide their understanding of brokerage, closure, trust, and status. Epistemic game theorists are interested in formal representations of interactive knowledge structures in scenarios where the outcomes of an individual's decisions depend on the decisions of other individuals that accommodate "all of the differences that (could plausibly) make a difference" to the outcome of an interaction.

Achieving closure in a (new) subnetwork that includes members of both of these subnetworks depends on building a language for representing epistemic states—an EDL of the form outlined in Chapter 2 and elaborated in later chapters—that is subtle enough to allow new and useful distinctions yet precise enough to work with more formalistic approaches to prediction and explanation, and that can function as a regulative schema for the interdisciplinary dialogue that makes up the new network.

A regulative schema of this kind must supply the new network with commonly held rules or norms for adjudicating the usefulness of members' contributions. Closure closes by *foreclosing*—in the sense of exclusion or disbarment—communicative acts that do not correspond to the set of commonly held communicative norms. It is only relative to such an (often) implicit set of exclusionary rules so that breaches and *faux pas* can be detected; this detection is essential to the mutual monitoring effect that network closure contributes to social capital.

Because the use of specialized language is almost always a tricky coordination game played among senders and receivers who "try out" and "critique" new ideas, the successful instantiation of this game depends on focal points—rules and norms by which the usefulness of communicative acts is gauged—that are themselves (almost) common knowledge among members of the community that makes up the network. It is for these reasons that we have spoken of and attended to an EDL first and foremost and only derivatively spoken of and attended to models and methods that its adoption enables.

Our Gambit. We have argued for the value of an empirical research program in "network epistemics" that aims to uncover the importance of complex epistemic states to what we mean by social capital and to the ensuing dynamics of networks. Social network theorists have a large accumulated base of empirical know-how surrounding the mapping of patterns of real interacting agents. Epistemic game theorists have a no less impressive set of tools for coherently describing the epistemic states of interacting agents. Bringing the two fields into mutually advantageous contact is nevertheless delicate: empirical correlates—and even interpretation—of the entities that populate formal models are not easily articulated.

Harsanyi's (1968a, 1968b) well-known "theory of types," for instance, is notoriously difficult to test empirically by mapping the type of agent onto a set of measurable variables; thus, its use is limited to studying the *effects* of certain assumptions about the rationality and conjectures of interacting agents rather than the descriptive accuracy of the assumptions themselves. Such limitations may not (always or yet) bother epistemic game theorists, but they bother social network theorists, who tend to be committed to a realist—rather than an instrumental—view of theories and models.

Our communicative bridge thus has to provide novel insight into the patterns of human interaction that are of interest to both network and epistemic game theorists. Having already rehearsed arguments for treating network "cohesion" through an epistemic lens, and shown its importance to the realization of brokerage and closure forms of social capital, we return to cohesion here but turn our attention to its role in the co-mobilization and coordination of networked agents. It is widely accepted among social network theorists that "network embeddedness" enhances the ability of agents to mobilize or coordinate their entire network or subnetworks.

Cooperation and collaboration, in turn, hinge sensitively on solving the sort of co-mobilization and coordination problems of central concern to epistemic game theorists. To the extent that embeddedness enables coordination and co-mobilization, then, the precise ways in which it does so deserve close attention—from both social network and epistemic game theorists.

Way(s) Forward: Why This Is Only a Beginning

We are as much at an end as we are at a beginning. If the foregoing is to serve as an application as well as an exposition of a theory and a set of models, then the EDL will be useful in furnishing a blueprint for inquiry into networks and interactions that generates its own "test cases" and "use cases," along with its own set of new questions and dilemmas.

There is, nevertheless, a domain of inquiry and analysis that this book—for reasons of compactness—does not touch on, even though the EDL seems tailor-made for it. This is the domain of schemes and procedures that individuals (and "agents"—their formal counterparts) may use to make inferences from what they know or directly believe to what they infer. Moving from state spaces comprising events to state spaces comprising propositions that have truth values and truth conditions makes possible questions such as "What is the calculus of inference—the 'logic'—that individuals are most likely to employ to synthesize new and valid propositions starting from propositions they believe or know to be true?" This question has several different forms, which take us in different directions.

Logical Form. What is the right logic or the right logics for representing the ways in which individual agents reason using propositions for the purpose of empirically studying behavior? Just as set theory and the probability axioms function as normative and prescriptive schemata for event spaces, so propositional first-order logic may be said to function as a normative schema for the procedures by which agents manipulate sentences. However, it is well known that first-order logic is a poor approximation for the grammatical form of natural language. For example, the axiom of choice states that any proposition is either true or false. But anyone, if asked "Is the king of France bald?"

will (correctly) point out that there is no king of France, whereas a language processor constrained by the axiom of choice would be mightily challenged. This does not even take into account the fact that modal, subjunctive, and epistemic logics seem to form an integral part of what humans do when they reason, in propositions, about the world and about the ways other humans reason about the world, as we have seen.

Fruitful inquiry in this domain will be informed by work in the logic design that traditionally has taken place outside of epistemic game theory, network sociology, or microinteractionist sociology—for example, artificial intelligence (Fagin et al. 1995), which tries to determine the "right" logic to ascribe to an individual by direct experimentation (building programs and applications and gauging their usefulness) and by formal work in logic and language design. Syntactic state spaces "let the genie out of the bottle," as they make possible—indeed, demand—inquiry that transcends the straitjacket of any specific logical form. Deviant logics, fuzzy logics, and many-valued logics may all have a role to play in the ensuing research.

Logical Depth. Quite aside from the most suitable logical form to ascribe to an agent is the logical depth to which that agent is supposed to be able or willing to reason. Recent work in rational choice theory (Lipman 1991) highlighted the problem that "logical omniscience" poses for producing realistic agent models. A logically omniscient agent (assume first-order logic) is supposed to know all of the logical consequences of what s/he knows. Thus, his/her knowledge should be closed under deduction. This is obviously an unrealistic requirement: an agent's knowing the basic algorithm by which subsequent digits in the decimal expansion of e are produced does not entail that she knows all of the digits of e or that she is (rationally) required to know them or come to know them.

At the other end of the spectrum is the equally unpalatable alternative of *imbecility*, wherein an agent does not know any of the consequences of what she knows (Moldoveanu 2011). Alice may know that *A entails B* is true and may know that *A is true*, but she is not presumed to know that *B is true* or to be somehow held accountable for knowing, by inference, that it is. So she should not be presumed to know that her dentist is expecting to see her today at 5:00 P.M. from the fact that she knows that today is Tuesday and the fact that she knows that her appointment with her dentist is on (this) Tuesday at 5:00 P.M.

There is, then, an opportunity—or perhaps a requirement—to take the matter of logical depth seriously when we build epistemic models of networked agents meant to represent humans, in a way that heeds the constraints of "no imbecility" and "no logical omniscience." And, since we are dealing with agents who may *choose* to reason to greater or lesser logical depths depending on the expected payoff(s) of doing so, we are well advised to make any model of inferential depth and reasoning we end up with responsive to micro-local incentives and constraints, in the same way that other models of choice are.

Informational Breadth: Awareness. In Chapter 2, we made a number of modeling choices regarding the representation of what agents know, how they know, what they know they know (or not), and what they do not know they do not know. We erred in favor of epistemic states at the individual level that are intuitive and easily interpretable in terms of measurement instruments. The representations we advanced were, however, not informed by a systematic account of the informational breadth of an agent's knowledge base. The problem of finding "the right" informational breadth of an agent's propositional state space has both theoretical and empirical ramifications.

On the theoretical side, the size of the propositional state space we deploy varies sensitively with the number of propositions we deem to be known, relevant, and so forth. That is because each proposition "about the world" generates a potentially very large number of propositions about what others know about the world (including what they know the agent knows and so forth). For this reason, "dimensioning" an epinet depends most sensitively on the number of propositions we allow into our state space.

On the empirical level, ascribing beliefs and knowledge to an agent is sensitively linked to the design of the instruments with which we measure epinets—surveys, questionnaires, direct observation of behavior, forced-choice experiments. Any empirical model of interacting and relating therefore depends sensitively on what we presume the individuals we model as agents know.

We have raised, potentially, at least as many questions in the last two pages as we answered in all those preceding them, which may befit both our aspiration to provide an "app" and our assurance that, in the epistemic realm, interesting questions are at least as important as the answers we find.

Glossary

Awareness (of a proposition by an agent): An agent's (second-order) knowledge of his/her knowledge of a proposition. More precisely, the agent's knowledge of the proposition Q: *I know P*. (Chapter 2)

Belief (in the truth of a proposition by an agent): An agent's credence of a proposition, P, to some degree that is less than full knowledge of the proposition. (Chapter 2)

Clout (of an agent): The fraction of agents in an epinet whose epistemic states change as a function of discovering that agent's epistemic state (provided it differs from their own). (Chapter 3)

Common belief (of a proposition by two or more agents): A state or situation in which each agent believes the proposition, P, knows that other agents believe it, and so forth, ad infinitum. (Chapter 2)

Common knowledge (of a proposition by two or more agents): A state or situation in which each agent knows the proposition, P, knows that other agents know it, and so forth, ad infinitum. (Chapter 2)

Coordinata (of an epinet): A set of propositions that are relevant to the coordinative activities of a network—that is, those propositions that need to be almost-common knowledge in the epinet for the network to successfully coordinate. (Chapter 3)

Coordinator (of an epinet): An agent who is known by most agents in the network to know what everyone else knows or believes. (Chapter 3)

Epinet ("epistemic network"): A directed graph whose vertices represent (1) individual agents (humans, humanoid, cyber agents) and (2) relevant propositions, and whose edges represent epistemic relations (knows that, believes that) between agents and propositions or between agents and their epistemic states regarding the propositions. (Chapter 2)

Epistemic centrality of
    Agents: The network centrality of an agent in an epinet; measures how well known to others in the network an agent's own epistemic states are. (Chapter 3)
    Propositions: The network centrality of a proposition, P, in an epinet; measures how known the proposition is, how known those who know it are for knowing it, and so on. (Chapter 3)

Epistemic preconditions for
    Co-mobilization (of two or more agents in a network): The set of epistemic states that is sufficient for co-mobilization. (Chapter 2)

Coordination (of two or more agents in a network): The set of epistemic states that is sufficient for coordination. (Chapter 2)

Fame (of an agent or proposition in an epinet): The size of a subnetwork of an epinet whose agents know that that agent has some positive property, P. (Chapter 3)

Glory (of an agent or proposition in an epinet): The fraction of agents in an epinet who know of all agents that know that that agent has some positive property, P. (Chapter 3)

Ignorance (of a proposition by an agent): An epistemic state in which an agent knows that s/he does not know the truth value of a proposition, P, but knows of the possibility that the proposition is true. (Chapter 2)

Immunity (of an epinet to an epistemic attack): The degree to which an epinet survives a malicious epistemic move by one of its agents—that is, a move meant to destroy or alter the epinet's epistemic structure. (Chapter 5)

Infamy (of an agent): The fraction of agents in an epinet who know that that agent has some negative property, N. (Chapter 3)

Knowledge (of a proposition by an agent): An intentional state connecting an agent, A, to a proposition, P, comprising the conditions that A believes P and that P is true. Unlike belief, knowledge of P implies the truth of P. (Chapter 2)

Knownness (of an agent): The fraction of agents in an epinet who know of that agent. (Chapter 3)

Mobilizer (of an epinet): An agent who knows what all or a majority of the other agents in the epinet know. (Chapter 3)

Move (by an agent in an epinet): The action taken by an agent that changes (1) the truth value of a proposition that is relevant to other network agents, (2) the epinet's interactive epistemic structure, or (3) the combination of (1) and (2). (Chapter 5)

Mutual knowledge or belief (of a proposition by two or more agents): An epistemic state in which each agent knows (or believes) that another agent knows (or believes) a relevant proposition, P. (Chapter 2)

Mutual knowledge or belief neighborhood (of a network): A subnetwork of agents for whom some relevant proposition, P, is mutual knowledge (or belief). (Chapter 2)

Notoriety (of an agent or proposition in a network): The fraction of agents in an epinet who know of all agents that know that that agent has some negative property, N. (Chapter 3)

Oblivion (of an agent vis-à-vis a proposition): An epistemic state in which an agent does not know the proposition, P, and also does not know that s/he does not know it. (Chapter 2)

Proposition: A grammatically correct statement that has a specified set of truth conditions (for instance, conditions that verify or falsify it), or a well formed formula of first-order logic or predicate logic that has a specified set of truth conditions. (Chapter 2)

Reach (of an agent in an epinet): The fraction of agents in an epinet whose epistemic states change as a function of discovering the epistemic state of that agent. (Chapter 3)

Renown (of an agent in an epinet): The fraction of agents in an epinet who know all agents who know of that agent. (Chapter 3)

Robustness (of an epinet): The invariance of the epinet to involuntary distortion, corruption, or omission of information during transfer. (Chapter 5)

Security conduit (of an epinet): A channel (i.e., singly linked subnetwork) of trust-linked agents whose identity is common knowledge among them. (Chapter 4)

Security corridor (of an epinet): A two-way security conduit. (Chapter 4)

Security neighborhood (of an epinet): A subnetwork of trust-linked agents whose identity is common knowledge among them. (Chapter 4)

Stability (of an epinet): The invariance of the epinet to deductions made by agents from what they already know about the epinet's structure. (Chapter 5)

Trust (epistemic model of): The epistemic relationship between two agents that safeguards the registration and passage of relevant information.

Trust in competence: A trusts in B's competence if A knows that if some relevant proposition, P, were true, then B would know it. (Chapter 4)

Trust in integrity: A trusts in B's integrity if A knows that if B knew some relevant proposition, P, then B would assert it to A. (Chapter 4)

Trust conduit (of an epinet): A channel (i.e., a singly linked subnetwork) of trust-linked agents. (Chapter 4)

Trust corridor (of an epinet): A two-way trust conduit. (Chapter 4)

Trust neighborhood (of an epinet): A subnetwork of trust-linked agents whose identity is *not* common knowledge among them. (Chapter 4)

Unawareness (of a proposition by an agent): An epistemic relation between an agent and a proposition, P, wherein the agent knows the proposition but does not know that s/he knows it (i.e., the proposition is not instantly recalled or easily accessible but is recognized if presented explicitly to the agent). (Chapter 2)

Notes

Chapter 2

Portions of this chapter originally appeared in Moldoveanu and Baum: "'I Think You Think I Think You're Lying': Interactive Epistemology of Trust in Social Networks." *Management Science* 57(2), 2011, pp. 393–412. Copyright 2011, Institute for Operations Research and the Management Sciences, 7240 Parkway Drive, Suite 300, Hanover, MD 21076 USA. Reprinted with permission.

Chapter 3

1. Degree centrality for faculty member i refers to the number of edges attached to the node—that is, the number of direct connections that i has. Betweenness centrality for faculty member i is $\sum_{jk} \sigma_{jk}(i)/\sigma_{jk}$, where σ_{jk} is the number of shortest paths between faculty members j and k, and $\sigma_{jk}(i)$ is the number of shortest paths from j to k that pass through i. Eigenvector centrality, if faculty member i is defined proportional to the sum of the eigenvector centrality of i's neighbors, is $e_i = \sum_{j=nn(i)} e_j/\lambda$, where $nn(i)$ denotes the set of neighbors of faculty member i, which can be rewritten in matrix form $A \cdot e = \lambda e$, where A is the adjacency matrix of the faculty network, and e represents the vector of faculty centrality scores. Thus, e is the eigenvector of A relative to the eigenvalue λ.

2. We identified the cliques in each network using the N-clique procedure implemented in Ucinet 6.0 (Borgatti, Everett, and Freeman 2002). An N-clique is one in which the geodesic distance between all nodes is no greater than N for paths in a network subgraph. We set $N = 1$, thus defining clique members as directly tied to each other, and we set the minimum clique size to three faculty members.

3. Google centrality (Page et al. 1998) is a computationally simplified form of eigenvector centrality, computable for very large networks such as the World Wide Web in short enough periods of time to be useful to typical users.

Chapter 4

Portions of this chapter originally appeared in Moldoveanu and Baum: "'I Think You Think I Think You're Lying'": Interactive Epistemology of Trust in Social Networks." *Management Science* 57(2), 2011, pp. 393–412. Copyright 2011, Institute for

Operations Research and the Management Sciences, 7240 Parkway Drive, Suite 300, Hanover, MD 21076 USA. Reprinted with permission.

1. We are grateful to Tim Rowley and Diederik van Liere for granting us access to the network data collected in the first phase, as well as for their assistance in the second phase with the collection of additional data used in the analysis of trust.

2. Betweenness for respondent i is $\sum_{jk}\sigma_{jk}(i)/\sigma_{jk}$, where σ_{jk} is the number of shortest paths from j to k, and $\sigma_{jk}(i)$ is the number of shortest paths from j to k that pass through respondent i (Freeman 1977).

3. Constraint for respondent i is $\sum_j (p_{ij} + \sum_q p_{iq} p_{jq})^2$, $q \neq i, j$, p_{ij} is the strength of respondent i's relationship with alter j, and p_{iq} and p_{jq} are the strengths of alter q's relationships with i and j, respectively (Burt 1992). When $p_{iq} p_{jq}$ is large, a strong third-party tie connects respondent i to alter j indirectly. Summing over q provides an assessment of the overall strength of third-party ties surrounding respondent i. Constraint varies from a minimum of p_{ij}, when alter j is disconnected from all of respondent i's other alters, to a maximum of 1, when j is i's only *alter*.

4. These factors were selected by the firm's senior management.

5. Ideally, this final item would have been separated into two: one focused on competence and the other on integrity. They were combined at the request of the firm's top management to shorten the survey.

6. Because we wanted to focus on significant ties, we did not include highly asymmetric reciprocal ties (i.e., where one respondent rated the tie of low significance; the other, of high significance).

7. Given the correlations among the variables, we report a set of hierarchically nested models to check whether multicollinearity was imposing a conservative bias on our estimates by inflating coefficient standard errors. The absence of such inflation is reinforced by variance inflation factor (VIF) statistics for each model, which reach a maximum of 1.34—well below the threshold of 10 (Belsley, Kuh, and Welsch 1980).

8. Again, neither model estimates nor VIF statistics reported for each model indicate multicollinearity concerns.

References

Albert, R., and A.-L. Barabási. 2002. "Statistical Mechanics of Complex Networks." *Reviews of Modern Physics* 74: 47–97.

Albert, R., J. Hawoong, and A.-L. Barabási. 2000. "Error and Attack Tolerance of Complex Networks." *Nature* 406: 378–382.

Arrow, K. J. 1974. *The Limits of Organization.* New York: Norton.

Aumann, R. J. 1976. "Agreeing to Disagree." *Annals of Statistics* 4: 1236–1239.

———. 1987. "Correlated Equilibrium as an Expression of Bayesian Rationality." *Econometrica* 55: 1–18.

———. 1989. "Notes on Interactive Epistemology." Unpublished manuscript.

———. 1999a. "Interactive Epistemology I: Knowledge." *International Journal of Game Theory* 28: 263–300.

———. 1999b. "Interactive Epistemology II: Probability." *International Journal of Game Theory* 28: 301–314.

———. 2001. "Game Theory." *New Palgrave Dictionary of Economics.* New York: Blackwell.

Aumann, R. J., and A. Brandenburger. 1995. "Epistemic Conditions for Nash Equilibrium." *Econometrica* 63: 1161–1180.

Austin, J. L. 1961. "Performative Utterances." In *Philosophical Papers,* edited by J. O. Urmson and G. J. Warnock, 233–252. Oxford: Clarendon.

———. 1962. *Sense and Sensibilia.* Edited by G. J. Warnock. Oxford: Oxford University Press.

Axelrod, R. 1984. *The Evolution of Cooperation.* New York: Basic Books.

———. 1997. *The Complexity of Cooperation: Actor-Based Models of Competition and Collaboration.* Princeton, NJ: Princeton University Press.

Ayres, I., and B. Nalebuff. 1997. "Common Knowledge as a Barrier to Negotiation." *UCLA Law Review* 44: 1631–1659.

Barber, B. 1983. *The Logic and Limits of Trust.* New Brunswick, NJ: Rutgers University Press.

Barney, J., and M. Hansen. 1994. "Trustworthiness as a Source of Competitive Advantage." *Strategic Management Journal* 15: 175–190.

Belsley, D. A., E. Kuh, and R. E. Welch. 1980. *Regression Diagnostics: Identifying Influential Data and Sources of Collinearity.* New York: Wiley.

Benjamin, B. A., and J. M. Podolny. 1999. "Status, Quality and Social Order in the California Wine Industry." *Administrative Science Quarterly* 44: 563–589.

Binmore, K., and A. Brandenburger. 1990. *Common Knowledge and Game Theory: Essays on the Foundations of Game Theory.* Oxford: Basil Blackwell.

Blau, P. 1964. *Exchange and Power in Social Life.* New York: Wiley.

Bonacich, P. 1987. "Power and Centrality: A Family of Measures." *American Journal of Sociology* 92: 1170–1182.

Borgatti, S. P., M. G. Everett, and L. C. Freeman. 2002. *Ucinet for Windows: Software for Social Network Analysis.* Harvard, MA: Analytic Technologies.

Brandenburger, A. 1992. "Knowledge and Equilibrium in Games." *Journal of Economic Perspectives* 6 (4): 83–101.

Burt, R. S. 1992. *Structural Holes.* Cambridge, MA: Harvard University Press.

———. 1999. "Private Games Are Too Dangerous." *Computational and Mathematical Organization Theory* 5: 311–341.

———. 2005. *Brokerage and Closure: An Introduction to Social Capital.* New York: Oxford University Press.

Burt, R. S., and M. Knez. 1995. "Kinds of Third-Party Effects on Trust." *Rationality and Society* 7: 255–292.

Butler, J. K. 1991. "Toward Understanding and Measuring Conditions of Trust." *Journal of Management* 17: 643–663.

Callaway, D. S., M. E. J. Newman, S. H. Strogatz, and D. J. Watts. 2000. "Network Robustness and Fragility: Percolation on Random Graphs." *Physical Review Letters* 85: 5468–5471.

Chwe, M. S. Y. 1999. "Structure and Strategy in Collective Action." *American Journal of Sociology* 105: 128–156.

———. 2000. "Communication and Coordination in Social Networks." *Review of Economic Studies* 67: 1–16.

———. 2001. *Rational Ritual: Culture, Coordination and Common Knowledge.* Princeton, NJ: Princeton University Press.

Clark, A. 1988. *Being There: Putting Brain, Body and World Together Again.* Cambridge, MA: MIT Press.

Coleman, J. S. 1988. "Social Capital in the Creation of Human Capital." *American Journal of Sociology* 94: S95–S120.

———. 1990. *Foundations of Social Theory.* Cambridge, MA: Harvard University Press.

Dekel, E., B. L. Lipman, and A. Rustichini. 1998. "Standard State-Space Models Preclude Unawareness." *Econometrica* 66: 159–173.

de Tocqueville, A. 2000. *Democracy in America.* Translated and annotated by S. D. Grant. Indianapolis: Hackett.

Durkheim, E. 1933. *The Division of Labor in Society.* New York: Macmillan.

Durrenmatt, F. 1994. *The Physicists.* Translated by James Kirkup. New York: Grove Weidenfeld.

Fagin R., J. Y. Halpern, Y. Moses, and M. Y. Vardi. 1995. *Reasoning about Knowledge.* Cambridge, MA: MIT Press.

Farrell, J. 1996. "Cheap Talk." *Journal of Economic Perspectives* 34: 26–41.

Frankfurt, H. 2005. *On Bullshit.* Princeton, NJ: Princeton University Press.

Freeman, L. C. 1977. "A Set of Measures of Centrality Based on Betweenness." *Sociometry* 40: 35–41.

Friedkin, N. E. 1983. "Horizons of Observability and Limits of Informal Control of Organizations." *Social Forces* 62: 54–77.

Friedland, N. 1990. "Attribution of Control as a Determinant of Cooperation in Exchange Interactions." *Journal of Applied Social Psychology* 20: 303–320.

Fukuyama, F. 1995. *Trust: The Social Virtues and the Creation of Prosperity.* New York: Free Press.

Gambetta, D. 1988. *Trust: Making and Breaking Cooperative Relations.* New York: Basil Blackwell.

Gettier, E. L. 1963. "Is Justified True Belief Knowledge?" *Analysis* 23: 121–123.

Golembiewski, R. T., and M. McConkie. 1975. "The Centrality of Interpersonal Trust in Group Processes." In *Theories of Group Processes*, edited by C. L. Cooper, 131–185. New York: Wiley.

Gould, R. V. 1993. "Collective Action and Network Structure." *American Sociological Review* 38: 182–196.

Granovetter, M. 1985. "Economic Action and Social Structure: The Problem of Embeddedness." *American Journal of Sociology* 91: 481–510.

Greene, W. 2000. *Econometric Analysis.* New York: Prentice Hall.

Grice, H. P. 1968. "Utterer's Meaning, Sentence-Meaning, and Word-Meaning." *Foundations of Language* 4: 225–242.

———. 1969. "Utterer's Meaning and Intentions." *Philosophical Review* 78: 147–177.

Harsanyi, J.C. 1967. "Games with Incomplete Information Played by 'Bayesian' Players I: The Basic Model." *Management Science* 14: 159–182.

———. 1968a. "Games with Incomplete Information Played by 'Bayesian' Players II: Bayesian Equilibrium Points." *Management Science* 14: 320–334.

———. 1968b. "Games with Incomplete Information Played by 'Bayesian' Players III: Basic Probability Distribution of the Game." *Management Science* 14: 486–502.

Hendricks, K., M. Piccione, and G. Tan. 1999. "Equilibrium in Networks." *Econometrica* 67: 1407–1434.

Hill, C. W. L. 1990. "Cooperation, Opportunism and the Invisible Hand: Implications to Transaction Cost Theory." *Academy of Management Review* 15: 500–513.

Hosmer, L. T. 1995. "Trust: The Connecting Link between Organizational Theory and Philosophical Ethics." *Academy of Management Review* 20: 379–403.

Jackson, M. O. 2005. "Allocation Rules for Network Games." *Games and Economic Behavior* 51: 128–154.

Kesselring, J. 1942. *Arsenic and Old Lace.* New York: Dramatists Play Service.

Krackhardt, D. 1987. "Cognitive Social Structures." *Social Networks* 9: 109–134.

———. 1999. "The Ties That Torture: Simmelian Tie Analysis in Organizations." *Research in the Sociology of Organizations* 16: 183–210.

Kramer, R. 1999. "Trust and Distrust in Organizations: Emerging Perspectives, Enduring Questions." *Annual Review of Psychology* 50: 569–598.

Kreps, D. M. 1990. "Corporate Culture and Economic Theory." In *Perspectives on Positive Political Economy*, edited by J. Alt and K. Shepsle, 90–143. New York: Cambridge University Press.

Kripke, S. A., ed. 2011. *Philosophical Troubles. Collected Papers Volume I*. New York: Oxford University Press.

La Rochefoucauld, F. de. 1912. *The Moral Maxims and Reflections of the Duke de La Rochefoucauld*. London: Methuen.

Lewis, D. K. 1969. *Convention: A Philosophical Study*. Cambridge, MA: Harvard University Press.

Lewis, J. D., and A. Weigert. 1985. "Trust as Social Reality." *Social Forces* 63: 967–985.

Lipman, B. L. 1991. "How to Decide How to Decide How to . . . : Modeling Limited Rationality." *Econometrica* 59: 1105–1125.

Loftus, E. F. 1979. "The Malleability of Human Memory." *American Scientist* 67: 312–320.

Mayer, R. C., J. H. Davis, and F. D. Schoorman. 1995. "An Integrative Model of Organizational Trust." *Academy of Management Review* 20: 709–734.

Mertens, J. F., and S. Zamir. 1985. "Formulation of Bayesian Analysis for Games with Incomplete Information." *International Journal of Game Theory* 14: 1–29.

Modica, S., and A. Rustichini. 1999. "Unawareness and Partitional Information Structures." *Games and Economic Behavior* 27: 265–298.

Moldoveanu, M. C. 2002. "Language, Games and Language Games." *Journal of Socioeconomics* 31: 233–251.

———. 2009. "Thinking Strategically about Thinking Strategically: The Computational Structure and Dynamics of Managerial Problem Selection and Formulation." *Strategic Management Journal* 30: 737–763.

———. 2011. *Inside Man: The Discipline of Modeling Human Ways of Being*. Stanford, CA: Stanford University Press.

Moldoveanu, M. C., and J. A. C. Baum. 2002. "Contemporary Debates in Organizational Epistemology." In *Blackwell Companion to Organizations*, edited by J. A. C. Baum, 733–781. Oxford: Blackwell.

———. 2011. "I Think You Think I Think You're Lying: The Interactive Epistemology of Trust in Social Networks." *Management Science* 57: 393–412.

Moldoveanu, M. C., J. A. C. Baum, and T. J. Rowley. 2003. "Information Regimes, Information Strategies and the Evolution of Interfirm Network Topologies." In *Research in Multi-Level Issues*, edited by F. J. Yammarino and F. Dansereau, 2:221–264. Oxford: Elsevier.

Moldoveanu, M. C., and H. H. Stevenson. 1998. "Ethical Universals in Practice: An Analysis of Five Principles." *Journal of Socio-Economics* 27: 721–752.

Morris, S., and H. Shin. 1993. "Noisy Bayes Updating and the Value of Information." CARESS Working paper 93-02, University of Pennsylvania.

Nov, O., and S. Rafaeli. 2009. "Measuring the Premium on Common Knowledge in

Computer-Mediated Communication Problems." *Computers in Human Behavior* 25: 171–174.

Oxley, J. E., J. Rivkin, and M. D. Ryall. 2010. "The Strategy Research Initiative: Recognizing and Encouraging High-Quality Research in Strategy." *Strategic Organization* 8: 377–386.

Page, L., S. Brin, R. Motwani, and T. Winograd. 1998. *The PageRank Citation Ranking: Bringing Order to the Web.* Working paper 0120, Stanford Digital Library Technologies.

Paul, G., S. Sreenivasan, S. Havlin, and H. E. Stanley. 2006. "Optimization of Network Robustness to Random Breakdowns." *Physica A* 370: 854–862.

Pfeffer, J. 1993. "Barriers to the Advancement of Organizational Science: Paradigm Development as a Dependent Variable." *Academy of Management Review* 18: 599–620.

———. 1995. "Mortality, Reproducibility, and the Persistence of Styles of Theory." *Organization Science* 6: 681–686.

Podolny, J. M. 1993. "A Picture Is Worth a Thousand Symbols: A Sociologist's View of the Economic Pursuit of Truth." *American Economic Review* 93: 169–174.

Powell, W. W., K. W. Koput, and L. Smith-Doerr. 1996. "Interorganizational Collaboration and the Locus of Innovation: Networks of Learning in Biotechnology." *Administrative Science Quarterly* 41: 136–152.

Putnam, H. 1981. *Reason, Truth, and History.* Cambridge: Cambridge University Press.

Rubinstein, A. 1986. "Finite Automata Play the Repeated Prisoner's Dilemma." *Journal of Economic Theory* 39: 83–96.

———. 1989. "The Electronic Mail Game: Strategic Behavior under 'Almost Common Knowledge.'" *American Economic Review* 79: 385–391.

Ryall, M. D., and O. Sorenson. 2007. "Brokers and Competitive Advantage." *Management Science* 53: 566–583.

Saloner, G. 1991. "Modeling, Game Theory, and Strategic Management." *Strategic Management Journal* 12 (S2): 119–136.

Samet, D. 1990. "Ignoring Ignorance and Agreeing to Disagree." *Journal of Economic Theory* 52: 190–207.

Savage, L. J. 1954. *The Foundations of Statistics.* New York: Wiley.

Schelling, T. C. 1960. *Strategy of Conflict.* Cambridge, MA: Harvard University Press.

———. 1978. *Micromotives and Macrobehavior.* New York: Norton.

Seidel, M. D., and J. D. Westphal. 2004. "Research Impact: How Seemingly Innocuous Social Cues in a CEO Survey Can Lead to Change in Board of Director Network Ties." *Strategic Organization* 2: 227–270.

Shakespeare, W. 1963. *Othello.* Edited by M. R. Ridley. London: Methuen.

Shin, H. S. 1993. "Logical Structure of Common Knowledge." *Journal of Economic Theory* 60: 1–13.

Uzzi, B., and J. Spiro. 2005. "Collaboration and Creativity: The Small World Problem." *American Journal of Sociology* 111: 447–504.

Van Maanen, J. 1995a. "Style as Theory." *Organization Science* 6: 133–143.

————. 1995b. "Fear and Loathing in Organization Studies." *Organization Science* 6: 687–692.

Wasserman, S., and K. Faust. 1994. *Social Network Analysis: Methods and Applications.* Cambridge: Cambridge University Press.

Watts, D. J., and S. H. Strogatz. 1998. "Collective Dynamics of 'Small-World' Networks." *Nature* 393: 440–442.

Weber, M. 1992. *The Protestant Ethic and the Spirit of Capitalism.* Translated by T. Parsons. London: Routledge.

Williamson, O. E. 1975. *Markets and Hierarchies: Analysis and Antitrust Implications.* New York: Free Press.

————. 1985. *The Economic Institutions of Capitalism.* New York: Free Press.

Index

Italic page numbers indicate material in figures and tables.

Albert, Réka, 133, 154
almost-common knowledge, 32, *33*, 43–44, 47, 61, 104–105
almost-common knowledge neighborhood, 43–44
anisotropy, network, 49
Arrow, Kenneth J., 97
Arsenic and Old Lace (Kesselring), 7, *8*, 37, *38–40*
ascription, 54–55, 136–137, 166–167
asymmetry in understanding, 128
Aumann, Robert, 3, 19, 22, 25–26, 161
Austin, J. L., 55
awareness: in *Arsenic and Old Lace*, 37; collective, 31–32; defined, 20, 36–37; epinet representation of, *23*, *33*; as individual epistemic state, 27–29; and informational breadth of knowledge, 167; levels of, 27–32; and positive introspection, 29; and trust in integrity, 102; and trust neighborhoods, 117. *See also* unawareness
Axelrod, Robert, 96, 124, 128
Ayres, Ian, 33–34

Barabási, Albert-László, 133, 154
Barber, Bernard, 94, 95
Barney, Jay B., 93
behavior: cooperative, mutual expectation of, 48, 100; opportunistic, 94

belief(s): degree of, 30; elicitation protocols for, 136; interactive belief hierarchy, 34–36; interactive hierarchies of, 34–36, 100; measuring, 136; states of, 30, 100. *See also* coherence of beliefs; common knowledge; level 1 beliefs; level 2 beliefs; level 3 beliefs; mutual knowledge or belief
Belsley, David A., 174n7
benevolence, 95–96
Benjamin, Beth A., 47
biases, 22; attribution, 22; simplification, 22
binariness, 103
Binmore, Kenneth F., 22
Blau, Peter M., 93
bootstrapping, 135
Brandenburger, Adam M., 19, 22, 32
brokerage: cohesion and, 52; of information, 52, 113, 116–118; requirements for, 51–52, 77; of trust, 51, 123
bullshitters, 151
Burt, Ronald S., 14, 48–49, 51–52, 54, 124, 138, 159
Butler, John K., Jr., 95

centrality: betweenness, 90–91, 106–107, 173n1; Bonacich, 47, 85; closeness, 89–90; coherence, cliques and, 74–80, *78–79*; coherence, trust and,

centrality (*continued*)
107–109, *108*, 128; degree, 89; eigenvector, 66, *67*, *75*, 91, 128, 173n1;
Google, 173n3; measures of, 85; *tout
court*, 128
cheap talk, 46, 136
Chwe, Michael Suk-Young, 15, 43, 46,
56, 58, 104–105
circle of trust, 117, 143
Clark, Andy, 162–163
cliques: and centrality, 74–75; and coherence, 76, *78–79*; common knowledge of membership in, 118; and
coordinata, 62; defined, 1–2; divisive
moves in, 146–148; *N*-clique procedure, 173n2; and pockets of common knowledge, 46–47, 105–106;
referral, 117; as security neighborhoods, 117–118, 143; as social pockets, 75–76, *78–79*, 105–106; as trust
neighborhoods, 117
closure, 52, 105, 129, 162–164
clout, 87, 90
coherence of beliefs, 90, 100; centrality
and trust and, 74–80, *78–79*, 107–
109, *108*, 116; as condition for coordination and mobilization, 104–105;
distinguished from coherence of
model, 137; distinguished from cohesion, 52–53, 65
cohesion: of brokered subnetworks, 51–
52; coordination and, 59–65; defined, 52; distinguished from coherence, 52–53, 65
Coleman, James S., 51, 113, 116
collaborative creative work, 14
commonality, 32–33
common belief. *See* common knowledge
common knowledge: assuming, 2, 60–61;
brokering, 159; in epinets, *33*, *45*;
inferring, 104–105; in neighborhoods, 118
communication: coded, 158; covert/
encrypted, 3, 147, 149; face-to-face
and non-face-to-face, 44, 60, 104;

"in confidence," 122; noise and distortion in, 123, 128; norms of, 54;
principles of, 55; reliability of, 60–
61; timing of, 128. *See also* lies
co-mobilization in networks, 14–15;
agent thresholds, 57; and cohesion,
56–59; epistemic preconditions for,
43, 57, 74; knowledge of rules of, 63;
mutual knowledge of, 47; and trust,
100
conductivity, 49, 90, 137–139, *139*. *See
also* superconductivity
confidence, level of, 24, 31, 50, 86–87,
99, 101
connectedness, 47, 63, 85, 89–91;
agent, 52
constraint, 106–116, *108*, *110–112*,
114–115
contrition, 124
conversational implicature, 55–56
coordinata, 62, 63–64, 84
coordination in networks, 43; backbone, 126; coordinative potential,
32; epistemic preconditions for, 19,
44, 56, 59–64, 74, 160; focal points
in, 84; mobilization, 46–47, 100;
problems of, 59–65; and trust, 100
coordinator, 62, 63, *64*, 66
cost-benefit calculations, 60
costs, transaction, 96
culture, 104–105, 107

Davis, James H., 95
Dekel, Eddie, 161
del Potro, Juan Martín, 87
density, of relationships, 105
distribution/sharedness, 31
Durkheim, Émile, 93
Durrenmatt, Friedrich, 7–11, *10*, *11*,
147
dynamics: and dynamic equilibrium
states, 132–134, 154; of social
networks, 158, 161, 164; strategic-
agentic vs. system-dynamic views,
154; of trust, 139–141, *140*

echoing, 52

edges/links, 32, 64, 142

EDL (epistemic description language): epinet graphic tool as, 23–24; knowledge states in a social network, 100–101; objectives/desiderata for, 20–23, 49–50; operationalizability, 21, 50; precision and subtlety of, 20–21, 49–50; primitives and kernels for, 24–33; primitives for, *23*, 24–33, 134, 157

empiricism, 157

enumeration, 25

epistemic bridge, 160

epistemic game theory, 25–26, 28

epistemic glue: and conversational implicature, 55; defined, 1–2; scholarship on, 3; use of epinets to describe, *41*, 41–42

epistemic qualifier, 30

epistemic state(s): collective, 31–33; complex, *81*; counterfactual, 124; defined, 15; epinet with, *33*, *45*; individual, 24–31; interactive, 46–47; network-level, 31–33, 44–49; noncoherent, 137; noninteractive, 20; simple and compound, *23*, 23–24; stability, robustness, and immunity, 152–155; trust as modal, 100. *See also* individuals' epistemic states; interactive epistemic states; subjunctive epistemic states

epistemic structures, defined, 2; modal, 57, 100, 101, 138, 168

epistemic tangles, 14

epistemic trails/wakes, 137–138

epistemology, realist vs. instrumentalist, 20–21

event spaces, 2, 77, 153

exformation, 14

explananda, 94, 156

expressivity, 55

Fagin, Ronald, 3, 166

fame, 21, 85–88, 90

Farrell, Joseph, 46

fault tolerance, 154

Faust, Katherine, 89

Fleischmann, Martin, 91

footprints, network, 52, 89

forced choice, data from, 26, 157, 167

foreclosing, 163–164

forgetting, defined, 2

fragility and robustness, 123–130

Frankfurt, Harry G., 151

Freeman, Linton C., 174n2

Friedkin, Noah E., 15

Friedland, Nehemia, 96

Fukuyama, Francis, 93–94

full common knowledge, 43–44, 60, 104

function: choice, 64; decay, 49; value, 15–16, 45

Gambetta, Diego, 94

games: Bertrand, 12; language, 54; prestructured, 152; private, 14, 54. *See also* prisoner's dilemma games

game theory: epinet advantages over, 133; epistemic, 25–26, 28; equilibrium in, 43, 132, 152–153, 156; and first-order logic, 53; and state space of events, 81; successful strategies in, 96; traditional, 2, 22, 33; "unbounded rationality" vs. "mechanistic social action" in, 133

generosity, 124

geodesics, 91, 173n2. *See also* superconductivity

Gettier, Edmund L., 24

glory, 21, 84–88

Golembiewski, Robert T., 93

gossip, 138

Gould, Roger V., 15

Granovetter, Mark, 97

Greene, William H., 113

Grice, H. P., 55

Hansen, Mark H., 93

Harsanyi, John C., 20, 50, 164

Hawoong, Jeong, 154
Hendricks, Ken, 46
Hill, Charles W. L., 96
holes, trust, 124–125
homeostasis, within an epinet, 153–155
Hosmer, Larue T., 97

ignorance, 29–30
imbecility, 166–167
immunity, 152–155
individuals' epistemic states: awareness,
    27–29; confidence, 31; connections
    between, 1; degree of belief, 30–31;
    in epinets, 19, 133, *135*, 152, 167;
    ignorance, 29; interactive and nonin-
    teractive, 20–21; knowledge, 24–27;
    oblivion, 30; unawareness, 29–30
infamy, 87–88
information: breadth of, 167; broadcast-
    ing, 16; cascades, 138; contagion,
    16; distortion of, 140; facts vs.
    rumors, 119; flow, 132, 137–138;
    games, 14; pathways, 118–122;
    sensitive, 119–120; spread of, 49,
    116–122
informativeness, 55
intent: vs. ability, 102; attacks with,
    154; and breaches of trust, 122, 125,
    147; certainty regarding, 60; vs. er-
    ror, 96, 144–145; lies, distortion
    and, 148–149; mapping behavior
    onto, 48; of moves, 148–149; palters
    and, 150–152
interaction and interdependence, 132
interactive epistemic states, 3, 19–20,
    157–160; in an epinet, 134–137,
    137, 152–153; and lies, 149–152;
    and trust, 98–104
interpretation, 77, 80, 134–136
introspection, 28–29; positive, 28;
    negative, 29
irrationality, resolving, 48

Jackson, Matthew O., 15, 46, 89
judgments, of value and of fact, 84

Kesselring, Joseph, 7, 37
Knez, Marc, 14, 48, 54
knowledge: defined, 24–27; distribution
    of, 31; as individual epistemic state,
    24–27; measuring, 136; relevance
    of, 24–25, 28, 104, 125–126; social
    pockets of, 75. *See also* almost-
    common knowledge; common
    knowledge; full common knowledge;
    mutual knowledge or belief
knowledge pipes, 119
knowledge states, 30
knownness, 47, 85, 87–88, 89
Kohlschreiber, Philipp, 87
Koput, K. W., 14
Krackhardt, David, 3
Kramer, Roderick M., 95
Kreps, David M., 104–105, 107
Kripke, Saul A., 3
Kuh, E., 174n7

La Rochefoucauld, Marquis de, 124–125
leading questions, 29
level 1 beliefs: about beliefs, 34; ac-
    curacy/coherence of, 65, 71–76, *75*,
    78–79; epinet of networked agents
    example, *135, 137, 139, 140*; faculty
    network example, 66, *67, 69, 71, 73,*
    74–76, *75*; palters and, 149–150;
    realists vs. constructivists, *83*; senior
    management network example,
    107–116, *111*
level 2 beliefs, 28, *41, 42*; about beliefs,
    34; accuracy/coherence of, 65, *71,*
    71–76, *75, 78–79*; almost-common
    knowledge and, 43–45, *45*, 57, 105;
    as collective/mutual, 32, *33*; depic-
    tion of, 66, *71*; epinet of networked
    agents example, *135, 137, 139, 140*;
    faculty network example, 66, *68,*
    72, 74–76, *75*; inference from, 104;
    realists vs. constructivists, *83*; senior
    management network example,
    107–116, *108, 110–112, 114–115*;
    trust and, 100–105, 107

level 3 beliefs, 105, 116; about beliefs, 34; accuracy/coherence of, 65, 71–76, *73*, *75*, *78–79*; almost-common knowledge and, 43–45, *45*, 61, 105; as collective/mutual, 32, *33*; epinet of networked agents example, *140*; faculty network example, 66, *68*, 74–76, *75*; realists vs. constructivists, *83*; senior management network example, 107–116, *108*, *110–112*, *114–115*; trust and, 100–105, 107
Lewis, David, 19
Lewis, J. David, 93, 94
lies, 148–149, 153–154; black, 149; pink, 149; white, 149
Lipman, Barton L., 161, 166
Loftus, Elizabeth F., 27
logic: abductive, 53; deductive, 53; deviant, 53, 166; first-order, 53; fuzzy, 53, 166; inductive, 53; many-valued, 166; propositional, 24, 165–166

Maxims (La Rochefoucauld), 124–125
Mayer, Roger C., 95
McConkie, M., 93
measuring epinets, 136, 154–155
Mertens, Jean-François, 20
messages, encrypted, 3, 147, 149
misattribution, 82–84, *83*
misunderstandings, 99
mobilization, 62, 105
mobilizer, 56–57, 62–63, *63*, 66
models: agent, 22, 35–37, 166; forward, 43; rational agent, 34–37, 60, 132–133, 162; rational choice, 36, 55, 133, 166; reverse, 43
Modica, Salvatore, 28–29
morality, 97
Morris, Steven, 60–61
moves and strategies, 144–152; auditable/inauditable, 146–147; clarifying, 148–149, 151; collusive, 146–148; declarative, 152; distortive, 140, 146, 148–152; divisive,

146–147; interrogatory, 152; sanctioning, 151–152; substantive, 151–152
mutual knowledge or belief, 32, *33*, 47, 57–58
mutual knowledge or belief neighborhood, 43, *45*, 76

Nalebuff, Barry, 33–34
Nash equilibrium, 19, 64
near-commonality, 32
network: anisotropy, 49; centrality, 74–75, *75*, 105, 113; cohesion, 53; coordinators, 62–64, *64*; diameter, 52; fragility, 126; mobilizers, 62–63, *63*; robustness, 126–127; self-discovery protocol, 58–59, *59*; spectroscopy, 65
networks: conspiratorial, 118; expert, 119; high-closure, 52; hub-and-spoke, 62; of interorganizational collaboration, 14–15; study of, 22. *See also* social networks
networks *tout court*, 15, 103
nodes, 15, 23–24, 32, 64, 158, 173nn1–2
noise, 96, 123–130 passim; colored, 128; white, 153–154
norms, attributed vs. shared, 98
notoriety, 88
Nov, Oded, 104

oblivion: in *Arsenic and Old Lace*, 7, 37; in bullshitters, 151; in a clique, 148; defined, 2, 20; epinet modeling of, *23*, 135, *135*, 152–153; as individual epistemic state, 30; interpretation, misattribution, and, 77–81; leading to missed transactions, 46; loss of, 136, 138, 140; in *Othello*, 5–6; in *The Physicists*, 9; in prisoner's dilemma game, 27; reference to *The Physicists*, 147; representing state of, 30; in semantic approach, 161; and status, 84

operators: contraction, 22; deletion, 22; distortion, 22; *knows*, 35
Othello epinets, 5–7
Oxley, Joanne E., 21

palters, 149–151
paradigm war, 82–84, *83*; constructivists in, *83*, 83–84; realists in, 82–84, *83*
perceptions, 27
Pfeffer, J., 82
Physicists, The (Durrenmatt), 7–11, *10*, *11*, 147
Piccione, Michele, 46
Podolny, Joel M., 47
Pons, Stanley, 91
Powell, W. W., 14
prisoner's dilemma games: finite-horizon, 48; between self-interested individuals, 104; trust in, 94, 104
propositions: coordinata as, 63–64; defined, 25; distinguished from raw qualia, 26; faculty-relevant, 66–74; interpretations of, 134; shared, 56; subjunctive forms of, 131; usefulness of, 4–5, 161; use of, 52–53, 161
Putnam, Hilary, 26

questionnaires/surveys, data from, 25–26, 50, 77, 131, 136, 157

Rafaeli, Sheizaf, 104
rationalism, 157
rationality: morality and, 97; un-bounded, 133
reach, 86–87, 90
recall, perfect and imperfect, 28–29, 37
reference, problems of, 25–26
regimes, trust, *120*, *121*
relativism, 84
renown, 88
Rivkin, Jan W., 21
robustness, 123–130, 152–155
Rubenstein, Ariel, 44, 59, 104

rules: allocation, 45–46; biconditional, 57, 101–102; co-mobilization, 57, 63; conditional, 57; decision, 64; mobilization, 57, 62; syntactical, 25, 53
rumors, 119, 121, 138
Rustichini, Aldo, 28–29, 161
Ryall, Michael D., 15, 21

salience, 24, 28
Saloner, Garth, 21
Samet, Dov, 25
Savage, Leonard J., 25
scaffolding, 162–163
Schelling, Thomas, 19, 32
Schoorman, F. David, 95
security conduit, 120–121, 123, 129
security corridor, 121–122, 123, 129
security neighborhood, 117–118, 126–127, 129, 143
Seidel, Marc-David, 16
self-defining truths, 150–151
sharedness, 31
Shin, Hyun Song, 60–61
sincerity, 55
Smith-Doerr, Laurel, 14
social capital: cohesion and, 52–56, 62–63, 65; defined, 51; epistemic states and, 77, 164; and mutual monitoring effect, 164; processes affecting, 138
social currency, information as, 90
social fabric, 127
social lubricant, 139
social networks, 43–49; coordinative backbone of, 126; as empirical measurement, 162; as epinets, 65–77, *67*, *68*, *69*, *70–71*, *72–73*, *75*; fragility and robustness of, 123–130
Sorenson, O., 15
specifying an epinet, 134; step 1: individual epistemic states, *135*, 135–136; step 2: interactive epistemic states, 136–137, *137*; step 3: trust and epistemic links, 137–139, *139*

Spiro, Jarrett, 14
stability, 152–155
states of the world, 25–27
state spaces: of events (game theory), 81; propositional, 29, 131, 144, 152, 167; semantic vs. syntactic, 25–26, 64, 131, 161, 166
status, 47, 84–91
strike, labor, 34–35
Strogatz, Steven H., 133
subconsciousness, defined, 20
subjunctive epistemic states: defined, 30–31; importance of, 124, 166; and trust, 57, 91, 127–129, 131, 138
sufficiency, logical, 57
superconductivity, 49, 91, 120–122, 129, 143
surveys/questionnaires, data from, 25–26, 50, 77, 131, 136, 157

Tan, Guofu, 46
theory of types (Harsanyi), 164
ties: conductiveness of, 90; density of, 52; formation of, 85; friendship, 3–9; reciprocated, 109–116, *110–112, 114–115*; redundancy of, 129; trustful-trusting, 94–101 passim, 118, *139*, 139–140, *140*
Tocqueville, Alexis de, 93
transitivity, 103, 139
trust: backbone of, 129–130; as a behavioral disposition, 94–95; breaches of, 99, 122–127; bridges of, 129; centrality, coherence, and, 107–109, *108*; in a clique, 46–47; as cognitive-moral entity, 97–98; as cognitive-rational entity, 96–97; defined, 21, 48–49, 97, 99; degree of, 118; importance of, 93–94; as influence on economic behavior, 93–94; and information pathways, 118–122; interactive epistemic states and, 98–104; as interpersonal entity, 95–96; making and breaking of, 124; measurement of, 21; and modal epistemic structures, 101–104; partitions of, 117–118; on rational vs. moral grounds, 99; scholarship on, 93–94; ties of, *121*, 122, 138, *139, 141; tout court*, 103; transitivity and, 103, 139. *See also* trust conduit; trust corridor; trust in competence; trust in integrity; trust neighborhood
trust conduit, 119, 120, *120, 121*, 122, 129, 153
trust corridor, 119–120, *120, 121*, 129, 143, 153
trust in competence, 99, 102–103, 124–125, 127
trust in integrity, 99, 101–102, 124–125, 127
trust neighborhood, 117–118, *120, 121*, 126–127, 129, 143
trustworthiness, 14, 16–17, 49, 95–98, 116, 140

Ucinet 6.0, 173n2
unawareness, 29–30, 156, 161
uncertainty, 29
unknown unknowns, 29
Uzzi, Brian, 14

validity, 24, 55, 156, 159
Van Maanen, J., 82

Wasserman, Stanley, 89
Watts, Duncan J., 133
Weber, Max, 93
Weigert, Andrew, 93, 94
Welsch, Roy E., 174n7
Westphal, James D., 16
Williamson, Oliver E., 94

Zamir, Shmuel, 20